Social Threat and Social Control

SUNY Series in
Deviance and Social Control

Ronald A. Farrell, Editor

Social Threat
and Social Control

Edited by
Allen E. Liska

State University of New York Press

Production: Ruth Fisher
Marketing: Bernadette LaManna

Published by
State University of New York Press, Albany

For information, address the State University of New York Press,
State University Plaza, Albany, NY 12246

Library of Congress Cataloging-in-Publication Data

Liska, Allen E.
  Social threat and social control / Allen E. Liska.
    p. cm.—(SUNY series in deviance and social control)
  Includes bibliographical references and index.
  ISBN 0-7914-0903-1 (CH : acid-free).—ISBN 0-7914-0904-X (PB :
acid-free)
  1. Social control. 2. Threat (Psychology) 3. Social conflict.
4. Social control—Case studies. I. Title. II. Series.
HM73.L57 1992
303.3'3—dc20   91-7550
                                                                        CIP

10 9 8 7 6 5 4 3 2 1

Contents

List of Illustrations

List of Tables

Preface

For some time, I have been interested in the study of social control systems, and in testing and elaborating the threat hypothesis of the conflict perspective to social and crime control. Starting in the early 1980s, I have published articles on how the criminal justice system (police size, arrest rates) responds (expands and contracts) to forms of social threat, especially threat to the interests of authorities; and my Ph.D. students have extended this perspective in their dissertations and subsequent articles to mental health and welfare systems.

Recently, I have come to realize that this research literature is theoretically dissipated. Studies are categorized by substantive forms of social control (imprisonment, arrests, lynching, mental hospitalization, social welfare), rather than by theoretical propositions; and to a large extent, these studies are isolated from each other. Researchers studying imprisonment are criminologists interested in prisons, not mental health or welfare; researchers studying lynching specialize in race relations or collective behavior, not imprisonment; researchers studying mental hospitalization are interested in mental health, not crime or welfare; and those studying welfare are experts in social services, not race relations or mental health. It is rare, indeed, for researchers studying one form of control to be aware of theoretically similar work on another form of control, and even rarer for them to interweave that work into their own. For the most part, research is not employed to test and elaborate theory; rather, theory is employed to loosely guide research and to interpret its findings, and explanatory variables are selected because they are readily accessible and/or amenable to a particular theoretical interpretation.

I have also come to realize that advances in these diverse research areas would be facilitated through their theoretical integration. I recently published a general review article in the *Annual Review of Sociology*, and organized a session, "Effects of Threat and Fiscal Crises on Patterns of Social Control," for the American Society of Criminology annual meeting, 1989. This book extends this work.

It focuses on the threat hypothesis of the conflict perspective. The goal is threefold: one, to use the threat hypothesis to organize and interrelate seemingly diverse literatures on social control; two, to use new data to resolve puzzles and crucial issues in these literatures; and, three, to use these literatures to develop and expand the threat hypothesis.

The book is organized into an introduction, three substantive sections, and a conclusion. Drawing and building on my earlier review article, the introduction places the book into a broader theoretical context. It begins by discussing the concept of social control, its historical development, and the expansion of crime control bureaucracies during the 1960s, 1970s, and 1980s. It then discusses the three major theoretical perspectives of social control: economic perspective, structural-functional perspective, and conflict perspective. As the book focuses on the threat hypothesis of the conflict perspective, the latter is developed in considerable more detail than are the other perspectives.

The book is divided into three substantive sections by forms of social control, ranging from lethal or fatal controls, to coercive controls, to beneficent controls. The first section, fatal controls, includes one chapter on lynching in the American South and one chapter on the police use of deadly force. The second section, coercive controls, includes one chapter on crime reporting, one chapter on the expansion and contraction of urban police departments, one chapter on arrest rates, and one chapter on prison admission rates. The third and final section, beneficent controls, includes one chapter on the linkages between the criminal justice and mental health systems and one chapter on the expansion of the welfare system. The concluding chapter discusses the implications of this body of research for the threat hypothesis.

Acknowledgments

Over the years I have received so much intellectual stimulation and support from so many people that it is hard to know where to begin and where to end an acknowledgment. I wish to particularly acknowledge the contributions of my colleagues, Richard Felson, Marvin Krohn, and Steve Messner who have read and commented over the years on so many of my papers and chapters; and I wish to acknowledge the contributions of the many graduate students with whom I have worked over the years. Four of them (Tom Arvanites, Mitch Chamlin, Barbara Warner, and Jiang Yu) have contributed chapters to this volume. There have been many others who have indirectly contributed to my thinking on social threat and social control, including Mick Benson, Bill Baccaglini, Rosemary Gido, Mark Reed, Andy Sanchirico, and Mark Tausig.

I also wish to acknowledge and thank the Harry Frank Guggenheim Foundation, which has supported my work on social threat and social control, and the National Institute of Aging, which supported my earlier work on the fear of crime, a precursor of this work.

Finally, I wish to thank Eileen Pellegrino who has typed many of the chapters and over the years has typed and edited so much of my work.

1

Introduction to the Study of Social Control

Allen E. Liska

This book focuses on the impact of social threat on the pattern and shape of deviance and crime control institutions, organizations, programs, and policies. This is an important subject of study for two reasons. One, the financial cost of supporting these institutions, organizations, programs, and policies around the world is staggering and has sharply increased in the West, particularly in the United States, since World War II. Two, these institutions, organizations, programs, and policies substantially affect the structure and organization of society and people's daily lives. While sociologists and other social scientists have only recently become interested in deviance and crime control, it is a special case of social control, a subject of which sociologists have had a long-standing interest. The discussion of deviance and crime control thus begins with a historical review of the sociological study of social control.

History of the Concept of Social Control

The concept of social control has a long history in the social sciences. Among sociologists the concept gained prominence at the turn of the last century when sociologists were confronted with the problem of social order in the emerging urban centers. To a large part, sociologists, like Ross and Cooley, attributed this to the absence of primary social relationships in urban society. These social relationships were thought to be the mechanism through which the social order is passed from one generation to another. From the turn of the twentieth century to about 1930, sociologists studied how ecological forces (industrialization and urbanization) created social conditions (social

1

mobility, weak primary relationships, migration, and cultural diversity), which in turn weakened social control, which increased deviance.
Sociologists studied a litany of institutions and organizations, such as
the family, education, law, religion, and occupations that could function as a source of social control in an urban environment and thereby
maintain the social order. Because social control was viewed as necessary for social order, during this era the study of social control was
equated with the study of sociology.

This era came to an end in the early 1930s when many sociologists
came to believe that urban centers were not necessarily disorganized
and lacking social order but were just organized differently than traditional rural agricultural societies. They argued, not that there was
less social control in urban than rural environments, but that similar
social control processes in urban and rural environments led to different types and forms of social order. They were interested less in the
degree or level of social control—implicitly assumed to be constant
across different forms of social order—than in the social conditions
that give rise to these different forms of social order. Perhaps one of
the best examples is Sutherland's theory of differential association. He
argued that deviance from the norms of the conventional society is
frequently in conformance to the norms of another social order in
conflict with the norms of the conventional order. Indeed, his theory
of deviance is a theory of how people are socialized into the norms of unconventional social orders and how these orders are passed on.

By the 1940s the structural-functional perspective had taken
hold in American sociology, and by the 1950s it assumed a dominant
position. Assuming a very high degree of normative consensus, order,
consistency, and integration, the perspective reduced the study of
social control to the study of acts of deviance that disrupt an otherwise integrated social system. Social control was generally defined as
those acts, relationships, processes, and structures that maintain
social conformity. There were numerous conceptual efforts to define,
refine, and categorize these acts, relationships, processes, and structures. Reiss (1951), for example, distinguished between personal and
social control. Nye (1958) emphasized the role of family relationships
for both types of control. These emphases and distinctions are reflected in the latter work of Hirschi (1969), who attempted to
delineate the social relationships (such as social attachment to
conventional others, commitment to conventional activities and roles,
and involvement in conventional activities and roles), that control
people from acting on their motives to deviate.

During the 1960s, the critique of the structural-functional perspective had a profound impact on the conceptualization of social control. Of interest here is the structural-functionalist assumption that social norms are reasonably clear and thus that norm violations are equally clear: they can be defined, and efforts to control them can be defined independently of the norms themselves. Hence, we can study the effectiveness of social control in actually controlling norm violations. Theories of the 1960s (Lemert 1951; Becker 1963; Scheff 1966) questioned these claims and turned the above question on its head. They argued that social norms are generally not very clearly defined; rather, they are frequently quite vague and dependent on situational circumstances. Indeed, what is deviant depends on what is negatively reacted to, what is not tolerated in social interaction, or what is sanctioned in social interaction. We learn about proper behavior, not by learning about abstract norms and then applying them to specific situations, but by observing what is tolerated and punished in specific situations. Hence, because deviance is defined in terms of social control, the latter not the former should be the focus of study. This perspective drew attention to the study of acts, particularly acts of punishment, that attempt to control social interaction. Numerous studies examined who gets arrested, prosecuted, and sentenced. To the extent to which social control acts, relationships, processes, and structures can be defined independently of deviance, the societal-reaction theorists argued that social control generally does not decrease deviance; it increases it. They proceeded to delineate the mechanisms by which this occurs.

In sum, the study of social control has been an integral part of sociology since its inception. Originally, the concept was defined as any structure, process, relationship, or act that contributes to the social order. Indeed, the study of social order and social control were indistinguishable. This conceptual problem was evident in the early Chicago perspective in which the concepts "social disorganization," "social control," and "deviance" were not conceptually distinguished. Deviance was thought to be the consequence of a lack of social control and was often used to measure its presence; areas of a city with high rates of deviance were assumed to have low levels of social control. In the late Chicago perspective, by the 1930s and 1940s, the level of social control was no longer a significant variable. It was implicitly construed as a constant and only the content was thought to vary. Areas of a city were thought to be differentially organized. Within the structural-functionalism of the late 1940s and 1950s, the study of social control was further allocated to the sidelines, dealing with residual problems of deviance in a social system assumed to be generally integrated and well functioning. However, by the early 1960s society was, again, assumed to be considerably less orderly and integrated and, again, the concept rose to the forefront, as both a dependent and an independent variable. Studies examined both its causes and consequences. Thus, by the mid-1960s, the intellectual ground had been laid for a renewed scholarly interest in the study of social control. We now turn to the social conditions that focused this interest into the study of crime control during the 1970s and 1980s.

Crime Control

By crime control we mean those activities authorized by a governmental unit that are intended directly or indirectly to reduce crime. By "authorized" we mean that the activities are legal—that is, they do not violate any laws. Legal activities to reduce crime can be engaged in by governmental organizations (the police), nongovernmental organizations (private police and security units of corporations), collective citizen groups, (the Guardian Angels), and citizens acting individually (purchasing secure locks).

Growth in Crime Control During the 1960s and 1970s

Since the middle 1960s large-scale social surveys (GSS, Harris, Gallup, NORC, NCS) have reported that a very high percentage of the U.S. population is concerned about crime and fears being victimized (Garofalo 1979; Skogan and Maxfield 1981; Yin 1985), and that this percentage has been steadily increasing since the mid-1960s. Using Gallup polls and the General Social Science survey, Stinchcombe et al. (1980) report that this percentage reached about forty-five percent in the middle-to-late 1970s with the major increase occurring between 1968 and 1974. More recent reports suggest that the figure has remained at this high level. Indeed, concern about crime and the fear of crime have reached such proportions that they themselves have become the subject of considerable study.

Perhaps in direct response to these public concerns, crime control activities and resources have also increased significantly since the 1960s, particularly from the mid-1960s to the mid-1970s. Consider the police. From 1950 to 1965 cities employed approximately 1.9 police officers per thousand population; but by 1975 that number had increased to 2.5. This trend was accentuated for cities over 250,000 in population. From 1950 to 1965 they employed approximately 2.4 officers per thousand population; but by 1970 that number increased to 2.8, and by 1975 it increased to 3.6, stabilizing thereafter at about 3.3. As might be expected, a similar trend is evident in police expenditures. The Bureau of Justice Statistics reports that police expenditures per capita adjusted for inflation, while increasing slowly from World War II to 1960, accelerated from the early 1960s to the late 1970s. From 1946 to 1962 it increased seventy-six percent, approximately 4.4 percent annually, but from 1962 to 1977 it increased 128 percent, approximately eight percent annually. Since then it has remained relatively constant. From the mid-1960s to the mid-1970s, the arrest rate also increased substantially. From 1965 to 1975 it increased from 3,695 to 4,455 per one hundred thousand population (twenty-one percent) for all crimes and from 622 to 1,061 (seventy-one percent) for index crimes, whereas for the previous five years and for the following five years the rate remained relatively stable.

Consider imprisonment. The Bureau of Justice Statistics reports that since World War II the prison population of the U.S. slowly increased from a low of 98 per one hundred thousand population in 1945 to 109 in 1950, 112 in 1955, 117 in 1960, and then briefly decreased to 108 in 1965 and 96 in 1970, perhaps reflecting the demand for young males made by the Vietnam War. After the war it sharply and steadily increased to 111 in 1975, 138 in 1980, and 201 in 1985. To give these figures even more meaning, consider the prevalence rate of imprisonment. For 1979, Langan and Greenfeld (1985) calculate that 0.18 percent of the U.S. population and as much as 1.66 percent of black males are imprisoned in any one day. By aggregating the probabilities of serving a first sentence at age thirteen through age eighty-four, they estimate the lifetime prevalence of imprisonment. Assuming the 1979 rates over a person's lifetime (they are already higher today), approximately 2.7 percent of the population, 5.1 percent of all males and 18.6 percent of all black males will experience imprisonment during their lifetime.

Starting with the War on Crime program, initiated by the Johnson administration and continued by the Nixon administration, billions of dollars have been funneled into the criminal justice system. Chapman et al. (1975) report that all levels of government spent about $3.3 billion for crime control in 1960, but by 1973 that figure had risen to $13 billion. This is just not a matter of inflation. Statistics show that an increasing proportion of the GNP was being allocated to crime control during those years. The Center for Research on Criminal Justice (1975) estimates that the proportion of the GNP spent on the criminal justice system increased from one-half percent in 1955 to a full one percent in 1971.

In sum, statistics show that crime control as measured by crime control activity (such as arrest and imprisonment rates), by the supporting infrastructure (such as police size), and by the expenditures to support them have steadily increased since World War II, and that the increase has accelerated since the early 1960s, particularly from the mid-1960s to the mid-1970s.

Consequences of Crime Control

This expansion of crime control is important because of its consequences for society. The most widely studied consequence is the deterrence of crime. Indeed, most research on crime control studies the effectiveness of control organizations and programs—particularly institutional forms of punishment—for deterring crime. Whether these organizations and programs do or do not control crime, they are an integral part of society and have numerous foreseen and unforeseen consequences for society.

Perhaps the structural-functionalists, starting with Durkheim, were among the first to recognize this. They have pointed out that crime, primarily through the societal reaction to it (such as punishment), functions to maintain the social order; that is, to maintain social boundaries and to build social solidarity and cohesiveness. Others have noted the negative consequences of crime control institutions and programs. First and foremost, they are enormously expensive. As just noted, the present criminal justice system in the U.S. consumes billions of dollars on policing, prosecuting, and sentencing people. Additionally, crime control, whether just or unjust, is always an intrusion into the daily lives of citizens. Many of its consequences have not been fully recognized. For example, only recently have scholars begun to discuss the economic consequences of penal work units, such as farms and road gangs, for local (Adamson 1984) and national (Connor 1972) economies, and the consequences of imprisoning a high proportion of young black males on the family structure of blacks.

In sum, because of the rapid expansion of crime control in the 1960s and 1970s and perhaps of a growing realization of its consequences for individuals and society, crime control has become the form of social control that has been most studied during the 1970s. To a large extent, these studies are isolated from the studies of other forms of deviance and crime control, such as the mental health system; and to a large extent, they use the individual as the unit of analysis, examining how various crime control activities, like arresting, prosecuting, and sentencing, are affected by the legal, psychological, and social characteristics of people. Because these microlevel studies are well organized and synthesized, constituting a clearly defined literature, they are not the subject of this book. Some studies use collectives—organizations and communities—as the unit of analysis, examining how deviance and crime control patterns are affected by social structures. Most of this research takes the form of historical case studies that illustrate rather than test sociological perspectives on deviance and crime control (Erikson 1966; Harring 1983); most of it focuses on only one organization, program, or policy of control within the criminal justice, mental health, or welfare systems; and most of these studies, isolated from each other, do not constitute a recognized body of research, "a literature," and their implications for a general macrotheory of deviance and crime control are not exploited. The general purpose of this book is to organize this research into a theoretical literature.

Theoretical Perspectives

Most of these studies can be organized within one of three theoretical perspectives: economic, structural-functionalist, and conflict.

Economic Perspective

Within this perspective, crime control research is generally macro-comparative and theory testing, and it constitutes a recognized body of research that bears on general economic theory. Hence, it cannot and should not be ignored by other social scientists.

The perspective (Becker 1968; Ehrlich 1973; Schmidt and Witte 1984) assumes that people have relatively stable preferences or interests, that they weigh the benefits and costs of behavior alternatives, and that they behave so as to maximize the ratio of benefits to costs. The study of crime control is always considered with regard to its impact on crime, particularly with developing policies and programs to control it. Crime control and crime are thus part of one general model composed of three equations that predict: (1) criminal behavior (crime generation equation); (2) crime control activities, such as arrests and convictions, that affect the cost of criminal behavior (production function equation); and (3) crime control resources, such as

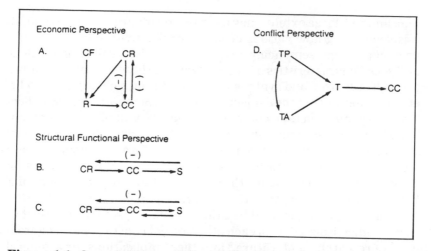

Figure 1-1 Casual structures underlying the three perspectives

Note: CF, community fiscal capacity; R, resources, CR, crime rate; CC, crime control; S, solidarity; T, threat; TA, threatening acts; TP, threatening people.

capital and labor, that affect the production of crime activities (demand equation). See figure 1.1A.

Criminal behavior is thought to be just like any other behavior. People engage in it when the ratio of benefits to costs is higher for it than for noncriminal alternatives. Effective crime control policies should decrease the benefits and increase the costs of crime, and/or increase the benefits and decrease the costs of alternatives to crime (Ehrlich 1973; Becker 1968). One major cost of crime is punishment. Crime rates (equation 1) are thought to be a negative function of the level of punishment, especially the severity and certainty of punishment (Blumstein et al. 1978; Cook 1977).

The level of crime control activity—the relative certainty of punishment—is conceptualized as a production function (equation 2). It is assumed to be negatively affected by workload (crime rates) and positively affected by resources (capital and labor). That is, given constant resources, as the crime rate increases, the proportion of crimes cleared by arrests, prosecutions, or convictions should decrease; and given a constant crime rate, as resources increase the proportion of crimes cleared by arrests, prosecutions, and convictions should increase. Research (Phillips and Votey 1981; Liska et al. 1985) examines the effect of capital investment (e.g., computer technologies), labor (e.g., police size and salaries), and the organization of labor (e.g., two-officer patrols and high-density patrolling) on crime control activities (e.g., the certainty of arrest).

Crime control resources (capital and labor) are viewed as a positive function of community fiscal capacity and workload, such as crime rates (equation 3). These resources are thought to be constrained by a community's fiscal capacity, in the sense that a rich community can afford more control per capita (as it can afford more social services in general) than can a poor community (Phillips and Votey 1981). Work in the 1950s and 1960s focused on the effect of a community's mean income, its tax rate, and intergovernmental transfers on crime control resources (Weicher 1970). By the 1970s, interest shifted to the effect of crime rates (workload) on resources. As crime increases, citizens are thought to demand more control services. They are willing to increase revenues and to support political candidates who advocate strong crime control (McPheters and Stronge 1974; Phillips and Votey 1981; Carr-Hill and Stern 1979). Indeed, much of the work during and after the 1970s has focused on estimating the reciprocal effects of crime rates and crime control resources.

In sum, economists approach this issue as part of a clearly specified model, linking crime rates and crime control, which can be derived from a general economic theory of behavior. Sociologists could learn much from the logical and empirical rigor of this work. Yet, the theory —particularly the three-equation model of crime and crime control— is built on some very questionable assumptions (Loftin and McDowall 1982), which direct research away from some fundamental questions.

Two assumptions, regarding interests and power, are particularly relevant to the study of crime control. First, crime is assumed to be more or less costly to all citizens, and thus all are assumed to be motivated and interested in controlling it. The power to influence crime control policy is equated with the vote, and elections are equated with a free market where information on candidates' policies is fully available (Becker 1968; Ehrlich 1973; Phillips and Votey 1981). In effect, people are thought to have similar and enlightened self-interests regarding crime control and equal power to influence policy. These assumptions depoliticize and direct attention to the aggregate demand for crime control and to the objective social conditions that influence that demand, such as crime rates and community resources.

The two assumptions should be considered very carefully. Interests and motivations to control crime are not self-evident. Indeed, they seem to be quite variable—varying over time, among societies, and among social statuses within societies. Such interests may vary with the rate of victimization experienced by each status and by the needs of each status to protect itself and its property. Perhaps those who can afford to live in low-crime neighborhoods and to insure their property against theft (the very rich), as well as those who have little to lose (the very poor), have a minimal interest in crime control, compared to those who have something to lose but cannot afford to protect it (the middle class). While the right to vote may be equally distributed in many Western societies, information on candidates' policies and the resources to influence them are generally not equally distributed. Economists appear to be generally unconcerned either in explaining the distribution of interests in crime control and the distribution of power to influence policy, or in taking these distributions into account in explaining variation in crime control among social units.

Structural-Functionalist Perspective

The structural-functional perspective traditionally conceives of society as integrated and orderly. It assumes that there is a general consensus on goals and values, that general needs for survival can be identified, that social structures (persistent patterns of behavior) function to maintain society's values, goals, and needs, and that social structures can be explained by these functions. Rapid change in the social structure is conceived as an extraordinary event which is brought about by an equally extraordinary event in the external environment of the society.

While "modern or neo" structural-functionalism may not make many of these assumptions, much contemporary social control theory and research is guided by them. The structure of crime control, as of any other behavior, is thought to maintain society's values, goals, and needs, particularly needs for social control, and it is thought to be explained by these functions. To the extent that the structure of crime control is effective—functional—it is assumed to persist and remain stable, only changing in response to extraordinary events in the external environment.

This perspective has some general similarities to the economic perspective. Both assume that there is a consensus and stability of values and goals (in economic terms, preferences and interests) and that persistent patterns of crime control come into existence and are maintained because they contribute to society's values and goals. While economists explicate the underlying processes in terms of enlightened self-interests and market mechanisms, structural-functionalists talk more vaguely about social values and hidden feed-

back mechanisms, frequently couched in teleological and evolution-
ary terms.

From the general structural-functional perspective three propositions can be identified regarding consequences, stability, and change
in punishment as a form of crime control.

Consequences. Durkheim (1938) noted various consequences of
punishment, including the maintenance of social solidarity, of a social
identity, and of social boundaries, as well as the control of crime.
Social systems are assumed to sustain the level of punishment required to maintain necessary social states, such as social solidarity
and social boundaries. Whether or not punishment controls crime is
of secondary importance to its other functions. Crime enters into the
analysis not as a negative social state to be controlled but as a stimu-
lant to crime control (punishment). Thus, crime is frequently thought
of as making positive contributions to society.

The "consequences" proposition has generated a loosely organized body of research composed of historical (Erikson 1966; Currie
1968; Connor 1972; Ben-Yehuda 1980), field-observational (Dentler
and Erikson 1959; Scott 1976), and laboratory-experimental studies
(Lauderdale 1976; Lauderdale et al. 1984). The historical and field-
observational studies tend to "illustrate" rather than to test the
proposition. Case studies are selected that illustrate how crime control either functions to increase boundary maintenance and solidarity
(Erikson 1966) or fails to do so (Ben-Yehuda 1980). For example,
Erikson describes in fascinating detail three crises in Puritan society
initiated by the immigration of culturally dissimilar groups. He argues
that these crises (Quaker persecution, Antinomian controversy, and
witchcraft hysteria) stimulated crime control, which in turn functioned to redefine moral boundaries and sustain social solidarity.
Theory-testing research is limited to a few laboratory and survey
studies. For example, Lauderdale's (1976) experimental research
shows that external threat increases both the rejection of deviants
and the affirmation of social solidarity; but it does not show that the
rejection of deviants mediates the effect of external threat on solidarity.

With the possible exception of Lauderdale's work, there is little
strong evidence that crime control in the form of punishment or the
general reaction to crime (or deviance) affects any social state—such
as social solidarity, social boundaries, or cultural identities—thought
to be important to group survival. Unless such effects are empirically
established, it is premature to become embroiled in a controversy over

whether or not patterns of crime and crime control can be explained
by their consequences.

   Change in punishment. Within the structural-functional perspective on crime control, social change tends to be treated as an
extraordinary event. Yet, from time to time, social systems, even those
that are predominantly stable, experience events (e.g., political movements, immigration, economic inflation and depression, and war)
that threaten the social order. According to this perspective, people
respond to these threats with acts that reaffirm and strengthen their
collective values and identity. In times of social stress, simple norm
infractions are magnified and take on great symbolic significance,
whereas in normal times they may just be ignored. Hence, during times
of stress we might expect little tolerance and considerable punishment for norm violations.

   Some support for this proposition can be found in historical
studies, especially in studies on witchcraft. Erikson (1966), Currie
(1968), and Ben-Yehuda (1980) interpret changes in the punishment
of witchcraft as a response to boundary crises precipitated by socially
disruptive events, such as an influx of culturally different people or a
technological revolution. Yet, as previously indicated, most of these
studies illustrate rather than test the theory. They are steeped in the
contextual detail of a particular time and place, making comparisons
across time and across studies difficult. Pivotal concepts, such as
"boundary crisis," are not clearly defined so that they can be operationalized across historical contexts.

   Inverarity (1976) attempts to test this general theory by examining the link between mechanical solidarity and repressive punishment. He examines a sample of parishes in post-Civil War Louisiana
that are assumed to have undergone a boundary crisis precipitated by
the Populist movement. Following Durkheim, he assumes that a social
crisis precipitates an increase in punishment only in parishes whose
mechanical solidarity is strong. Measuring mechanical solidarity as
the percentage of blacks, the level of urbanization, and the level of
religious homogeneity, and measuring repressive punishment as the
number of lynchings, he reports support for the hypothesis: mechanical solidarity coupled with a social crisis increases repressive punishment. This work has been extensively criticized, perhaps because it
claims to be one of the few rigorous tests of the functional thesis (Pope
and Ragin 1977; Wasserman 1977; Bohrnstedt 1977; Bagozzi 1977;
Berk 1977). For example, critics have questioned whether the post-

Civil War Populist movement in Louisiana really constituted a boundary crisis and whether the above indicators constitute a valid operationalization of mechanical solidarity.

Stability of punishment. Within the structural-functional perspective, functional patterns of behavior are assumed to persist (remain stable), and since punishment is assumed to be functional, it too is assumed to be stable. This reasoning leads to an interesting corollary. Assuming that the overall level of punishment is stable, then as the crime rate increases, only the most serious crimes can be punished and the less serious ones must be ignored. Indeed, Durkheim (1938) argued that even the social definition of crime expands and contracts in relationship to the general volume of undesirable behavior. He described this in what has come to be known as the society of saints parable (1938:68–69):

> Imagine a society of saints, perfect cloister of exemplary individuals, crimes, properly so called, will there be unknown; but faults which appear venial to the layman will create there the same scandal that the ordinary offense does in ordinary consciousness. If, then, this society has the power to judge and punish, it will define these acts as criminal and treat them as such.

Considerable theory-testing research, stimulated by the work of Blumstein and his colleagues, has addressed this issue. Their work has two interrelated thrusts: documenting the stability of punishment and identifying the causal processes that underlie it.

Blumstein and associates (Blumstein and Cohen 1973; Blumstein et al. 1976; Blumstein and Moitra 1979) use time series techniques to examine the stability of imprisonment rates in the United States from 1926 to 1974, in Canada from 1880 to 1959, and in Norway from 1880 to 1964. They argue that imprisonment rates in these countries are generated by a stationary process; that is, the observed statistical variation in punishment over time can be modeled as statistical variation around a constant mean. In a reanalysis of these data, Rauma (1981a) argues that while a stationary process may indeed generate these observations, there is just as much evidence that a nonstationary process generates them. Furthermore, he (1981b) argues that a univariate time series analysis can tell us very little about the causal processes, as specified by Durkheim and others, that underlie whatever level of stability is observed.

In a second related research thrust, Blumstein tries to show how stability in punishment is maintained by continual adjustments in the type of behavior punished. In one study, Blumstein and Cohen (1973) examine the relationship between crime and arrest rates for serious and nonserious crimes in the United States. Their findings suggest that as the general crime rate increases, the arrest rate of nonserious crimes decreases, and as the crime rate decreases, the arrest rate of nonserious crimes increases, thereby maintaining a stable general arrest rate. In a second study, Blumstein et al. (1976) analyze the flow rates between conformists, criminals, and prisoners in Canada. Making certain assumptions about the stability and state of the prison population, they deduce flow rates among these groups that generally approximate the observed rates.

In short, Blumstein and his associates have attempted to model the social process that underlies the stability of punishment. The model, however, is underidentified. They circumvent this problem by studying either the outcomes of the process (univariate time series) or by providing "guesstimates" of some of the parameters. Their work takes us further than we have been before and has stimulated considerable debate (Rauma 1981a). What is needed now is research that measures more of the model variables and empirically estimates more of the model parameters.

Continuing in the Blumstein tradition, Berk et al. (1981) have also attempted to identify the equilibrium mechanism that underlies the stability of punishment. Assuming that the punishment rate varies somewhat around a specific level that is functional for a given society —the system target—then the growth rate of punishment is a simple function of the growth rate of the population. If for some reason punishment rates exceed the target, responding to changes in the external environment, future growth rates in punishment should decrease; and if rates fall below the target, furture growth rates should increase. Growth rates of punishment are then the "mechanism" by which societies adjust the punishment rate to system targets. Berk et al. (1981), using a time series of imprisonment rates in California from 1851 to 1970, find no empirical support for this equilibrium hypothesis.

Generally, research leaves considerable doubt that the punishment rate in social systems is stable over time and that this stability is sustained because it is somewhat functional. Moreover, research suffers from theoretical ambiguity in conceptualizing the social process underlying stability—an ambiguity that can be traced to Durkheim. Theorists and researchers alike assume that societies have certain requisites for survival, such as solidarity and boundary maintenance, and that a level of punishment persists because it functions to maintain these needs; but neither Durkheim nor recent researchers such as Erikson, Blumstein, Rauma, or Berk clearly specify the social process by which a level of punishment persists that maintains a system's requisites for survival. Instead, research examines the logical consequences of the punishment stability assumption. Assuming that punishment is stable, Blumstein and Cohen (1973) suggest that if the crime rate is high, then only the most serious crimes can be punished; and Berk et al. (1981) imply that if the punishment rate is high, then the punishment growth rate will be low. These relationships are construed as the dynamic mechanisms by which stability is sustained. This is correct, but only in a logical or definitional sense. If the relationship between the rate of punishment and the growth of that rate is negative, then of course the punishment rate will tend toward stability. Yet the study of such relationships does not shed light on the substantive causal processes by which this stability is sustained—that is, those causal processes by which the consequences of punishment, such as solidarity or boundary maintenance, influence punishment so as to sustain a stable level of punishment.

Some researchers (Erikson 1966; Berk et al. 1983), and to a lesser extent even Blumstein and Cohen (1973), argue that the observed stability of punishment may simply reflect stability in the processing capacity of control systems. For example, stability in the prison population may simply reflect stability in prison size. In a recent paper, Berk et al. (1983) argue that the constraints of prison capacity operate through the many daily admission and release decisions of criminal justice administrators. This explanation should be regarded with some caution. Considerable research shows that the capacity of control systems is not necessarily stable; rather, it may expand and contract in response to social conditions (Currie 1986; Connor 1972). More importantly, this explanation of punishment stability is unrelated to the logic of structural-functionalism. That is, if the capacity of a control system is stable, thereby limiting and stabilizing the level of punishment, then the postulation of unobservable goals, targets, and needs to explain stability is quite unnecessary. Blumstein et al. (1976: 319-20), apparently unsatisfied with an explanation in terms of system capacity, argue "that social forces accounting for stability include more than simple prison-cell capacity.... More fundamental considerations of social structure are probably at work. If too large a portion of society is declared deviant, then the fundamental stability of society will be disrupted. Likewise, if too few are punished, the identifying values of society will not be adequately articulated and reinforced, again leading to social instability."

It is interesting that Erikson, Blumstein, and Berk made references both to unobservable targets, goals, and needs, and to the
capacity of the social control system in order to explain the stability of
punishment. Emphasis on the latter links their research to an explicit
causal mechanism missing in the former, and emphasis on the former
links their work to a general theoretical framework missing in the
latter.

    Feedback loops and system estimation. In contemporary econo-
mics and much sociology the problem of identifying causal processes
consistent with a traditional functional explanation has been dealt
with by postulating causal feedback loops (Stinchcombe 1968). Consider just one possible consequence of punishment, "social solidarity."
Based on the structural-functional tradition, it is reasonable to assume that crime positively affects punishment, which positively affects solidarity, which in turn negatively affects crime (see figure
1.1B). Changes in any one of the variables, brought about by changes
in various exogenous variables, vibrate through the system and
dampen over time; and because the causal loop consists of both
positive and negative causal effects, the system tends toward long-
term stability. For example, an increase in crime, brought about by an
increase in unemployment, increases punishment, which increases
solidarity, which in turn decreases crime. Alternatively, the emergence of an external threat, like a war, may increase solidarity, which
decreases crime, which decreases punishment, which in turn decreases solidarity. In both cases the initial random shock to the system
is counteracted by the feedback loop and dampened over time.
    The system can be further complicated by postulating additional
feedback loops. The system in figure 1.1C has two feedback loops, an
internal loop and an external loop. In addition to indirectly decreasing punishment through decreasing crime, solidarity may directly increase punishment. To put it simply, as solidarity increases, the resolve
to control crime may increase. The inner loop amplifies the effect of an
initial random shock on the system, and the outer loop controls it. The
net effect depends on the relative strengths and time lags of the two
loops.
    While complex feedback loops make it difficult to see intuitively
the outcome of random shocks to a causal system and make the
parameters of the system difficult to estimate, explicit feedback loops
with a control structure transform the traditional teleology of func-
tionalism into a testable causal theory (Stinchcombe 1968). Assumptions about unobservable needs, goals, and targets are rendered

unnecessary, and functional theories simply become special cases of causal theories.

Also, making explicit the causal logic underlying the assumed stability of punishment clarifies the interrelationships between the three propositions regarding consequences, change, and stability. Much theory and research on each proposition is not integrated with work on the other propositions. Yet, these interrelationships are significant in estimating each proposition. Indeed, for models B and C in figure 1.1, estimates of the specific causal paths will be biased unless the model as a whole is considered. For example, estimates of the effect of crime rates on crime control will be biased unless the indirect effect of crime control on crime rates is controlled.

This sensitizes us to the structure of random shocks. In the language of simultaneous equation modeling, random shocks constitute exogeneous variables and can thus serve as instruments to identify the structural coefficients linking the endogenous variables. Identification of models (1.1B) and (1.1C) requires that some of the exogenous variables (random shocks) affect one but not the other endogenous variables. Thus, in studying feedback systems it is not only important that we study external variables that shock the system, but that we study those exogenous variables that shock only some endogenous variables in the system.

Conflict Perspective

While both the economic and structural perspectives have been important for studying and understanding deviance and crime control, since the mid-1960s the conflict perspective has been *the* dominant perspective for organizing and stimulating macroresearch on deviance and crime control. The remainder of this chapter and book focus on this perspective.

Similar to the economic perspective, the conflict perspective (Turk 1969; Quinney 1977; Spitzer 1975; Beirne 1979) assumes enlightened self-interests, especially on the part of economic elites; contrary to the economic perspective, the conflict perspective assumes an uneven distribution of self-interests in crime control and an uneven distribution of power to implement self-interests into social policy. Theory and research focus on how these distributions of interests and power come into being, persist, and influence deviance and crime control, particularly lawmaking and enforcement. Lawmaking is assumed to reflect the interests of the powerful; those activities are criminalized that threaten their interests. Assuming that the violation of some laws is more threatening than the violation of others, the conflict perspective asserts that those laws that most protect the interests of the powerful are most enforced. Assuming that law violations are more threatening when committed by some people than by others, the perspective asserts that laws are most enforced against those people who most threaten the interests of the powerful. Hence, the conflict perspective asserts that the greater the number of acts and people threatening to the interests of the powerful, the greater the level of deviance and crime control—the threat hypothesis (see figure 1.1D)

Perhaps the major advantage of the threat hypothesis is that it broadens the study of deviance and crime control from just the criminal justice system to other institutions and organizations, such as the mental health and welfare systems. Indeed, considerable research from this perspective has examined both the mental health and welfare systems as alternative forms of controlling threatening acts and people.

Perhaps the major problems with the threat hypothesis are the definitional and theoretical linkages. Concerning the former, the major concepts like "the powerful," "interest," and "threat," are not clearly defined nor measured. For example, while the concept "the powerful" is generally interpreted as "elites" and "authorities," these concepts, too, are not well defined in contemporary conflict theory. This is a significant issue because that which is threatening to some elites and authorities is not necessarily threatening to others. Concerning just political authorities, that which threatens one level (city, state, and nation) may not necessarily threaten another. Within levels of government, that which threatens one branch (judicial) may not threaten another (legislative). Even within branches of government (executive), that which threatens one unit (police) may not necessarily threaten another (prosecutor). Hence, in defining acts and people as threatening in a heterogeneous complex society, it is necessary to specify the authorities or elites in question.

Because the critical causal variables are not well defined theoretically and operationally, and are not clearly linked to each other in the form of propositions or a causal model, the relevant research literature is also not well defined and integrated. Consequently, studies are categorized by substantive forms of control (lynching, imprisonment, arrests, hospitalization, welfare), rather than by theoretical propositions. Researchers studying imprisonment are criminologists interested in prisons; researchers studying lynching are specialists in race relations or collective behavior; researchers studying mental hospital admissions are interested in mental health; and researchers studying welfare are experts in social services. Conflict theory and the threat hypothesis in particular are employed to loosely guide research and to interpret findings, and explanatory variables are selected because they are readily accessible and/or generally amenable to a conflict interpretation. They are tied together by their focus on similar structural variables assumed to represent a threat to the interests of authorities. Some studies refer to the level and distribution of threatening people (percentage of unemployed, percentage nonwhites, and degree of income inequality) and some refer to the level and distribution of threatening acts (crime and civil disorders). Yet, it is not clear, theoretically, how the level and distribution of these acts and people generate a threat to the interests of different authorities and how that threat leads to specific forms of control.

I now briefly review some of these seemingly diverse research literatures (see figure 1.1D). They are arranged by the level of force, ranging from the stick (fatal controls) to the carrot (beneficent controls). They include studies of police use of deadly force and public lynching; studies of the criminal justice system, including crime reporting, police size, arrest rates, and prison admission rates; and studies of the welfare and mental health systems.

Fatal control

Fatal control refers to those forms of social control where the threatening population is killed—the most extreme form of control. This book examines two forms of fatal controls: police homicide of citizens and lynchings.

While lynching is certainly not an official form of control, the distinction between official and unofficial forms of controlling the black population was not always clear in the South from the Civil War to World War I. Vigilante groups were common, and some were supported and linked with local crime control agents.

A few lynching studies have been stimulated by Blalock's hypothesis (1967) that links racial discrimination to the percentage of nonwhites. He argues that as the percentage of nonwhites increases, they constitute a growing economic and political threat to whites. Economically, nonwhites compete for jobs, and politically, they compete for power. Racial discrimination—economic and political—is conceptualized as an attempt by whites, the ruling racial group, to control a threatening nonwhite population. Lynching is simply part of this pattern.

A few studies (Reed 1972; Inverarity 1976; Corzine et al. 1983) link the rate of lynching to the percentage of blacks in southern counties. Corzine et al. (1983) further report that the relationship is nonlinear with an increasing slope (power-threat hypothesis) and that the relationship is strongest in the deep South, particularly after the voter registration drives in the 1890s. They argue that these relationships support a threat hypothesis. Blacks, historically, have been perceived as more of a threat in the deep South than in other regions, and racial conflict was accentuated in the voter registration drives of the late nineteenth century. Inverarity's (1976) findings were immediately questioned in a controversial exchange by Pope and Ragin (1977), Wasserman (1977), Bohrnstedt (1977), and Berk (1977); and Reed (1972), and Corzine et al.'s (1983) findings have recently been challenged by Tolnay, Beck, and Massey (1989). They argue that support for the power-threat hypothesis (increasing slope) is contingent on a few outlier cases, a truncated sample, and an inappropriate measure of lynching. When the few outliers are deleted or when the sample is not truncated, the data provide no support for a nonlinear relationship (power-threat hypothesis) and only some support for a linear relationship (threat hypothesis).

In chapter 2 of this book, Tolnay and Beck review and elaborate the threat hypothesis as it applies to lynching in the Reconstruction and post-Reconstruction periods of the South. They conceptually distinguish sources of threat (political, economic, and status) and threatened social classes (old aristocrats, capitalists, poor whites). They theoretically specify when black concentration leads to each source of threat, differentially experienced by each class, and they theoretically specify that the relationship between each source of threat and lynching depends on the effectiveness of other forms of social control.

Considerable research on homicide by police has been conducted (Fyfe 1982); however, only a few macrostudies bear on the conflict perspective model in figure 1.1D. The findings are mixed. Using states as the unit of analysis, Kania and Mackey (1977) report a substantial and statistically significant correlation between the rate of homicides by the police and various measures of poverty, conceptualized as indicators of the presence of a threatening population. Yet, they also report a statistically insignificant correlation between such homicides and riots, a clear indicator of threatening acts. Sherman and Langworthy (1979), using cities, report a negative relationship between homicides by police and unemployment, also conceptualized as an indicator of threat. Perhaps the strongest support for the threat hypothesis comes from Jacob and Britt (1979). Using states as the unit of analysis and controlling for various other variables, such as violent crime, they report that economic inequality, conceptualized as an indicator of threat, shows a statistically significant effect on homicides by police.

In chapter three of this book Yu and myself expand this line of work. We examine the relationship between racial and economic structures of cities and the police use of deadly force against both whites and nonwhites, and we explore the implications of these findings for the threat hypothesis.

Coercive control: criminal justice system

Coercive control refers to the activities of social control agents that physically constrain peoples' behavior (arrests and imprisonment). Studies examine both these activities and the infrastructures that support them. For two coercive control bureaucracies (police and prisons), this book examines the primary control activity (arrest, imprisonment) and their capacity to perform that activity (crime reporting, police size, prison size).

Crime Reporting. Crime reporting by citizens is a critical component in activating the criminal justice system. Black and Reiss (1970) report that the vast majority of reported crimes are reported by citizens and that only a very small number are discovered by police. Considerable microresearch shows that demographic, social, and psychological variables affect the reporting of crime to the police. Reporting seems to be affected by class, race, and gender; the relationship between the offender and the victim; the seriousness of the crime; and the victim's fear of crime. Our concern is the variation in crime reporting across macrounits and the extent to which it is affected by social threat as specified by the threat hypothesis. In chapter 4 of this book, Warner examines the extent to which the variation in crime reporting by social class and race across macrounits is affected by the relative presence and distribution of threatening people and acts.

Police. To a large extent, the volume of crime control is limited by the processing or carrying capacity of the police department, which is a direct function of its size, that is, numbers and expenditures per capita. The rapid expansion of police size during the 1960s and 1970s stimulated considerable attention to this issue.

Three studies (Jacobs 1979; Jackson and Carroll 1981; Liska et al. 1981) examine police size in the United States from 1950 to 1970. They use civil disorders as an indicator of the presence of threatening acts and use the percentage of poor, percentage of nonwhites, income inequality, and degree of racial segregation as indicators of the presence and distribution of threatening people.

They report that civil disorders have no effect on police size. This is not surprising. If civil disorders affect police size, the process probably operates at the regional or national level. Disorders in any one city may affect police size, not only locally but also in comparable and neighboring cities.

They report no effect of the percentage of poor but a substantial effect of the percentage of nonwhites. This effect is stronger in 1970, following the civil disorders, than in 1960, and it is stronger in the South than in the non-South. Interestingly, Jackson and Carroll (1981) report that as the percentage of nonwhites increases from ten to 40 percent, its effect increases at an increasing rate, but as the percentage increases above forty percent its effect decreases. They argue that as the percentage approaches fifty percent, nonwhites are no longer a minority; they are approaching a majority large enough to achieve political power and authority, and nonwhite authorities are supported, not threatened, by a nonwhite majority.

Empirical support for the effect of income inequality on police size is inconsistent. Jacobs (1979) reports a positive effect, but Jackson and Carroll (1981) are unable to replicate his results. Liska et al. (1981) report that segregation has a negative effect on police size, which like the effect of the percentage of nonwhites, is stronger in the South than in the non-South and increases from 1950 to 1970. They argue that the segregation of problematic populations such as non whites into urban ghettos functions as a vehicle of social control, thereby lessening the need for more overt forms of social control.

Using data from the 1980s, Greenberg et al. (1985) question many of these findings. They find no income inequality effect, and they find that the strength and form (linear and nonlinear) of the percent nonwhite effect is contingent on geographical region and year (1960, 1970, and 1980).

Attempting to resolve these inconsistencies, Chamlin (1989) and Jackson (1989) have recently developed interesting directions of research. Chamlin (1989) argues that changes in social composition (e.g., percent nonwhite and income inequality) may be more threatening to authorities than high static levels of these compositions. He reports that changes in police size from 1972 to 1982, while not affected by static levels, are significantly affected by changes in many of these variables, such as property crime rates, percent nonwhite, and racial segregation. Jackson reports that in western and southern cities, the percentage of Hispanics has more effect on police size than does the percentage of blacks; that both the percentage of Hispanics and the percentage of blacks have stronger effects in large than in small cities; and that the curvilinear effect of the percentage of non-whites (decreasing slope after 40 percent) is also more evident in large than in small cities. She argues that the threat associated with the presence of minorities has decreased since the 1960s—which was marked by racial disorder—and is ameliorated by informal social control in small cities.

In chapter 5 of this book, she synthesizes the last two decades of research on the effect of minority group size and concentration on police size (expenditures for salaries and capital goods, and officers per capita) and examines how the strength and form of the effect is contingent on social context.

Liska and Chamlin (1984) and Liska et al. (1985) extend this work on police size to the study of actual crime control activities, such as arrests. Clearly, the arrest rate of nonwhites is higher than that of whites. However, contrary to the threat hypothesis (that an increase in the proportion of nonwhites increases people's sense of threat and thus the arrest rate of nonwhites), the findings show that an increase in the percentage of nonwhites decreases the arrest rate of nonwhites. Liska and Chamlin argue that the latter occurs because as the percentage of nonwhites increases, the victims of nonwhite offenders also tend to be nonwhite. Nonwhite victims may be less able to define their misfortunes and victimizations as crimes deserving of police attention; crimes between nonwhites may be treated more as personal than as legal problems by police. Hence, not only may nonwhites be linked with the threat of crime, they may also find authorities insensitive to their legitimate needs for protection from crime. In chapter 6 of this book, Chamlin and Liska extend this analysis to arrest rates of the 1980s.

Prison. Conflict theorists explain the development of prisons during the seventeenth, eighteenth, and nineteenth centuries as a strategy of authorities to control the urban masses of immigrants and migrants and to manage the labor supply. A capitalistic system needs a ready supply of laborers who respect private property. Prison segregates those who do not respect property rights from the ranks of labor (a divide-and-conquer strategy) and instills moral (Ignatieff 1978) and work (Foucault 1978) discipline in the masses. Rusche and Kirchheimer (1939) argue that during times of economic depression prisons absorb the unemployed and during times of prosperity they provide a ready supply of labor. Developing this theme, contemporary conflict theorists emphasize the threat that unemployment poses to the social relationships of production.

While much debate has ensued over the explanation of this hypothesized relationship between unemployment and imprisonment, only a few studies have systematically examined it. Most of these, using time series analysis, yield consistent results but suffer from methodological problems which leave the results inconclusive. For example, Yeager (1979) studies the relationship in the United States from 1952 to 1974; Greenberg (1977) studies it in Canada from 1950 to 1972; and Box and Hale (1982) study it in England and Wales from 1949 to 1979. All report a positive relationship between unemployment and imprisonment rates, controlling for crime rates. These studies share one major limitation: the time series from World War II to the mid-1970s (about twenty-five to thirty years) is a relatively short period in which to examine unemployment cycles and covers a peculiar period of time characterized by neither a major war nor an economic depression. Indeed, Jankovic (1977), using a series in the United States from 1929 to 1974, reports that the positive relationship between unemployment and imprisonment rates does not hold during the depression and war years. His analysis highlights the fact that prisons can only absorb a small proportion of the population. In "normal" times they can absorb a significant portion of the unemployed, but when the rate of unemployment reaches epidemic proportions, such as during a depression, they can absorb only an insignificant proportion of them. Studying a long time series from 1851 to 1970 including four depressions, Berk et al. (1982) observe a positive relationship between depressions and the growth in imprisonment rates; because they do not control for the crime rate, however, the underlying causal process remains unclear.

Additionally, it is not at all clear how unemployment explains the substantial growth in the rate of imprisonment in the United States since the early 1970s, during which time the unemployment rate has varied. Using a cross section of states and controlling for crime rates, Galster and Scaturo (1985) find little empirical support for a positive effect of unemployment on the imprisonment rate for any year from 1976 to 1981.

To resolve some of these inconsistencies, Inverarity and McCarthy (1988) distinguish the social meaning of unemployment between competitive and monopoly economies and between competitive and monopoly sectors of mixed economies. They argue that with the development of competitive capitalism a new system of control was needed to maintain competitive wages and incentives to work and to control those who perform no useful role during downturns of the business cycle. The prison system plays that role. With the development of monopoly capitalism the costs of production can be passed on to the consumer; therefore, higher wages can provide an incentive to work and welfare can be used to ease the pains of downturns in the business cycle. The prison system is less important for social control. Contemporary economic systems include some sectors that are predominantly competitive and some that are predominantly monopolistic. Inverarity and McCarthy report that unemployment has a stronger effect on imprisonment in the competitive than the monopolistic sectors.

In chapter 7 of this book, Inverarity develops the theoretical underpinnings of the unemployment—imprisonment hyposthesis. He grounds the hypothesis in both action and structural theories; he examines the social meaning of unemployment in plantation economies, competitive capitalism, and monopoly capitalism; and he examines the link between economic systems and forms of social control.

Beneficent Constraints

Mental Asylums. To a large extent, the emergence of mental asylums in the West has been interpreted within the threat hypothesis. Foucault (1965) argues that the asylum was yet another mechanism of controlling the urban masses of seventeenth-century Europe. Davis and Anderson (1983) report, for example, that during the seventeenth century one French asylum confined between five thousand to six thousand persons, including orphans, beggars, the unemployed, indigents, the idle, vagabonds, petty criminals, and the mad. Rothman (1971) and Davis and Anderson (1983) argue that during the nineteenth century mental asylums also emerged in the United States to control the newly arrived urban immigrants. These historical studies equate the emergence of the asylum with the emergence of both the urban police and the prison. They are responses by authorities to the threat of urban disorder that is associated with the large-scale processes of urbanization, industrialization, and capitalism. However, other than hypothesizing that asylums and prisons emerged during similar times in response to similar social conditions, these studies do not explore how these two control bureaucracies function together to control threatening populations and acts. Are they independent, competing, or functional alternatives?

In the 1950s and 1960s considerable debate occurred on the medicalization of social problems, particularly crime. Conrad and Schneider (1980) argue that during the first half of the twentieth century psychiatrists medicalized social problems. They located the cause of many social problems, such as crime, in the psychological malfunctioning of people, and they argued that the solution of these problems lies in the psychiatric treatment of these people by medical specialists in treatment centers. Consequently, during the twentieth century the population of mental asylums in the United States significantly increased to about one-half million by the mid-1950s (Morrissey et al. 1982); as a point of comparison, the prison population in the United States was less than two hundred thousand for the same time period (Bureau of Justice Statistics).

By the mid-1960s this trend started to reverse. First, as a consequence of the pharmacological revolution, many troublesome people could be controlled by drugs without commitment; secondly, because of the costs associated with large-scale asylums, the federal and state governments encouraged the emergence of local community-based mental health centers; and, third, the civil rights movement through a series of court cases tightened the standards and procedures for admission to asylums. Since that time the asylum population has significantly decreased, while the prison population has significantly increased, so that by the late 1970s the asylum population was down to one hundred and fifty thousand and the prison population was up to three hundred thousand. These trend reversals in asylum and prison populations stimulate questions of the extent to which prisons and asylums are functionally alternative bureaucracies for controlling threatening populations and acts.

The recent deinstitutionalization of asylums has provided opportunities for crucial tests of the functional-alternative hypothesis. Because of deinstitutionalization, many asylums are no longer operating at full capacity, thereby providing space for the overflows of other control bureaucracies, such as prisons (Melick et al. 1979). Various researchers (Steadman 1979; Arvanites 1988) examine how threatening populations that in the past might have been admitted directly into asylums are now first processed into the criminal system; then, some of them remain in local jails and others through various mechanisms, such as "Incompetent to Stand Trial" and "Not Guilty by Reason of Insanity," are channelized into asylums. In effect, the United States may have moved from the medicalization of crime and the

criminal to the criminalization of mental illness and the mentally ill.
    In chapter 8 of this book, Arvanites reviews this literature, focusing on the mechanisms by which the recent deinstitutionalization of the mental health system is driving the recent expansion of the criminal justice system.

    Welfare. Welfare is frequently conceptualized within conflict theory as a form of social control. Piven and Cloward (1971) have stimulated considerable controversy by arguing that the welfare expansion in the United States during the middle and late 1960s was a response to the urban riots during that period—an attempt to pacify an economically deprived and threatening population.
    Various studies provide some support for this thesis. In what is perhaps the first major systematic study, Isaac and Kelly (1981) report that no relationship between riots and welfare exists at the city level, but that a strong relationship exists at the national level from 1947 to 1974. They argue that the political processes affecting welfare policy operate at the national level; it is federal policy that drives the welfare system. Jennings (1983) arrives at a similar conclusion, although he respecifies Isaac and Kelly's model and changes the measures of some of the variables. Schram and Turbett (1983) report that riots affect welfare policy in two stages. Riots during the mid-1960s prodded the federal government to liberalize welfare policies generally; these policies were then most likely to be implemented in the late 1960s and early 1970s by those states that experienced the most rioting. Hicks and Swank (1983) argue that because the media gives local riots national visibility, their effects are national in scope and that riots are not the only sources of threat to which the welfare system responds. Using a national time series, they report that the national welfare caseload is affected by local threats, including local riots, crime rates, and the use of legal services. This series of studies by Isaac and Kelly (1981), Jennings (1983), Schram and Turbett (1983), and Hicks and Swank (1983) suggests that local riots have national effects.
    In chapter 9 of this book, Chamlin reviews the research on welfare as a response to both social threat and social need and capacity (developmental hypothesis) and challenges the above conclusion. He argues that the original Pivan-Cloward thesis focuses on the welfare expansion from the 1960s to the 1970s, whereas most research examines cross-sectional levels of state or city welfare. The causes of the recent expansion may be significantly different than the causes of cross-sectional variation. Chamlin examines the extent to which

changes in local caseloads from 1960 to 1970 are sensitive to changes in both local social threat and social need.

Focus of the Book

In sum, the conflict theory of deviance and crime control consists of a set of loosely interrelated and ideologically charged ideas. Major concepts such as interest and power are not clearly defined independent of what they are supposed to explain; thus, the definitions frequently yield tautological propositions. That is, norm and law formulation and enforcement, thought to be explained by ruling-class interests, are frequently used to infer those interests in concrete historical cases (Quinney 1977; Beirne 1979). Consequently, conflict theory is only loosely linked to research in various substantive areas, and conflict research on social control consists of a loosely interrelated set of studies, more linked to various substantive "sociology of" areas, such as race relations, criminology, stratification, and penology, than to each other. Conceptual integration across these substantive areas and a tightening of theoretical and epistemic connections are clearly needed.

This book, then, focuses on social control from the conflict perspective, particularly on the threat hypothesis of the perspective (see figure 1.1D). The goal is threefold: one, to use the threat hypothesis to organize and interrelate seemingly diverse literatures on social control; two, to use new data to resolve puzzles and crucial issues in these literatures; and, three, to use these literatures to develop and expand the threat hypothesis.

As a working strategy toward these goals, this book categorizes social control patterns along a dimension ranging from the stick (deadly force) to the carrot (beneficent controls). It categorizes the macrocauses of threat into actions (crime and riots) and people (the proportion of nonwhites and the unemployed, and the degree of racial segregation and income inequality); and it emphasizes the central role of "threat" in conceptually organizing and integrating the above macroconditions and in linking them to various forms of social control (see figure 1.1D).

Explication of the causal structure underlying the threat hypothesis of conflict theory serves two important functions. First, tightening theoretical linkages between various and diverse research literatures (e.g., welfare, arrests, and lynching) enlarges the empirical scope of the theory to include various forms of control and stimulates researchers to examine the interrelationships among these forms. A few researchers have hypothesized that some forms of deviance and crime control are functionally equivalent; that is, they perform similar control functions, and, therefore, as one form increases the others decrease. Recently, the functional-equivalence hypothesis has been examined in regard to legal executions and lynchings (Phillips 1987; and Beck et al. 1989), the criminal justice and welfare systems (Chamlin 1987), the criminal justice and mental health systems (Steadman et al. 1984; Arvanites 1988), and the criminal justice, welfare, and mental health systems (Inverarity and Grattet 1987). Also, the perception of threat by authorities may not necessarily lead to all forms of control; some forms require economic resources. Both imprisonment and welfare cost money—a special instance of the classic "guns and butter" issue. To the extent that social units expend their economic resources for imprisonment, they may not be able to afford welfare. Additionally, some types of threat may lead to specific forms of control. Some research (Kluegel and Smith 1981) suggests that authorities and the public believe that some categories of the poor (nonwhites) are less deserving of financial support than are others (whites)—the respectable poor. Hence, an increase in the proportion of nonwhite poor may lead to more forceful forms of control (such as arrests) rather than to more beneficent forms (such as welfare).

Second, tightening epistemic and theoretical linkages clarifies the implications of research for theory. Because of loose linkages, social control research has generally not had much feedback on either the threat hypothesis or conflict theory. After two decades of research, the threat hypothesis is not much different than originally formulated in the late 1960s. That is, the theory has not grown and developed as a result of this research; research has been used not to test and develop the hypothesis, but to illustrate it.

The book is organized into three main sections: The section on fatal control includes a chapter on police homicides of citizens and a chapter on lynchings. The section on coercive control includes a chapter on citizen reporting of crimes, a chapter on police size, a chapter on arrest rates, and a chapter on prison admission rates. The final section on beneficent controls includes a chapter on mental asylums and a chapter on welfare. Each of the chapters explicates the threat hypothesis as it applies to a specific form of social control and evaluates it through both a review of the relevant literature and an analysis of new data. The concluding chapter discusses the implications of this body of work for the threat hypothesis, specifically, and for the conflict theory of social control, generally.

Part I

Fatal Controls

Toward a Threat Model of Southern Black Lynchings

Stewart E. Tolnay and E. M. Beck

When Lillian Smith (1944) alluded to "strange fruit" in the title of her novel, she was referring to the image of a lynch victim dangling at the end of a rope. Southern states produced a bountiful harvest of such fruit after the Civil War. In the Deep South, alone, roughly nineteen hundred blacks were lynched between 1882 and 1930. During this period, the intensity of lynching ebbed and flowed, reaching its zenith in the 1890s, surging again in the 1920s, and fading significantly after 1930. Moreover, lynchings exhibited considerable unevenness in their geographic distribution within the Deep South. Most were concentrated in a swath running across South Carolina, Georgia, Alabana, and Mississipi—corresponding closely with the Black Belt of those states.

Many attempts have been made to explain the temporal and geographic distributions of lynchings during this violent era of southern history (e.g., Beck and Tolnay 1990; Beck et al. 1989; Corzine et al. 1983, 1988; Hovland and Sears 1940; Inverarity 1976; Mintz 1946; Reed 1972; Tolnay and Beck 1990; Tolnay et al. 1989a; Young 1927-28). However, this literature has failed to produce a coherent and cohesive set of propositions that inform us about the most important social forces responsible for the lynching phenomenon. We still know excruciatingly little about who lynched, why they lynched, or why they stopped lynching. Ayres (1984:238) has summed up well the extent of our ignorance about lynching: "The triggers of lynching, for all the attention devoted to it by contemporaries, sociologists, and historians, are still not known." Still, it may be possible to identify a general, common thread that runs through the commentary of contemporary observers of the lynching era, and subsequent inquiries by social scientists. This "thread" represents the rather broad consensus that the lynching of southern blacks was largely a response by some members of the white community to *perceived threats* from the black population. The nature of these threats is diverse, ranging from the fear of black criminals to the fear of black voters. As we reach a better understanding of these perceived threats we should also move closer to a better understanding of lynching.

In many respects, southern whites during this era considered themselves to be a population under siege. Before the Civil War, the large black population was rigidly controlled by the institution of slavery. Extraordinary authority was vested in slave owners, and was buttressed by the political and legal machinery of the Old South. With Emancipation came a significant challenge to white southerners. Suddenly, nearly four million southern blacks were transformed from personal property to potential *competitors*. As rivals, they threatened the political and economic hegemony enjoyed by whites. And, if successful, blacks threatened the superior status position which whites took for granted as members of the dominating caste. To counteract these potential threats, southern white society required measures to "control" the black population—measures which could be as effective as slavery had been. "Jim Crow" legislation, disenfranchisement, judicial discrimination, debt peonage, and violent intimidation were included in the repertory of social control techniques implemented by white southerners. It is within this context that lynching can be viewed as an instrument of social control over a "threatening" southern black population.

In this chapter we: 1) explore alternative "threat explanations" for black lynchings; 2) examine evidence supporting them; 3) assess their probable utility, and 4) suggest some directions for future tests of the race-threat model of black lynching. To facilitate this endeavor, we implicitly assume lynching to be a social control technique exercised by macro level social units, in response to the socioeconomic conditions prevailing within those units. We are less concerned with the motives of *individual* lynchers or lynch mobs, or with the "psychology" of lynching. We shall also focus on lynchings within Deep South states, since some evidence suggests different lynching histories for the Deep and Border South (e.g., Beck et al. 1989; Corzine et al. 1983; Reed 1972). Finally, our attention is confined to the lynching of *blacks*, since it is the black population which represented a potential threat to white southerners.

Black Lynchings as Social (Not Crime) Control

Judging from the reporting of lynchings in southern newspapers, and the frequent defenses of lynching advanced by southern politicians and editorial writers, it was an unfortunate (though understandable) response from a white community besieged by a criminal black population. Through the mythology of black retrogression, black males were widely portrayed as sexually driven "brutes" with a special affinity for white women (Williamson 1984). At the same time, the dominance and popularity of theories of scientific racism legitimized the image of blacks as an inherently defective race, prone to violence and criminal activity (e.g., Hoffman 1896; Smith 1905). According to the popular conception of southern lynchings, then, whites lynched to defend themselves against victimization from black criminals. Lynching served two important functions in white society. First, it assured the swift punishment of offenders who might otherwise be acquitted or treated leniently by a court system believed to be slow and ineffective. Second, it sent a message to the larger black community which communicated the potential cost for criminal activity.

If one accepts the "popular justice" arguments used by southern whites to explain and justify lynching, then a better understanding of the lynching phenomenon should be sought among alternative causes of *black criminality*. In fact, however, there are aspects of the southern lynching record which suggest that the true explanations for lynching are probably far more complex and insidious than the "popular justice" myth espoused by the southern white community. First, black criminals were not treated leniently by the southern criminal justice system. Rather, they were exposed to the same discriminatory treatment in the courts as in other spheres of southern society. For example, statistics on legal executions in the South clearly indicate that blacks were especially vulnerable to the death penalty (Tolnay et al. 1989b). Raper (1933) even referred to the execution of blacks as "legal lynchings"—a sentiment echoed by President Truman's Committee on Civil Rights (Shapiro 1988:368). Second, many lynch victims were taken from police custody by mobs, often after conviction. So, clearly, whites lynched even after the "wheels of justice" had begun to grind. Third, many victims were lynched for extremely trivial offenses, such as speaking disrespectfully to a white person, or for no reason at all. It is difficult to consider such victims as serious criminal threats to the "law abiding" white community. Finally, in many cases the lynching ritual included torture and mutilation that far exceeded the punishment required for black law violators.

By raising these points we are not denying that *some* lynchings could have been episodes of popular justice in reaction to crimes committed by blacks. Rather, they suggest that the white community was responding to social forces that transcended the threat of criminal victimization by the black population. Indeed, there were a number of reasons for the white community also to be threatened by the non criminal activity of southern blacks. In many respects, blacks threatened whites simply by actively participating in southern life, and by pursuing a share of society's scarce resources: property, power, and status. Such pursuit meant that competition with whites for the same scarce social resources was inevitable. Therefore, the "threat perspective" of black lynchings, as we will examine it in this chapter, considers lynching to have been a social control measure in the larger, sociological sense, rather than in the narrower, criminological sense.

Theoretical Bases for the Threat Perspective of Lynching

Threat interpretations of black lynching emanate from the broader family of "conflict" theories of social control (see e.g., Phillips 1986; Quinney 1977; Turk 1969). These theories begin with the premise that coexistent minority and majority groups differ significantly in the power and resources they command in society. The majority group enjoys greater access to power and resources, and takes whatever steps are necessary to perpetuate its advantage over the minority group. When the perceived threat from the minority group increases, the intensity of the majority group's repression of the minority will also increase. A commonly used indicator of the threat presented by a minority group is its size in relation to the dominant group's population. Thus, conflict theories of social control predict a *positive* association between the relative size of the minority population, and repressive measures by the majority to protect its privileged social position. A conflict perspective has been used to examine a wide variety of social control techniques, including size of the police force, certainty of arrest, and the use of deadly force by the police.

Blalock (1967) maintains that there are three dimensions of majority privilege that are jeopardized by a threatening minority group: economic, political, and status. Although he chooses not to deal with the status dimension, he argues that political threats and economic competition should produce somewhat different relationships between minority concentration and discriminatory efforts by the majority group. In both cases, the minority group's population concentration should be *positively* related with the majority group's discriminatory efforts, as conflict theory argues. However, when majority-minority competition is primarily economic in nature, the relationship should become weaker as minority concentration increases. When competition is primarily political, Blalock expects the relationship to intensify at higher concentrations of a minority population.

Blalock's "Power Threat" and "Economic Competition" hypotheses provide a valuable direction in our search for the underlying causes of discriminatory behavior by the majority. However, tests of the conflict orientation of social control that focus too heavily on the relative size of the minority population are in danger of overlooking the importance of heterogeneity within the majority group itself. Generally, the majority population will not be monolithic; rather, it will be stratified along class lines. The different classes may have divergent interests in the nature of majority-minority relations—as well as in the repressive social control techniques used against the minority. Specifically, it is possible for a large minority population to be threatening to the interests of one class in the majority hierarchy, but beneficial for another class.

Two variants of the conflict perspective recognize the possibility of divergent class interests in the use of violent persecution as social control of southern blacks. According to the more orthodox Marxist orientation, repression of the black minority was primarily in the interest of the white elite of merchants and planters (Bloom 1987). The white power structure benefited from the presence of a large, subservient, cheap labor force. The character of the southern social structure after Emancipation was strongly influenced by the white elite to assure that its political and economic interests were served. A web of legal and social arrangements effectively restricted the mobility of black laborers, and severely limited their ability to redress grievances against white employers (Mandle 1978). And, when necessary, violent tactics such as lynching were used by the white elite to supplement these arrangements (White [1929] 1969:103). Moreover, according to the orthodox Marxist argument, a virulent racist atmosphere and the violence it spawned served the interests of the white elite in another way as well. Intense antagonisms between poor whites and blacks precluded a coalition of laborers that might otherwise have risen in opposition to powerful whites and threatened their hegemony in southern society.

Bonacich's (1972, 1975) Split Labor Market Theory of racial antagonism paints a somewhat different picture, while maintaining a conflict orientation. According to Bonacich, the postwar South was composed of three primary classes: white planters and employers, higher-priced white laborers, and cheaper black laborers. The primary concern for white planters and employers was to hire workers as cheaply as possible to guarantee larger profits. The goal of white workers was to extract the highest wage possible for their labor. A bountiful supply of cheaper black laborers served the interests of the white elite, but frustrated the efforts of white labor. As long as the supply of workers was adequate, white employers had little incentive to intimidate black laborers. On the other hand, the economic competition between white and black labor created racial tensions which led to efforts by white laborers to restrict economic competition from blacks. Although Bonacich does not stress racial violence by white laborers as a strategy for achieving their objectives, it is a logical implication of her theory.

A threat perspective of southern lynchings must, inevitably, identify some dimension(s) of conflict between whites and blacks over their relative access to society's scarce resources. In short, whites attacked when they believed that blacks were threatening their privileged access to those resources. However, the precise nature of this conflict, and its manifestation in racial violence, must be considered within the context of the southern social structure. That society was doubly stratified by caste and class. As a result, the lines of social conflict ran in two, largely orthogonal, directions. The caste line tended to unite all whites against all blacks, while class divisions within the white community separated the economic interests of poor and well-to-do whites. An ever-present danger for the white elite was the evaporation of the caste line, which would increase the likelihood of a coalition between white and black labor. At the same time, however, lower-class whites also had a vested interest in the integrity of the caste line, since it assured them a basis for their claim of superiority over blacks. As we examine more closely the ways in which the black population "threatened" southern whites, it is useful to keep in mind the importance of the class issues identified by the traditional Marxist and Split Labor Market theories, *and* the importance of the caste system that divided the South racially.

How Southern Blacks "Threatened" Southern Whites

Southern whites were fond of commending local blacks for "knowing their place" and for not being "uppity." These compliments can be translated roughly to mean that local blacks did not expect more from southern society than southern whites were willing to give. Insolent blacks who did not "know" their place aspired to a larger piece of the southern pie, and bridled at the obstacles constructed by whites. Such blacks were threatening as they pursued greater access to political power, economic success, and enhanced social status. We shall treat these as three separate sources of competition between white and black southerners, though, of course, they were not completely independent.

Lynching and political competition. During Reconstruction, the southern political scene was radically transformed by the increased participation and representation among blacks (Kousser 1974; Woodward 1966). In some areas, emancipated slaves comprised an actual numerical majority of the population, and, therefore, represented a significant political challenge to the southern political order. For the first time in southern history, blacks were elected to positions at all levels of government. Not only did this threaten to weaken the grip on southern politics traditionally enjoyed by the white elite, but it also insulted poor whites who themselves had been marginal to the southern political process (Kousser 1974).

Southern whites eventually responded to this political threat by designing and implementing a variety of restrictive voting statutes that effectively disenfranchised the black population by the early 1900s (Kousser 1974; Woodward 1966). Until disenfranchised, however, black voters were occasionally the "wild card" of southern politics. Where the black vote could not be purchased, or neutralized through fraud, whites sometimes resorted to violent intimidation. There can be little doubt that murder and lynching were occasionally employed to reduce the political threat from the black population. For example, political competition was an underlying cause of the pre-election riot in Wilmington, North Carolina in 1898, as evidenced by the instructions of the soon-to-be mayor to white voters (Shapiro 1988:74), "Go to the polls tomorrow and if you find the negro out voting, tell him to leave the polls, and if he refuses kill him; shoot him down in his tracks. We shall win tomorrow if we have to do it with guns." But, is there enough evidence to conclude that political competition was one of the most powerful social forces behind the broader bloody history of black lynchings after Emancipation, as some have hypothesized?

While few contemporary observers of the lynching era placed great emphasis on black political competition, it has received more intensive scrutiny from modern researchers than any other possible underlying cause of black lynchings. Most investigators have attempted to test Blalock's (1967) hypothesis that political competition between majority and minority groups should produce a *positive* association between minority population concentration and discrimination, with an increasingly strong relationship as percent minority increases. Reed (1972) found support for Blalock's Power Threat hypothesis within Mississippi counties; and Corzine et al. (1983) presented more general support for the entire Deep South (especially before disenfranchisement). In both cases, lynching increased steadily in frequency with percent black, but rose very sharply in counties with over eighty percent black population. However, Tolnay et al. (1989a) subsequently cast serious doubt on the evidence offered by Reed and Corzine et al. After a variety of conceptual and methodological errors were corrected, neither Reed's nor Corzine et al.'s findings could be replicated. Considering the problems associated with prior tests of the "political threat" model of lynchings, however, both hypotheses must be considered viable—though still unsupported—explanations of southern black lynchings.

In fact, there is some reason to believe that political competition between southern whites and blacks may have played only a relatively minor role in black lynchings after the Reconstruction period. It is true that the large black population in southern states represented a *potentially* serious numerical threat to the politically dominant white population after Emancipation. However, it is also the case that southern whites were quite effective at quickly neutralizing black political participation—even before the widespread adoption of restrictive voting statutes. For instance, Kousser (1974) has shown that black participation in presidential elections, even before disenfranchisement, was pitifully low. Such evidence has led Williamson (1984:229) to conclude that, "After Reconstruction black voting never threatened white supremacy in the South as a whole, nor was it ever an active threat in a given state for very long. The threat of black voting was spotty and it was sporadic. When it arose, white politicians dealt with it locally and relatively quickly." It is understandable, then, that Ayres (1984:239) minimizes the political dimension to black lynchings, and observes, "Very few observers, whatever their race, region, or politics, pointed to political coercion as the direct cause of lynching."

In sum, it is premature to accept *or* to reject a political threat model of black lynchings. At certain times, and in specific areas, blacks were able to exert political power that threatened the political hegemony of the southern white elite. And, in those instances, whites sometimes resorted to violence to intimidate black voters. We still do not know, however, whether those were relatively isolated events, or were repeated frequently enough to represent a significant part of the lynching story.

Lynching and economic competition. The economic position of many rural whites deteriorated significantly during the 1890s and early in the twentieth century. The image of the southern white yeoman farmer quickly gave way to an image of the southern white share-cropper shackled by the crop lien system. For example, between 1900 and 1930 the number of white tenant farmers in the South increased by sixty-one percent, while blacks experienced only a twenty-seven percent increase (U.S. Bureau of Census 1975:465). As a result, despite their membership in the superior caste, more rural whites began to sink to the same disadvantaged economic position as blacks. And, for the first time, sizeable numbers of southern white farmers found themselves in direct economic competition with southern black farmers.

To whites on the brink of economic oblivion, blacks scraping a living from the same exhausted soil were all too obvious competitors for an already shrunken economic "pie." Black tenants farmed land that otherwise might have been tilled by whites. Black owners occupied farms that could have been purchased by whites, after they mustered the necessary resources. And black laborers took jobs that might have gone to whites, while working for wages *below* that expected by whites. It is not difficult to imagine how marginal rural whites could have felt economically threatened by local blacks.

The declining economic fortunes of many rural whites, along with modest progress by some rural blacks, created a situation ripe for confrontation. As a response to economic stress and black competition, lynching could have served two different kinds of purposes for poor whites. First, lynching of blacks may have been a simple aggressive response to frustration as Hovland and Sears (1940) claimed. That is, blacks served as a convenient, and vulnerable, target against which whites could express their anger and frustration created by blocked economic ambitions. Or, second, the lynching of blacks could have served a more *instrumental* purpose to improve the economic position of whites *vis-à-vis* blacks.

Two contemporary observers of the lynching era believed that competition between white and black labor did result in black lynchings. Arthur Raper (1933:31) claimed that mob violence against blacks was sometimes part of "organized efforts of the whites to displace

Negro laborers with unemployed whites." Walter White ([1929] 1969: 11-12) also saw an important economic motive to black lynchings, and observed "the majority of Southern whites in the rural South were and are sinking into an economic morass which makes them the prey of Klan organizers, anti-evolution mountebanks, mob hysteria, and every manner of charlatanry."

The discussion of economic motives for black lynchings, thus far, has emphasized competition between white and black laborers. Put crudely, poor whites lynched poor blacks because they represented an economic threat. This perspective identifies the white lower class as the primary instigators, and beneficiaries, of black lynching (consistent with Bonacich 1972). Such an emphasis overlooks the possibility that the white elite also had economic motives for lynching blacks. As mentioned above, white planters and employers likely benefited from the presence of black workers who were cheaper than white labor. Contrary to the perspective of white labor, therefore, black laborers represented an opportunity for larger profits to white employers—not a threat to econo..iic security. So, how could the white elite benefit economically from mob violence against blacks?

As long as white and black workers remained rigidly divided by the caste line, white planters and employers could use the presence of black labor to maximize profits and to hold down the wages of whites. A perennial threat to the white elite, however, was the potential for the caste line to weaken, resulting in the formation of an opposition coalition of white and black labor, as was threatened during the early stages of the Populist movement. Therefore, it was in the interest of the white elite to guarantee the integrity of the southern caste system —especially its ability to preclude the development of common interests between whites and blacks.

Some writers have emphasized the motives of the white elite in their interpretations of black lynchings. For example, Bloom (1987) argues that racism and terror primarily served the interests of the southern white elite by driving a wedge between black and white workers. He writes (1987:5), "For most of the second half of the nineteenth century, black and white labor were not primarily in competition with each other. They existed mainly in different geographical locations...the upper class created the atmosphere that promoted attacks on blacks and often actually carried out lynching and other forms of terror." Shapiro (1988:219) echoes this sentiment when he notes, "When those committed to racial subordination saw the possibility of blacks and whites coming together for common purposes, their response most often was to reach for the gun and rope." Others (e.g., White [1929] 1969) focused less on the white elite's efforts to prevent a coalition of white and black labor, and stressed instead the use of violence to maintain order and obedience among the black work force.

Clearly, there is ample reason to believe that blacks may have been lynched because they represented an economic threat to white southerners. And, it is very likely that poor whites and the white elite alike attempted to neutralize these threats by resorting to mob violence. However, their specific motivations were obviously quite different. Unlike the case of the political threat represented by southern blacks, economic explanations of lynching have received virtually no empirical attention.[1] Once again, we must consider the economic threat model to be a potentially useful candidate for explaining black lynchings, but a model that is, as yet, untested.

Lynching and status competition. The premier indicator of "status" within southern society during the late nineteenth and early twentieth centuries was one's race. Southern culture was transfixed with the notion of race supremacy, and virtually all other aspects of southern society must be considered with this in mind. In principle, all whites were superior to all blacks, and the rigidity of the caste line separating the races assured even the poorest of whites this one taste of superiority. For many white southerners, the sanctity of the caste line that perpetuated this ubiquitous distinction was critically important for it guaranteed that at least *somebody* in southern society occupied a *lower* social position. Anything that threatened the integrity of the caste line was certain to be vigorously, and possibly violently, opposed.

One factor contributing to the white southerner's obsession with the caste boundary was the emergence during the latter part of the nineteenth century of scientific theories which purported to prove the inferiority of the black race. Natural and physical scientists amassed evidence of racial differences in cranial capacity, anatomy, and behavioral characteristics to document the innate inferiority of blacks and the superiority of whites (e.g., Hoffman 1896). This "scientific" evidence established a legitimate basis for the long-standing conventional wisdom that viewed blacks as an inferior race. Eventually, this scientific racism metastasized to the popular media where it was greeted with enthusiasm by the white public (Newby 1965).

Scientific racism also raised the white southerner's consciousness of another potential threat from the black population—that interracial reproduction could contaminate the superior white gene pool. Racial amalgamation was suddenly viewed in a new light, and became an even more terrifying prospect for southern whites. It is small exaggeration to describe the southern whites' preoccupation with miscegenation and racial amalgamation as a regional paranoia. Virtually every aspect of social life, when it concerned blacks, was ultimately considered in relation to its potential to promote sexual contact between the races. This concern is expressed very well by William Benjamin Smith (1905:7–8) in *The Color Line: A Brief in Behalf of the Unborn*, when he warns, "If we sit with Negroes at our tables, if we entertain them as our guests and social equals, if we disregard the colour line in all other relations, is it possible to maintain it fixedly in the sexual relation, in the marriage of our sons and daughters, in the propagation of our species?"

While there was near unanimity among whites that the caste line must be maintained at virtually any cost, there is reason to believe that this concern was particularly salient to lower-class whites. All classes could share in the fear that racial amalgamation could biologically contaminate the superior race, but the elevated status guaranteed to whites by the caste boundary was particularly critical for the lower class. As we have noted above, there was a large and growing constituency of poor whites in the South that occupied an economic niche very similar to that occupied by most blacks. This similarity created a dissonance for the poor whites who could see little difference between themselves and blacks in terms of their basic standards of living at the same time that their caste membership told them they were socially, morally, biologically, and intellectually superior. Without a clear economic claim to superiority, the caste division became even more important as a source of status differentiation.

Did whites lynch blacks to maintain a sharp caste boundary between the races, in response to status threats from the black population? Certainly, many blacks were lynched for relatively trivial reasons that indicate an effort by southern whites to etch the caste boundary more indelibly in the minds of the black population. Lynchings for such offenses as "speaking disrespectfully to whites," "failure to give way to a sidewalk," or "acting like a white man," are suggestive of such a purpose. Also, many lynchings involved hideous forms of torture and mutilation that served as reminders that the white caste was free to exercise unencumbered control over the black population (see for example, Ginzburg 1988; NAACP [1919] 1969). Lynchings were frequently followed by public exhibition of the victim's body (often after mutilation) with the clear purpose of reminding the black population of their subservient "place" in the southern social hierarchy and the consequences if they forgot. These aspects of the lynching record are strongly suggestive of white response to a black population that threatened their status advantage in southern society.

Once more, little effort has been expended to examine the importance of caste maintenance as a motivation for black lynchings. Although not by specific design, Inverarity's (1976) research on the relationship between "boundary crises" and the use of lynching as "repressive justice" touches a theme closely related to the status version of the race-threat framework. According to Inverarity, the Populist movement in Louisiana in the 1890s created a social disruption that led to lynchings in an effort to help restore solidarity to the southern white community via the very visible punishment of a common enemy, black Louisianians. However, Inverarity's work has been severely criticized (Bagozzi 1977; Pope and Ragin 1977; Wasserman 1977), indicating the need for additional work on this issue.

Testing the status threat hypothesis may prove especially problematic since it will be difficult to separate the unique effects of status threats from those of economic and political threats. For instance, political and economic competition from the black population are hypothesized to increase the use of lynching as social control; but we would also expect the status of southern whites (especially lower-class whites) to be most seriously threatened where political and economic competition is keenest.

Alternative Social Control Measures

As the above discussion indicates, the basic assumption of the threat model of black lynchings is that whites lynched to counteract some type of competition from the black population. However, there was a variety of other social control techniques available to the dominant caste that could have achieved the same objective as mob violence. To the extent that those alternative methods of social control were effective, then, we would expect lynching to have been less common. In fact, it is possible that lethal sanctioning was a last resort to which southern whites turned when the other, less drastic techniques proved ineffective at eliminating the political, economic, and status threats they perceived from southern blacks.

We have already alluded to the effectiveness of disenfranchisement as a strategy for neutralizing political competition from the black population. By 1910, virtually every southern state had instituted some type of restrictive voting statute that drastically reduced the number of registered blacks and the number of black voters. Disenfranchisement was not a subtle process. It was explicitly designed and implemented to eliminate black political influence. For instance, while campaigning in 1906 for the governorship of Georgia, Hoke Smith asserted that, "Legislation can be passed which will... not interfere with the right of any white man to vote, and get rid of ninety-five percent of the Negro voters" [quoted in Henri 1975:22]. By 1908, such legislation *was passed* in Georgia, including a literacy test, a property test, an understanding clause, and a grandfather clause (Kousser 1974:239). Little work has been done to assess the impact of disenfranchisement on black lynchings. In a recent inquiry, Beck et al. (1989) inferred a relatively strong, short-term, impact in North Carolina, but not in Georgia. This issue deserves a more exhaustive investigation, however.

White southerns also instituted an impressive repertory of techniques to retard black economic progress, and thereby reduce the economic threat. In the *Roots of Black Poverty* (1978) Jay Mandle describes very well the social barriers that were erected to reduce economic and geographic mobility among southern blacks, including obstacles to land ownership, denial of credit for investment, debt peonage, and constriction of employment opportunities outside of plantation agriculture. In addition, educational opportunities for southern blacks were deliberately restricted by inadequate investments in facilities and teachers for blacks. As late as 1930, it was the rule for southern counties to fund black schools at about one-fifth to one-tenth the level of white schools (Johnson 1941). If lynchings really were the result of economic competition between whites and blacks, then they should have occurred less frequently where economic discrimination effectively neutralized the black economic threat. Virtually no effort has been made to determine whether this expectation can be supported empirically.

Southern culture included an abundance of reminders to the black population of their inferior and subordinate social status. The intricate web of Jim Crow restrictions officially reduced the black population to second-class status by forcing them to use separate and inferior facilities for transportation, accommodations, dining, and entertainment (Woodward 1966). Southern folkways complemented these legal restrictions by informally specifying behavioral expectations for blacks. Most importantly, these prescribed extreme deference when blacks interacted with whites, and forbade any intimacy between black males and white women. If these dimensions of southern culture successfully relegated blacks to their "place," then race-based status threats would have been minimized. It is even possible that they may have significantly reduced the salience of status threats that had their roots in economic and political competition, as discussed earlier. Again, however, no effort has been made to explore this possibility.

A final set of alternative social control techniques that may have mitigated the need for lynching can be found in the extremely discriminatory system of southern criminal justice. We have already referred to the view, by some, that legal executions of southern blacks were often little more than "legal lynchings" (e.g., Raper 1933; Shapiro 1988). If this is true, then legal executions may have served the same social control function as lynchings—in response to perceived threats from the black population. Indeed, a recent analysis by Tolnay et al. (1989b) provides preliminary evidence that this may have been the case. For instance, black executions in the Deep South, before disenfranchisement, were more common in counties where economic competition from blacks was more intense. Second, black executions were more common in Deep South counties with larger concentrations of black population. After disenfranchisement, however, both of these relationships virtually disappeared. There is little evidence, however, that legal executions served as a "substitute" for lynching as a social control of southern blacks (Beck et al. 1989; Massey and Myers 1989).[2]

Clearly, southern whites exploited an impressive arsenal of social control techniques to reduce the intensity of competition from the "threatening" black population. Lynching was only one of these, albeit one of the most extreme. The relationships among these various techniques is undoubtedly extremely complex. They may have been complementary, or they may have reinforced one another. Efforts to examine empirically the validity of the "threat perspective" of southern black lynchings should consider the possibility that these alternative methods of social control obviated, or reduced, the need for lynching. Thus, where possible, they should be included in empirical models to "test" the threat perspective—a subject to which we now turn.

Modeling the Threat Perspective of Black Lynchings

It should be clear by now that relatively little quantitative work has been done to assess the usefulness of the threat perspective of black lynchings. Repeatedly, we have pointed out the need for additional work on important issues related to the threat perspective

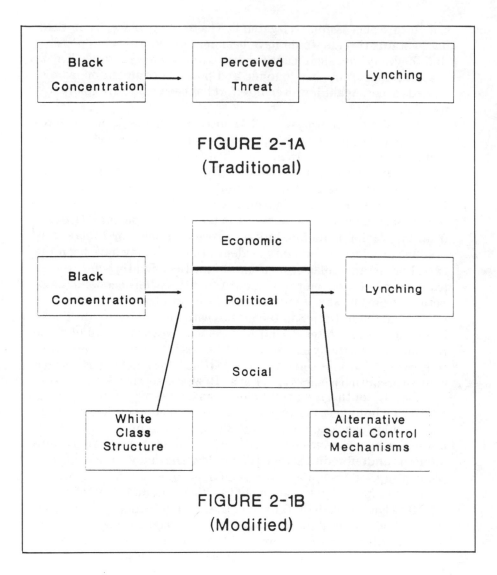

Figure 2-1 Traditional and modified conceptual models of threat perspective of black lynchings

or the inadequacy of the research that has been done. In this section, we provide a general critique of the direction previous research has taken, and offer some thoughts on what might be done differently in the future—in light of the issues raised in this chapter.

The basic conceptual model that has been used to test the threat perspective of southern black lynchings is reproduced in figure 2.1A. In brief, higher concentrations of the black population are expected to increase the frequency of black lynchings, and they are thought to do so by creating perceptions of some type of "threat" within the white population (e.g., Corzine et al. 1983; Inverarity 1976; Reed 1972; Tolnay et al. 1989a). In addition to the fact that this model has produced discrepant findings regarding the threat perspective, the model itself suffers from some rather serious problems.[3]

First, to date, the exact perceived threats operating have remained largely unmeasured. Political competition, economic competition, and status threats typically have not been included, specifically, in the empirical tests of the threat perspective.[4] Thus, inferences of the type of threat operating (if any) generally have been based on Blalock's expectations of certain types of nonlinearities in the relationship between minority concentration and discrimination (Blalock 1967). However, Blalock (1967) warned that contaminating influences may alter or even obscure the form of the relationship between minority concentration and discrimination. Later, he reiterated this concern by noting (1989:633), "It is extremely doubtful that the data on lynchings...are adequate to distinguish among these several nonlinear forms...." In sum, inferences of a significant relationship (either linear or nonlinear) between black concentration and lynching are consistent with the general expectations of the threat perspective, but virtually silent on the precise threat in operation.

Second, the conceptual model represented by figure 2.1A fails to consider the potential importance of alternative social control mechanisms discussed in the previous section. As noted earlier, lynching was not the only strategy available to southern whites for reducing black competition, and to the extent that other mechanisms were successfully exercised, lynching should have been less "necessary." Thus, for example, the presence of alternative social control measures may have determined partially whether white perceptions of a threatening black population were translated into mob violence.

Third, the model in figure 2.1A implicitly assumes that the white population is monolithic in character. That is, a proportionately large black population is believed to threaten whites, and therefore result in lynchings—*regardless of the nature of the white population.* As we pointed out earlier, the southern white population was itself stratified along class lines, and class very likely determined whether the presence of a large black population was "threatening" or "beneficial." It is naive to assume that all southern whites responded to a large black population in the same way.[5]

In recognition of these shortcomings in the model portrayed in figure 2.1A we propose the revised model in figure 2.1B as a more appropriate conceptual framework to guide future research. Only a cursory discussion is required to highlight its advantages over the prior model. Most importantly, the model in figure 2.1B specifically identifies the different types of perceived threats that might motivate the white population to lynch blacks. They are consistent with those discussed in the body of this chapter (political, economic, status), and avoid inferences based on the form of the relationship between minority concentration and lynching, alone. Secondly, the model allows for the possibility that black population concentration can mean substantially different things for different segments of the white population, thereby determining the extent to which the black population is perceived as threatening. This incorporates southern white class structure into the model, which was extremely important in shaping southern race relations. Finally, the model also recognizes that the same level of perceived threat may be translated into lynchings in one setting but not in another, depending on the success of alternative techniques of social control for reducing the threat.

While figure 2.1B is consistent with the general theoretical framework developed in this chapter, there are certainly alternative model specifications that might be entertained. We can illustrate some of these competing conceptual models by restricting our focus to "perceived threat," "alternative social control measures," and lynching. For these alternative models it is assumed that a larger concentration of black population increases perceived threat, but that this translation is shaped by class-specific interests in the white population. But, these processes are not included in the models, for ease of presentation.

Figure 2.2A presents a rather simple reformulation of figure 2.1B. In this case, both lynchings and alternative social control measures are affected *positively* by the level of perceived threat in the white population. In turn, the wider use of alternative measures of social control *reduces* the need for extreme and extralegal control, such as lynchings. Unlike the model presented in figure 2.1B, figure 2.2A suggests that alternative social control measures have an *additive* rather than *interactive* effect on black lynchings.

A somewhat different model specification is presented in figure 2.2B. Perhaps the alternative social control measures have no independent impact on lynchings. Rather, they too are responsive to the white perceptions of a race threat; but, in return, their effective implementation moderates the level of perceived threat. In contrast to figure 2.2A, this model specification implies that alternative measures

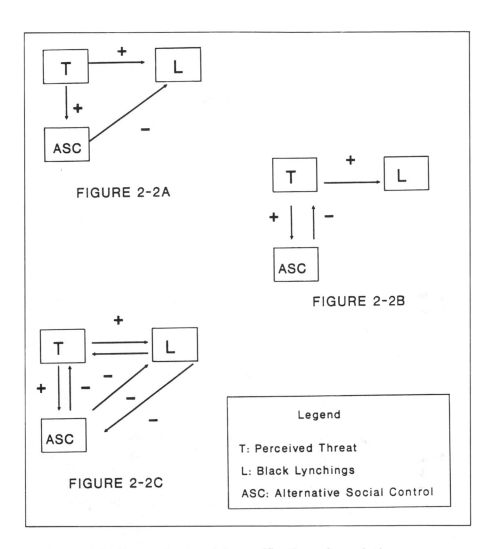

FIGURE 2-2A

FIGURE 2-2B

FIGURE 2-2C

Legend

T: Perceived Threat

L: Black Lynchings

ASC: Alternative Social Control

Figure 2-2 Alternative model specifications for relations among threat, alternative social control, and lynchings

of social control have only an *indirect* influence on lynchings, via their effect on perceived threat.

Finally, figure 2.2C includes all possible causal connections among these key variables. In addition to the linkages described in previous figures, figure 2.2C suggests a negative feedback from lynchings to perceived threat. That is, when lynchings take place, they reduce concern within the white population by demonstrating that the threatening black population can be controlled. In a similar fashion, and for much the same reason, lynchings might also have a negative, reciprocal effect on alternative social control measures.

Only through careful empirical analyses will we be able to choose among the many plausible model specifications that can be used to explain southern lynchings. However, it is extremely important that researchers realize that any empirical analysis of southern lynchings advocates some kind of conceptual or theoretical model. And, it is far preferable to have the conceptual model correspond as closely as possible to the actual dynamics of southern society during the lynching era, while also being as specific as possible.

Conclusion

A common thread running through previous treatments of lynchings is that mob violence was a reaction by southern whites to perceived threats from the black population. We have drawn from prior research, and from the historical record, to articulate more precisely what those "threats" were, how they operated, who perceived them, and when they were translated into lethal social control. This is necessary work if we hope to outline the basic contours of a race-threat model of black lynchings, as we have attempted to do in figure 2.1B.

We began this exploration by noting the lack of a coherent and cohesive set of propositions that inform us about the most important social forces contributing to the lynching phenomenon. The race-threat model is capable, we believe, of yielding such a set of propositions. We do not pretend to have enumerated those propositions in this chapter, but it is hoped that this discussion provides the necessary raw material for the more formal development of the race-threat model.

Specifying and Testing the Threat Hypothesis: Police Use of Deadly Force

Allen E. Liska and Jiang Yu

The conflict perspective assumes that law formulation and enforcement reflect the interests of the powerful. Those activities that threaten their interests are criminalized and those laws that most protect their interests are most enforced, particularly against those people who most threaten their interests. Hence, it follows from the perspective that the greater the number of acts and people that threaten the interests of the powerful, the higher the level of crime control—the threat hypothesis.

Much conflict research on crime control has studied the police as the first line of crime control authorities. Macrostudies (Jacobs 1979; Jackson and Carroll 1981; Liska et al. 1981; Greenberg et al. 1985; Jackson 1986, 1989) have examined the effect of threatening acts (crime and riots), threatening people (percentage of nonwhites and poor), and threatening distributions of people (racial segregation and income inequality) on police size and police crime control activities, such as arrests.

This chapter extends the threat hypothesis to the police use of deadly force, that is, the police homicide of citizens. While a rare activity, it is socially significant, and such incidents receive considerable attention in the mass media. During times of economic, racial, or political tension, incidents, particularly those that involve the underclass, carry considerable political and cultural meaning. They are frequently interpreted as political events, or as acts of callous discrimination; consequently, they frequently spark collective actions and disturbances, including official investigations, civil suits, mass demonstrations and protests, and even riots. Sherman (1983) cites numerous such consequences in case studies of New York, Miami, and Kansas City.

Although police homicide is generally not thought of as a crime control activity, it is officially defined as an activity that sometimes occurs, or sometimes is even necessary, in the pursuit of legitimate crime control activities. For just about all police homicides are thought to be the outcomes of situations perceived to be threatening by the police; indeed, just about all police homicides are officially defined as "justifiable homicides," described by the FBI as the "killing of a felon by a peace officer in the line of duty." Consequently, we might well expect police homicides to be affected by the presence and distribution of both threatening acts and threatening people.

Recently, some research on the use of deadly force by the police has appeared (Fyfe 1982); unfortunately, most of this is descriptive and atheoretical. That which bears on the threat hypothesis is at the microlevel, examining the extent to which police homicide within a social unit is affected by the social characteristics of the victim. While this is certainly a worthwhile question, our concern at the macro level is with the variation of police homicides between, not within, social units. To what extent does the police homicide rate vary between social units, and to what extent can this variation be explained by the threat hypothesis?

We have been able to locate only a few relevant macro studies, and the findings are mixed. For states, Kania and Mackey (1977) report a statistically significant correlation between police homicide and various indicators of poverty, some of which can be conceptualized as indicators of the number of threatening people (e.g., percentage of the population on welfare, receiving food stamps, and without a high school diploma); but they also report a statistically insignificant correlation between police homicide and riots (a clear indicator of threatening acts). For cities, Sherman and Langworthy (1979) report a negative correlation between police homicide and unemployment (an indicator of threatening people). For states, Jacobs and Britt (1979) report that economic inequality and violent crime show statistically significant effects on police homicide.

Some related research on lynching has also appeared. While lynching is certainly not a police activity, in the South from the Civil War to World War I the distinction between the activities of official and unofficial control agents was not always clear. Vigilante groups were common, and some were supported and interlinked with local crime control agents. We examine these studies here because many of them have been stimulated by the threat hypothesis, particularly Blalock's hypothesis (1967) linking social discrimination to the percentage of nonwhites. He argues that as the percentage of nonwhites increases, they constitute an increasing economic and political threat to whites. Nonwhites compete for jobs and political power. Racial discrimination is a tactic of whites to control a threatening nonwhite population, and lynching is simply part of this pattern. Supporting the threat hypothesis, a few macro studies link the rate of lynching to the percentage of blacks in local populations, generally southern counties (Reed 1972; Inverarity 1976; and Corzine et al. 1983). Supporting the power-threat hypothesis, Corzine et al. (1983) further report that the relationship is nonlinear with an increasing slope. Tolnay et al. (1989), however, question both these data and analyses.

Our research further extends this work by explicating and directly examining the process underlying the race threat hypothesis as it applies to police control activities, particularly to the police homicide of citizens. While Blalock (1967) argues that minorities are frequently perceived as posing a political and economic threat, others argue that minorities are frequently perceived as posing a criminal threat. Turk (1969) argues that culturally and racially dissimilar subordinate groups are perceived by authorities as threatening to the social order. While a relatively small dissimilar subordinate group may not be perceived as posing much of a threat, a relatively large dissimilar group, composing twenty to thirty percent of the population, may be perceived as very threatening and as posing a substantial problem of social control. In particular, research suggests that nonwhites in the contemporary United States are perceived by many people and authorities as posing a criminal threat. Swigert and Farrell (1976) report that whites and authorities hold criminal stereotypes of nonwhites as dangerous; Lizotte and Bordua (1980) report that whites perceive the proportion of nonwhites in a neighborhood as an indicator of the crime problem; and Liska et al. (1982) report that the percentage of nonwhites in a city substantially affects the fear of crime for both whites and nonwhites.

Assuming that police homicide grows out of threatening situations (Fyfe 1982) and that nonwhites are associated with dangerous street crime in contemporary American culture, the race threat hypothesis predicts that the percentage of nonwhites positively affects the threat perceived by police and thereby the police homicide rate. The effect of racial segregation on the perceived threat to police is much less clear. Some researchers (Liska et al. 1981) argue that racial segregation, by isolating nonwhites in urban ghettos, functions as a mechanism of social control and thereby decreases the perceived threat to authorities. While this may be true for higher authorities, it is not necessarily true for police. Segregation may increase the perceived threat for those who work in racially segregated ghettos, while decreasing it for those who work outside these ghettos. Hence, we focus on the percentage of nonwhites.

We suspect that three processes underlie the percent nonwhite effect. One, because nonwhite offenders are perceived to be more threatening (dangerous and unpredictable) than white offenders, nonwhite offenders are killed by police at a higher rate than white offenders; an increase in the percentage of nonwhites increases the ratio of nonwhite to white offender crime; and, therefore, an increase in the percentage of nonwhites increases the overall police homicide rate. Statistically, this process yields an aggregation effect. Two, nonwhite offender crime may also create a general climate of threat that permeates police interaction with white, as well as nonwhite, offenders, and which in turn increases the police homicide of both whites and nonwhites; therefore, an increase in the percentage of nonwhites increases both white and nonwhite police homicides. Three, just the day-to-day presence and visibility of nonwhites may be sufficient to create a generalized climate of threat to police; therefore, independent of the racial composition of crime, an increase in the percentage of nonwhites increases both white and nonwhite police homicides. Statistically, the second and third processes yield contextual effects.

In sum, research on police size, arrest rates, and lynching rates suggests that racial structures of crime and people contribute substantially to the perceived threat of social authorities, including the police. Our research focuses on the use of deadly force by police. This is an important social phenomenon, frequently leading to official investigations, lawsuits, demonstrations, and riots; and it provides an opportunity to extend the race threat hypothesis because the use of deadly force is thought to "grow" out of situations perceived to be threatening by the police. Yet, we have been able to locate only a few multivariate studies of the police homicide rate that directly bear on the threat hypothesis. In this chapter we explicate and examine the social processes that underlie the race threat hypothesis of the police use of deadly force.

Procedures

Police Homicides

Data on police homicide are taken from either the Vital Statistics of the United States or police records (Matulia 1985). In one of the first large-scale studies of police homicides, Sherman and Langworthy (1979) collected data from both the Vital Statistics and police records of thirty-two cities. They report that while police records show about double the number of incidents than the Vital Statistics do, the two indexes correlate at .56 and show similar relationships with other variables. These relationships are somewhat stronger for police records data than for the Vital Statistics data, suggesting that the latter may contain more measurement error.

While there may be less measurement error in police records than in the Vital Statistics, both data sources imperfectly measure the true rate. Assuming that the sources of measurement error for the Vital Statistics are not highly correlated with the sources of error for the police records,[1] we use their common variance, or covariance, to model the measurement error and thus to adjust the estimated parameters of the structural model for measurement error. Data from the Vital Statistics are taken from tapes, "Mortality Detail Files," provided by the National Center for Health Statistics through the ICPSR.[2] Data from the police records of cities over 250,000 in population for 1970 to 1979 were collected through a questionnaire sent to police executives (Matulia 1985) in a study sponsored by the National Institute of Justice. Because police homicide is a rare event, rates should include more than one year. We used 1975 to 1979 for both data sources so that all homicides in the indexes occurred during or after the year 1975 for which data on most casual variables were collected.

Threatening People

Previous research on police size, arrest, and deadly force has examined economic and racial structures, particularly income inequality, the percentage of nonwhites, and racial segregation. We examine all three. Income inequality (1970) is measured by the Gini index which expresses the average difference in income between all pairs of individuals in a city relative to the average income of that city. It is taken from the U.S. Census. The percent nonwhite (1975) is also taken from the U.S. Census. Racial segregation (1970) is measured by a dissimilarity index that describes the extent to which the racial composition of city blocks reflects the racial composition of the city as a whole (Sorenson, Taeuber, and Hollingsworth 1975).

Threatening Acts

The percentage of nonwhites may be related to the police homicide rate, not because nonwhites themselves are perceived to be threatening by the police, but because their presence may be associated with acts that are perceived to be threatening by the police. Research by Kania and Mackey (1977), Hawkins and Ward (1970), Sherman and Langworthy (1979), and Fyfe (1980) report a substantial relationship between police homicides and the overall homicide rate (see Langworthy 1986, for an exception). We computed four indexes of threatening acts which vary by the level of threat, especially to the police: index crime, violent index crime (homicide, rape, assault, and robbery), homicide, and homicide of the police. The first three indexes (1975) are computed from data available in the *Uniform Crime Reports* and are standardized by population, and the fourth index (1975 to 1979) is computed from data available in *Police Officers Killed and Assaulted* and is standardized by population and police size.[3]

Threatening Acts by Threatening People: Interracial and Intraracial Crime

Crime by race of the offender and the victim, while not available in the UCR, can be computed from the National Crime Survey of cities (NCS). The survey interviewed approximately ten thousand households in each of twenty-six major cities, from 1972 to 1975, asking crime victims to identify the race of the offender. This is possible for robbery, rape, and assault, three of the four index violent crimes. For each of these three crimes we construct interracial and intraracial crime rates: white offender-white victim, white offender-nonwhite victim, nonwhite offender-nonwhite victim, and nonwhite offender-white victim.[4]

Other Control Variables

Police size (1975), while not the focus of this research, is included because conflict theory suggests that it affects the level of crime control activities and because research shows that it is related to percent nonwhite, segregation, and income inequality. It is measured as the number of police employees per capita, available in the UCR. Population size (1975) is also included because research suggests that it is related to racial and economic structures and to a reliance on formal means of social control (Fischer 1976).

Analysis

The analysis consists of three parts. Controlling for various indicators of threatening acts and for other variables, the first part examines the effects of threatening people on the overall police homicide rate in a measurement model using both the Vital Statistics and the police survey data. The sample is composed of forty-five cities. These are the cities included in the Matulia survey (N = 57) minus those for which police homicide data could not be located in the Vital Statistics (ten cities) and for which police homicide data from the survey and the Vital Statistics are very inconsistent (two cities). To examine the two contextual processes, the second part disaggregates police homicide by race and examines the effects of threatening people on the police homicide of whites and nonwhites. Because the survey data do not report police homicide by race, the analysis is limited to the Vital Statistics data for these forty-five cities. To compare the relative strengths of the two contextual processes, the third part estimates the extent to which the racial composition of violent crime mediates the effect of the racial composition of cities on the police homicide of whites and nonwhites. This analysis is limited to those twenty-two cities of the sample for which racially specific violent crime rates can be computed.[5]

Results

Distributions

Clearly, there is considerable variation in police homicide of citizens between cities. The Vital Statistics show a mean of 1.4 and a standard deviation of 1.6 per 100,000 population for the five-year period, and the police survey shows a mean of 3.5 and a standard deviation of 2.6 per 100,000 population for the five-year period. Consistent with Sherman and Langworthy's (1979) finding, the survey rate is about double the Vital Statistics rate and the two indexes correlate .45. Both distributions, particularly the Vital Statistics, are skewed with a few cities showing very high rates; hence we estimate all equations using natural log transformations of these distributions.[6]

Structural-Measurement Model

Using maximum likelihood methods (ML), we estimate four structural-measurement models.[7] The first includes all of the causal variables and uses total index crime as the measure of threatening acts; the second includes just those causal variables that are substantially significant (dropping population and income inequality); the third also includes just those causal variables that are substantially significant and uses the violent index crime as the measure of threatening acts; and the fourth also includes just those variables that are substantially significant and uses homicide as the measure of threatening acts. ML (Maximum Likelihood) estimates of the models are presented in table 3.1, columns one to four, respectively.

The general pattern of results is clear. Percent nonwhite by far shows the strongest effect; segregation and police size show moderate effects; crime rates show an effect which is contingent on the degree of violence; and income inequality and population size show little to no effect. The structural R^2 equals about .75 for all four models, and the X^2/df ratio for all four models is very small and statistically insignificant, suggesting that all four models reproduce the observed correlations.

The most significant finding is that percent nonwhite shows a very substantial and statistically significant effect on police homicide, controlling for population size, police size, segregation, income in-

Table 3.1 Standardized Maximum Likelihood Estimates of the Threat Models of Police Homicide as a Latent Variable

	Models			
	1	2	3	4
Population	.12[c]	—	—	—
Inc. Inequality	.00	—	—	—
Police	-.25[b]	-.18[c]	-.22[c]	-.18[c]
Segregation	.24[a]	.22[a]	.23[a]	.18[b]
Percent Nonwhite	.70[a]	.66[a]	.62[a]	.45[b]
Total C.R.	.05	.01	—	—
Violent C.R.	—	—	.10	—
Homicide Rate	—	—	—	.27[c]
R^2	.76	.75	.74	.74
X^2/df	0.52	0.79	0.72	0.71

a = 2.0 times SE; b = 1.5 times SE; c = 1.0 times SE

equality, and threatening acts (measured by the total index crime rate, the violent index crime rate, and the homicide rate). While the effect drops when the homicide rate is used as the measure of threatening acts, it is still substantial (beta = .45) and statistically significant, and is much larger than the homicide rate effect (beta = .27), providing support for the threat hypothesis.[8]

We have thus far assumed that the threat hypothesis implies a linear relationship between percent nonwhite and police homicides. However, Blalock (1967) has interpreted the general threat hypothesis to imply a nonlinear relationship between percent nonwhite and lynching. He argues that economic and political threats posed by nonwhites lead to a positive relationship with a decreasing slope associated with economic threats and an increasing slope associated with political threats. Additionally, as the percentage of nonwhites approximates fifty percent, nonwhites assume more positions of political power and positions in the police department; thus, they are no longer viewed as a threat by authorities. To examine the data for a percent nonwhite-police homicide increasing or decreasing slope, we first examine scattergrams of the relationship with police homicide, aggregated and disaggregated by race, in its natural metric. (A log transformation tends to linearize many curvilinear relationships.) Scattergrams show no evidence of a departure from linearity. We also estimate polynomial equations. The square terms are not statistically significant. In sum, we find no evidence of a departure from linearity.[9]

The segregation effect is also substantial and statistically significant; and the direction of the effect, as expected, is inconsistent with findings on police size and arrest rates. That is, some research (Liska et al. 1981 and Liska and Chamlin 1984) shows that segregation negatively affects police size and arrest rates, but we find that it positively affects police homicide. Segregation, functioning as an informal control of the nonwhite population, may decrease the perceived threat to higher authorities, leading to decreases in formal controls, like police size and even arrests; but segregation may also both heighten the perceived threat and lessen the restraint of those police who work the streets of urban ghettos, leading to increases in police homicide.

A somewhat unexpected finding is that income inequality shows no effect, whereas Jacobs and Britt (1979) report a statistically significant effect. There are a number of differences between our and their analyses that may account for these inconsistent results. Most importantly, they use states and we use cities as the unit of analysis. The variance in income inequality among cities within the contemporary United States may be too small to be theoretically meaningful. For our sample of forty-five cities, income inequality shows a mean of .362 and a standard deviation of only .026.

Many theories assume that more police per capita results in more police activities per capita. This assumption has not been supported in regards to crime control activities such as arrests (Liska and Chamlin 1984), and it is clearly not supported in regard to police homicide. Indeed, police size seems to substantially decrease police homicide. Other things being equal, like the crime rate that is controlled here, police may feel more in control and less threatened on the street when working in large rather than small departments; perhaps there are more two-person patrols, better communication between street patrols and departmental headquarters, and more back-up in larger departments.

To what extent may these findings be biased due to multicollinearity among the independent variables? A review of the bivariate correlations, the determinants of the correlation matrixes, and the variance inflation factors suggests little evidence of multicollinearity in models 1, 2, and 3. In model 4, however, percent nonwhite and the homicide rate are substantially correlated (.79). While this is certainly reason for caution, it does not necessarily mean that the pattern of findings is wrong or even misleading. Belsley et al. (1980) have devised a sophisticated test (conditioning index and variance decomposition) for diagnosing the presence of multicollinearity and for assessing the degree to which it degrades OLS estimates. They find that conditioning indexes over thirty are a cause for caution, and they state "that OLS estimates shall be deemed degraded when more than fifty percent of the variance of two or more coefficients is associated with a single high conditioning index...." We have applied both tests to model 4. Neither criterion is exceeded: hence, it seems safe to conclude that while there is evidence of collinearity, it probably does not degrade the OLS estimates of model 4. To observe the degree of estimate sensitivity to model specification, Hanushek and Jackson (1977) suggest varying slightly the model specifications and observing the change in the parameter estimates. We do this by comparing the parameter estimates of models 1, 2, 3, and 4. Note that both the sign and the magnitude of the estimates of model 4 are very similar to both the sign and magnitude of the estimates of models 1, 2, and 3, as well as to the simple correlations, again suggesting that while caution is in order, the pattern of findings cannot easily be dismissed.

In sum, the analyses show that the percentage of nonwhites strongly and linearly increases police homicide, that segregation and general homicide rates moderately increase police homicide, that police size moderately decreases police homicide, and that other crime rates, population, and income inequality do not affect police homicide.

Disaggregation by Race

One problem with the above analysis is that the observed percent nonwhite effect may reflect two distinct statistical effects (aggregate and contextual), which reflect different causal processes. The Vital Statistics data show that the mean police homicide rate of nonwhites (2.41 per 100,000 population over these five years) is about three times the mean of whites (0.77 per 100,000 population over these five years). Hence, as the percentage of nonwhites increases, the aggregate police homicide rate increases. This is a statistical aggregate effect. If an increase in the percentage of nonwhites causally increases the police homicide of both whites or nonwhites (contextual effect), this cannot be observed in the aggregate police homicide rate. To more clearly examine the social processes underlying the threat effect, it is necessary to disaggregate police homicide by race.

This is only possible for the Vital Statistics; the survey data provide no racial identifiers. Thus in the disaggregate analysis we are unable to build a measurement model, thereby adjusting for measurement error. We expect more random variance in the structural model and by implication lower standardized coefficients. For the structural-measurement models (reported in table 3.1) the R^2s are high (.75) for the structural models and low for the measurement models (about .15 for the Vital Statistics measure and .50 for the police department measure). To examine the effect of random measurement error, we first reestimate structural model 1 not disaggregated by race using only the Vital Statistics data. The estimates (table 3.2, col. 1) compare nicely with these in table 3.1 and the R^2 (table 3.2, col. 1) is the same as the R^2 of the Vital Statistics measure in the structural-measurement model.

We next estimate the structural equations disaggregated by race: first, including the total index crime rate (model 1); second, including just those variables whose effects are substantially significant (model 2); third, substituting the violent index crime rate for the total index crime rate (model 3); and, fourth, substituting the homicide rate for the violent index crime rate (model 4). The results for all four models provide support for the contextual processes underlying the threat hypothesis. As the percentage of nonwhites increases, the police homicide of both whites and nonwhites increases. The effects are substantial and statistically significant and are independent of threaten-

Table 3.2 Standardized and Unstandardized (in parentheses) OLS Estimates of the Threat Models of Police Homicide (Vital Statistics) by Race

	MODEL 1			MODEL 2		MODEL 3		MODEL 4	
	Total	Whites	Nonwhites	Whites	Nonwhites	Whites	Nonwhites	Whites	Nonwhites
Population	.01	.07	.09	—	—	—	—	—	—
	(.000006)	(.0004)	(.0009)						
Inc. Inequality	-.03	-.15	-.01	—	—	—	—	—	—
	(-.93)	(-4.00)	(-.60)						
Police	-.18	-.40	-.18	-.31	-.16	-.22	-.06	-.32	-.19
	(-.11)	(-.235)b	(-.18)	(-.18)c	(-.15)	(-.13)	(-.070)	(-.19)c	(-.19)
Segregation	-.02	-.11	.11	—	—	—	—	—	—
	(-.002)	(-.009)	(.014)						
Percent Nonwhites	.53	.59	.51	.45	.52	.52	.60	.58	.61
	(.026)a	(.028)a	(.042)a	(.021)a	(.042)a	(.024)a	(.048)a	(.027)b	(.049)a
Total CR	-.14	-.15	-.16	-.14	-.21	—	—	—	—
	(-.005)	(-.005)	(-.010)c	(-.005)	(-.013)c				
Violent CR	—	—	—	—	—	-.21	-.24	—	—
						(-.030)	(-.058)c		
Homicide Rate	—	—	—	—	—	—	—	-.15	-.11
								(-1.06)	(-1.38)
R²	.15	.13	.21	.10	.19	.10	.17	.09	.15

a = 2 times SE; b = 1.5 times SE; c = 1.0 times SE

Table 3.3 Standardized and Unstandardized (in parentheses) OLS Estimates of the Effect of the Racial Composition of Crime As a Mediator of the Effect of Percent Nonwhite on Police Homicide by Race ($N = 22$)

	TOTAL		WHITES		NONWHITES	
Percent Nonwhite	.66	.64	.61	.40	.74	.64
	(.029)[a]	(.027)[b]	(.026)[c]	(.017)[c]	(.046)[c]	(.040)[b]
Police	- .10	- .12	- .21	- .24	- .12	- .14
	(- .057)	(- .068)	(- .12)	(- .14)	(- .099)	(- .12)
Violent CR	- .08	—	- .14	—	.12	—
	(- .011)	—	(- .020)	—	(- .025)	—
NWNW CR	—	- .02	—	.18	—	.05
	—	(- .002)	—	(.022)	—	(.010)
R^2	.29	.29	.17	.17	.35	.34

a = times SE; b = 1.5 times SE; c = 1.0 times SE
CR = Crime rate; NWNW = Nonwhite offender-nonwhite victim crime for robbery, assault and rape

ing acts as measured by general crime rates, violent crime rates, and homicide rates.[10] While the standardized coefficients show that the impact of percent nonwhite on police homicides, relative to that of other variables, is similar for whites and nonwhites, the unstandardized coefficients show that a unit increase in percent nonwhite produce twice the increase in nonwhite than white police homicides.

Like the aggregate analysis, the disaggregate analysis shows a moderate negative effect of police size on both the police homicide of whites and nonwhites and no effect of population size and income inequality on either the police homicide of whites or nonwhites. And unlike the aggregate analysis, the disaggregate analysis shows no effect of either segregation or homicide rates on the police homicide of either whites or nonwhites. This difference between the aggregate and disaggregate analysis probably lies in the inability to control for random measurement error in the disaggregate analysis, which uses just the Vital Statistics data. The small to moderate effects of segregation and the homicide rate, evident in the estimates of the aggregate structural-measurement model, may be obscured in estimates of the structural disaggregate model.

Racial Composition of Crime

Clearly, the effect of the percentage of nonwhites is the most consistent finding. It is strongly evident in the aggregate structural-measurement models where random measurement error in police homicide is controlled, and it is strongly evident in the disaggregate structural models for both whites and nonwhites where random measurement error is not controlled. The consistency of the findings supports the threat hypothesis and the contextual process underlying the hypothesis.

Because the percentage of nonwhites constrains the racial composition of crime, the observed percent nonwhite effect on the police homicide of whites and non-whites may reflect the effects of nonwhite offender crime (threatening acts by threatening people) and/or just the presence of nonwhites (threatening people). In this analysis we examine the extent to which the percent nonwhite effect on the police homicide of whites and nonwhites is mediated by racially specific crime rates: nonwhite offender-nonwhite victim (NW-NW), white offender-nonwhite victim (W-NW), nonwhite offender-white victim (NW-W), and white offender-white victim (W-W).

We first examine the correlations between each of these racially specific robbery, assault, and rape rates (W-W, W-NW, NW-W, and NW-NW), and police homicide of whites and nonwhites. Only the correlations between NW-NW (robbery, assault, and rape) and the police homicide of whites and nonwhites are substantial, statistically significant, and in the predicted direction. We combine the three NW-NW crime rates, as the correlations between them range from .68 to .78, and we examine the correlation between the NW-NW crime rate and percent nonwhite. The strong correlation ($r = .78$) clearly suggests that the percentage of nonwhites affects the racial composition of crime.

We next estimate (using OLS) the effect of percent nonwhite, police size, and the violent crime rate (the variables used in table 3.2) on the police homicide of whites and nonwhites for the subsample of twenty-two large cities for which data on interracial and intraracial crime are available (see table 3.3). The effects of the causal variables are generally similar to those for the full sample of forty-five cities. To observe the extent to which the NW-NW violent crime rate mediates the effect of the percentage of nonwhites on the police homicide of whites and nonwhites, we substitute the NW-NW violent crime rate for the violent crime rate and reestimate the equations. The results are reasonably clear. The NW-NW violent crime rate has no independent effect on the police homicide of either whites or nonwhites; it cannot, therefore, mediate the effect of percent nonwhite on the police homicide of either whites or nonwhites. The correlation between the NW-NW violent crime rate and the police homicide of whites and nonwhites comes about because of the correlation between the NW-NW violent crime rate and the percentage of nonwhites. It is the percentage of nonwhites, not the NW-NW violent crime rate, that affects the police homicide of both whites and nonwhites.[11]

Discussion

The conflict perspective conceptualizes the actions of crime control agents as efforts to control acts and people that are perceived to threaten their interests and/or the interests of higher authorities. Focusing on nonwhites and the poor as threatening people, research has reported relationships between the percentage of nonwhites, racial segregation, and income inequality, and patterns of crime control, such as police size and arrest rates. In a study of the police homicide of citizens, we attempt to extend this research by explicating and testing the social processes that underlie the threat hypothesis.

Although a rare activity, police homicide is a socially significant activity imbued with cultural and political symbolism. Incidents receive considerable attention in the mass media and frequently lead to collective social actions, including investigations, demonstrations, civil disturbances, lootings, and riots. It is indeed curious that actions of such significance for the social order have been ignored by sociologists.

The threat hypothesis is examined in three analyses. In a structural-measurement model we find that percent nonwhite strongly and linearly affects the overall police homicide rate, controlling for income inequality, segregation, population, police size, and threatening acts measured by different indexes of violent crime. While supporting the threat hypothesis, this analysis does not distinguish aggregation effects from contextual effects. The aggregate effect hypothesis assumes that because nonwhites are more threatening than whites, nonwhites are killed by police at a higher rate than whites; therefore, an increase in the percentage of nonwhites increases the overall police homicide rate. The contextual effect hypothesis further assumes that nonwhite offender crime and the day-to-day visibility of nonwhites create a general climate of threat that influences interaction between police and whites as well as between police and nonwhites; therefore, as the percentage of nonwhites increases, the police homicide of both whites and nonwhites increases. The analysis of the

Vital Statistics data, disaggregated by race, strongly supports the contextual threat hypothesis. Finally, the contextual hypothesis entails two related processes. One process associates a climate of threat with the presence and day-to-day visibility of nonwhites, and the other associates a climate of threat with a high rate of nonwhite offender crime. The analysis of a subsample of cities suggests that nonwhite offender crime does not mediate the effect of the percentage of nonwhites on the police homicide rate of whites or nonwhites, which implies that threat as perceived by the police is associated with just the presence and day-to-day visibility of nonwhites.

Analyses of police homicides, arrests, and police size suggest that the activities of crime control authorities should not be treated as causally homogeneous, as suggested by conflict and other perspectives. The activities reflect different causal processes. Police size may reflect deliberate decisions of local political and economic elites to expend resources in order to maintain and preserve the social order and their position in it. Arrest rates may reflect deliberate decisions of middle and upper-level police bureaucrats in response to victim and community pressure to control crime. Police homicide, on the other hand, may reflect emotional responses to street situations in which police feel threatened and have little time to calculate alternative courses of action. Most police homicides occur when police interrupt a robbery or burglary in progress or intervene in a social disturbance, including family quarrels, fights, and assaults. Because of cultural beliefs linking nonwhites to street violence and crime, police may feel particularly threatened in neighborhoods and cities where the percentage of nonwhites is relatively high.[12]

In conclusion, the conflict perspective assumes that the activities of crime control agents and organizations reflect the interests of the powerful, interpreted as authorities or elites; the more their interests are threatened, the higher the level of activity. Conflict theorists have yet to develop this proposition in a heterogeneous, complex post-industrial society, where there are multiple layers and systems of authorities and where that which is threatening to one layer and system is not to another. Drawing on recent research on police, we explicate the processes underlying the threat hypothesis and test them as an explanation of police homicide rates. We have not emphasized threat to elites and have not viewed police activities as simply serving the interests of elites; rather, we have emphasized threats to the police themselves and have explained the macrovariation in police homicide as the outcome of a climate of perceived threat associated with the percentage of nonwhites.

Part II

Coercive Controls

4

The Reporting of Crime:
A Missing Link in Conflict Theory

Barbara D. Warner

Within the past decade, conflict theory has been increasingly criticized on a variety of fronts. First, research findings from the 1960s and 1970s that suggested prejudiced responses by the police and the courts, the food on which much of conflict theory grew, have been seriously questioned. Research in the 1960s and early 1970s often emphasized that the large differences between both socioeconomic and racial groups in terms of *arrests* were usually not found in self-report studies of juveniles, suggesting that *crime* did not vary by socioeconomic status or race, only that arrests did. However, as self-report surveys were revamped to include more serious offenses and to eliminate other problems, and as data from victimization surveys became available, class and race differences in criminal involvement reflected in official reports began to be viewed as real, and not simply aspects of discretionary control (cf. Elliott and Ageton 1980; Elliott and Huizigna 1983; Hindelang 1976, 1978; Langan 1985).

Likewise, more recent studies examining sentencing differences among racial and income groups, which control for legal characteristics, began to show that differences between these groups were mostly attributable to differences in type of crime, characteristics of the crime, or arrest histories of the offender (cf. Hagan 1974; Cohen and Kluegel 1978; Blumstein 1982). Other studies suggest that although real sentencing differences related to nonlegal characteristics may have occurred in the 1960s, such sentencing discrimination no longer exists (cf. Pruitt and Wilson 1983). In addition, studies have found no significant differences across racial or income groups in the rankings of crime seriousness (cf. Sellin and Wolfgang 1964; Rossi, Waite, Bose, and Berk 1974; Levi and Jones 1985), suggesting a level of societal

71

agreement contradictory to conflict theory.

Most recently, however, conflict theory (along with other structural theories) has been criticized for its lack of attention to process issues (Liska and Tausig 1979; Liska, Chamlin, and Reed 1985; Sampson 1985; Gottredson et al. 1988). As a structural theory, conflict theory has paid little attention to the issue of *how* social structural arrangements actually affect aspects of social control. Research examining only the structural *sources* of power rather than the *processes* of power cannot lead to critical tests of conflict theory, as many of the structural relationships hypothesized within a conflict perspective may be used to support other theoretical perspectives as well (Liska and Tausig 1979: p. 205).

In a similar vein, Sampson (1985) has criticized macrolevel theories for not disaggregating individual effects from macrosocial effects. He suggests that findings which have previously passed for macrosocial effects "may well have been individual effects in disguise" (p. 649). Sampson also points out that theorized differential effects for different groups have generally not been addressed in macrolevel theories, making it unclear as to whether the theories have been supported or not.

The study presented here will attempt to address several of these issues. First, in accordance with the literature that suggests limited amounts of discretionary control on the part of the police, this chapter raises the question of whether discretionary practices may still exist, but be in the hands of certain groups of citizens through differential practices of reporting crime. Second, the analysis is disaggregated by race and income in order to further specify the processes through which any hypothesized structural variables may produce their effect.

The Reporting of Crime

The importance of the reporting of criminal behavior has been emphasized in studies of both police behavior and victimization. These studies suggest that the reporting of crime may be the most influential decision in the criminal justice system. They have shown that those who report crime are the true "gatekeepers" of the criminal justice system (Hindelang 1976; Hindelang and Gottfredson 1976; Gottfredson and Gottfredson 1980). In most criminal matters, it is the citizenry, not the police, who determine what crimes and which criminals are "let in" for further processing in the system.

Studies of police behavior by Black and Reiss (1970; Black 1971; and Reiss 1971), and more recently by Lundman and his colleagues (1978, 1980) have emphasized the almost entirely *reactive* (i.e., police respond to requests for assistance rather than initiate action) nature of police work. The kinds of problems police examine as well as the disposition of these problems are strongly shaped by the citizens who report the incidents to the police (cf. Lundman 1980). Although police take a proactive (i.e., police-initiated) role in some situations such as traffic violations and vice, these incidents are not at the heart of the legal system. As Black (1971) states, "Where the police role is most starkly aggressive in form, the substance is drably trivial, and legally trivial incidents provide practically all of the grist for arrest in pro-active police operations" (p. 1092).

Studies of the police done by Black and Reiss in the late 1960s showed that the police in most cases do not act as independent agents. Reiss (1971) reports that eighty-six percent of police mobilizations were originated by citizens. Lundman (1980) reports that almost ninety percent of police-citizen encounters are citizen initiated, when traffic violations are excluded. Similar findings are indicated in victimization surveys. Hindelang (1976) found only three percent of reported victimizations came to the attention of the police by direct police knowledge, i.e., as a result of a police officer being "on the scene". Thus, in the vast majority of crimes, if the police had not been contacted by a citizen, the criminal justice system would not have been involved. The citizen, then, through the reporting of crime, carries a great deal of control over the use of the criminal justice system. Black (1970) has referred to complainants as the

> prime movers of every known legal system, the human mechanism by which legal services are routed into situations where there is a felt need for law. Complainants are the most invisible and they may be the most important social force binding the law to other aspects of social organization. (p. 747)

Central to the issue of citizen reporting of crime, as Black (1971) points out, is that what becomes known and acted upon as a crime is first filtered by the community.

> [M]ost criminal cases pass through a moral filter in the citizen population before the state assumes its enforcement role. A major portion of the responsibility for criminal-law enforcement is kept out of police hands. Much like courts in the realm of private law, the police operate as moral servants of the citizenry. (p. 1104)

The hesitancy of conflict theorists to pay sufficient attention to the role of the citizenry within the legal system, and alternatively, to emphasize the police officer as an arm of the state with relatively little attachment to the community, has been unfortunate. Through its emphasis on those delegated to carry out the law and its subsequent neglect of those who mobilize the law, conflict theory has ignored one of the most crucial decisions in the criminal justice system. It therefore seems essential that the role of the citizen, through the reporting of crime, be examined in order to develop a clearer understanding of the social control of crime.

Social Threat and Crime Control

Macrosociological studies examining crime control have often focused on the threat hypothesis. The threat hypothesis assumes that the relationship between authorities and subjects is generally one of established dominance and deference. However, in times of extensive change (such as migration from rural to urban areas, technological unemployment, or increased numbers of minority groups), this accepted relationship and the normal social order may become questioned.

> As long as people accept the inevitability of their social order, and operate within it with little or no questioning of why it should be at all, authority is secure... [W]hen the response to authority is no longer one of conditioned deference the authorities are increasingly likely to be forced to meet resistance. The more aware subjects become of the authority relationship, the less automatic their behavior, the more likely they are to question the very existence of the relationship. Authority is unquestioned power; questioned authority implies the inevitability of tests of strength to determine whether the social relationship will continue and whether in the same form and with the same ordering of related parties. (Turk 1969:44–45)

Therefore, in times of extensive change or under conditions that may lead to the questioning of authority relations, those in power will increase coercive control to maintain the present order. Studies examining the threat hypothesis have analyzed the variance in police force size (Jacobs 1979; Liska, Lawrence, and Benson 1981), municipal expenditures for policing (Jackson and Carroll 1981) or arrest rates (Liska and Chamlin 1984; Liska, Chamlin, and Reed 1985; Williams and Drake 1980) in relation to threatening populations (e.g., percent nonwhite), threatening conditions (e.g., income inequality), and threatening behaviors (e.g., riots). Although these studies have frequently reported support for the threat hypothesis, they have been lax in their presentation of the actual processes involved.

The basic model tested in these studies is that of a direct effect between the independent variables (e.g., income inequality, percent nonwhite, and segregation) and police force size, expenditures, or arrest rates. Once a relationship is found it is often assumed that the mechanism through which the independent variables operate is the state's (or some elite group's) control of the police. This process, however, is often not investigated, but assumed. For example, Jacobs (1979) finds that economic inequality and the number of drug and liquor stores (as well as the percent black and the crime rate in 1970) are significantly and positively related to the size of the police force. From these results he concludes that "an unequal distribution of economic resources *will give elites* both the ability to control the coercive apparatus of the state and a vital need to maintain order so that ongoing relationships can be sustained" (Jacobs 1979: 922–23, emphasis added). Although Jacobs acknowledges that many groups benefit from increased police size, he states that the police department will be strongest when conditions are such that economic elites can influence police force size. No evidence, however, is presented on any particular group's influence.

The process through which structural variables representing conflict have an effect has important implications for conflict theory, and to some extent the validity of conflict theory can be seen to lie upon the empirical support found for the process involved. Note that if the effect of percent nonwhite and income inequality on arrest rates or police force size is due only to increased pressure on public officials by elites (as conflict theory assumes), the theoretical implications are very different than if the effect of these variables is due to increased pressure brought by all segments of society. The main proposition within the threat hypothesis is that particular situations (e.g., large percentages of nonwhites and income inequality) are perceived as threatening to the normal social order by elites, and that these elites will bring about increased coercive control. Implicit in this proposition is the assumption that less powerful groups, in situations where their role in the social order can be seen as subservient to the interests of the powerful, will not wish to maintain the normal social order. The process issues that follow from this proposition are: (1) elites, once threatened, are willing and capable of taking steps to maintain order; and (2) members of non elite groups are neither willing nor capable of taking steps to maintain that order. Although some research has begun to examine the first of these issues, the latter has not been examined at all.

In a series of studies on threat conditions and crime control, Liska and his colleagues (1981, 1984, 1985) argue that increases in the percent nonwhite increase the interracial/intraracial ratio for white victimization and increase the fear of crime among whites, which whites are able to parlay into increased police force size and crime control. Results from Liska et al. (1981) suggest that the percent nonwhite does affect fear of crime among whites and increases the interracial crime ratio for whites. However, they do not present comparable data for nonwhites (how does the percent of nonwhites affect fear of crime and victimization for nonwhites?) and thus cannot suggest that the percent nonwhite affects whites any differently than nonwhites, or that whites have any more reason to attempt or to succeed in affecting police force size.

Liska and Chamlin (1984) and Liska, Chamlin, and Reed (1985) strengthen the previous argument by examining racial segregation. Liska et al. (1985) find a significant interaction effect between percent nonwhite and segregation on arrest rates. They argue that the weaker effect of percent nonwhite on arrest rates in more segregated cities is due to the decreased visibility of nonwhites to whites. Liska and Chamlin (1984) also find that segregation has a strong inverse effect on arrest rates suggesting some support for the threat hypothesis.

The process involved in the effect of income inequality has been less thoroughly examined. Liska and Chamlin (1984) suggest that although their findings support conflict theory's premise that economic inequality exacerbates conflict and leads the dominant group to increase coercion in order to maintain order, more research documenting this process is necessary.

> [A]lthough the formulation and enforcement of numerous laws may be explained in terms of ruling class interests (Chambliss and Seidman 1982), the control of urban street crime seems to be in the interests of all economic classes. Indeed, it may be even more in the interests of the blue-collar and lower middle than of the upper class, which can afford to reside in relatively safe neighborhoods, locate businesses in these neighborhoods, and insure its property against theft. (p. 393–94)

Thus, although some progress has been made in examining the underlying processes assumed in conflict theory, especially by Liska and his colleagues, much is left to be done. In particular, virtually no attention has been given to the second assumption of the threat hypothesis. These studies have only examined the role of half of the relationship involved, that is, the effect of threat conditions on authorities or elites. The extent to which the non ruling classes are involved in norm-upholding (assumed by conflict theorists to be negligible) has not yet been examined. The assumption that crime control activities and therefore the criminalization of the poor and blacks is due entirely to the fears and interests of the ruling class may not be realistic. As Greenberg and his colleagues (1983, 1985) have pointed out, we must acknowledge the very real fears among the working and middle class, both black and white, in regard to crime. In reference to crime control studies of police, Greenberg, Kessler, and Loftin (1985) state that "conflict theorists have failed to show that urban black populations are strongly opposed to the police. Evidence of such opposition would strengthen a conflict interpretation of the relationship between race and police force size" (p. 650).

The reactions of the citizenry to crime, in terms of reporting under varying social conditions, seems an ideal way in which to more fully test and clarify the threat hypothesis. In order to do this, the reporting of crime to the police by different social groups will be examined in relation to two indicators of social threat: income inequality and percent nonwhite.

In summary, conflict theory has been used in studies of crime to attempt to explain and predict crime control patterns. In particular, it has examined, as the most prominent reaction, police reactions to crime. Unfortunately, conflict theory has thus far ignored the seminal role of citizen's reactions to crime in terms of mobilizing the criminal justice system. Examining the social conditions under which crime is more or less frequently reported is critical in understanding the implications of conflict theory in mobilizing crime control. The reporting of crime is one plausible process through which threat conditions may affect official responses to crime. Furthermore, examining which groups of people report crime under threat conditions is fundamental to the testing of the underlying assumptions of the processes involved in the threat hypothesis.

Therefore, the following two issues will be examined. First, do threat conditions affect the citizenry's reporting, thereby establishing a process through which threat conditions may affect police behavior (arrests) and police force size (through increased requests for police service)? And, second, to what extent is this process in line with conflict theory—that is, is this process one in which "elites" are predominantly managing crime control?

Since it is being assumed that the reporting of crime is the actual first step in bringing about formal social control, it is suggested that those same variables that have been hypothesized in other studies using the threat hypothesis to explain police force size and arrest rates should affect the reporting of crime in the same manner.

In this study it will be hypothesized that areas with high percentages of nonwhites and high income inequality will have higher rates of reporting crime than areas with low percentages of nonwhites and low income inequality. Two other variables, which may be related to the reporting of crime and may not be orthogonal to the independent variables being tested, need to be included also in a test of this hypothesis in order to avoid model misspecification and biased estimates (Hanushek and Jackson 1977). These variables are the seriousness of the crime and the crime rate. Gottfredson and Hindelang (1979), in an examination of Black's theory of law, pointed to the overriding importance of the seriousness of an offense in relation to whether or not it is reported to the police. Others have found that the amount of crime in an area is related to the residents' willingness to call the police (Macoby, Johnson, and Church 1958; Conklin 1971, 1975).

Although arguments could be made for a variety of different levels of analysis (e.g., the nation, the state, the city, or the neighborhood), this study uses the neighborhood as the primary level to which most of the independent variables are aggregated. Characteristics of one's neighborhood may be more appropriate for predicting threat, in that where one lives may be more important than more general city, state, or national characteristics.

The first hypothesis, regarding the effects of neighborhood characteristics on reporting, is as folows:

> H1: The percent nonwhite and the income inequality of a neighborhood positively affect the reporting of crime, controlling for the area crime rate and the seriousness of the crime.

A simple test of this hypothesis, however, is not sufficient to examine the "genuineness" of any significant relationships at the aggregate level. Since one of the concerns here is with who mobilizes crime control, the data will be disaggregated by race and income. This disaggregation of effects will allow for the examination of the underlying processes implied in conflict theory. That is, it is necessary to not only determine whether the percent nonwhite or income inequality affects the reporting of crime, but also—and more importantly—to determine whether these variables affect "elites" differently and to a greater extent than they affect others.

Conflict theory implicitly hypothesizes that the effects of "threat" variables on the reporting of crime will be strongest for the middle and upper-income groups and for whites. Therefore, the following hypotheses shall also be examined.

> H2: For white victims, percent nonwhite should positively affect whether a crime is reported controlling for the crime rate and the seriousness of the incident.

> H3: For middle and upper-income victims, income inequality should positively affect whether a crime is reported controlling for the crime rate and the seriousness of the incident.

> H4: For nonwhite and lower-income victims, percent nonwhite and income inequality should *not* affect whether a crime is reported, after controlling for the crime rate and the seriousness of the incident.

Methodology

In order to examine the contextual effects of neighborhood level racial and economic characteristics on individuals' decisions to report or not report a crime to the police, the national level incident file of the National Crime Survey (NCS) was used. For the crimes of burglary and assault, data from 1974 and 1975 were combined to establish a large enough sample of persons victimized. For robbery, a much less common crime, data from 1974 to 1977 were combined. These early years were chosen so that the data would be as close as possible in time to the data on neighborhood characteristics included in the NCS data files. Since the information on neighborhood characteristics contained in the NCS data are based on 1970 census figures, the years closest to 1970 were chosen.

Operationalization of variables. The dependent variable examined in relation to the neighborhood data is whether the respondent reported the incident to the police. If the incident was reported to the police by either a household member or someone else, the variable was coded "1"; if the incident was not reported to the police, it was coded "0". If the police were on the scence at the time of the incident, thereby negating the need for reporting, the incident was not included in the analysis.

The independent variables examined in these equations are measures of both neighborhood and personal characteristics. The neighborhood variables that are included in the NCS data file are based on the 1970 census housing records. Neighborhoods, as defined in the NCS national sample data, are based on areas of about five thousand individuals in the vicinity of the household. The neighborhood variables examined in terms of conflict theory's threat hypothesis are the ratio of the black population to the total population and the Gini index of income concentration.

Control variables for the seriousness of the incident and the race, income, and education of the respondent were also included in these analyses. In order to control for the seriousness of the incident, two things were done. First, separate equations were estimated for each of the three crimes being examined (robbery, burglary, and aggravated assault). In addition, attempts to control for seriousness within the different crime types were also made by including three control variables. These variables were concerned with whether a weapon was used, whether medical attention was needed for injuries received, and the estimated monetary amount of (property and cash) loss. The monetary amount of loss was used as a control variable in both the burglary and the robbery equations. Whether a weapon was used was included in the assault and the robbery equations; and whether medical attention was needed was used in the assault equation.

Other control variables that were included in the analyses were the respondent's income, race, education level, and the crime rate. The first three of these control variables are fairly straight-forward, the fourth control variable—crime rate—deserves further comment. Although it was impossible to estimate a crime rate for each specific neighborhood (as respondents were not identified by a neighborhood variable), some approximation of the crime rate was necessary. Therefore, a crime rate was computed for the closest geographic area available. In this data set, that was the primary sampling unit. The primary sampling units are either SMSAs or counties, and therefore are clearly larger than neighborhoods. However, it is difficult to ascertain just how wide one's net is in terms of awareness of crimes, and it was felt that including this measure would be better than including no measure of the crime rate.

The crime rate (actually several different crime rates) was computed for each primary sampling unit by dividing the number of persons victimized in each primary sampling unit by the number of persons sampled in that primary sampling unit. Crime rates were computed for three crime groupings (total victimizations, household victimizations, and personal victimizations) for 1974 and 1975.[1] Correlations between the three victimization rates were quite high (.95 –

.99), making the decision to use total victimizations, household victimizations, or personal victimizations relatively insignificant. Therefore, total victimizations was chosen as this was the most inclusive measure. The rates of total victimizations for 1974 and 1975 across all primary sampling units were correlated at .988, and therefore only the 1974 rates were used.

In analyzing these data, special concern was given to separating structural and individual level effects. This is important in order to establish true structural effects as well as to clarify the underlying causal processes involved. The separating of individual and contextual (i.e., group-level) effects can be done by either including in the equation the individual-level variable along with the group-level variable (e.g., respondent's race as well as percent of the city that is black), or equivalently, creating separate equations for different groups. These analyses used separate equations for different racial and income groups. The analyses were based on the first victimization of each six-month period of all surveyed individuals reporting victimizations for robbery, burglary, or assault.

Since the dependent variable in these equations is a binomial, or a binary choice variable, the assumption of OLS regression that the error terms are independently and identically distributed (homoscedasticity) comes into question and the probability thus arises that coefficients derived from OLS regression, although unbiased, may not be efficient (Pindyck and Rubinfeld 1981). Therefore, logistic regression, which is based on a cumulative logistic probability function rather than a linear function, was used.

The basic equation examined was:

$$\text{Log of Odds of Reporting} = a + bx^1 + bx^2 + bx^3 + bx^4 + bx^5 + bx^6 + bx^7 + bx^8 + bx^9 + e$$

where

x_1 = Ratio of black population to total population
x_2 = Gini index of income concentration
x_3 = Race of respondent
x_4 = Family income
x_5 = Crime rate
x_6 = Presence of a weapon[2]
x_7 = Extent of injury[3]
x_8 = Monetary amount of loss[4]
x_9 = Education level[5]

This equation was estimated for each of the three different crimes (robbery, burglary, and assault), and for each of these crimes, the equation was estimated for four different groups of victims (whites, nonwhites, low-income and middle and upper-income) as well as for all groups combined.[6]

Results

The rates of reporting for the victims included in these analyses (i.e., victims without missing data) are presented in table 4.1. The overall rate of reporting is highest for robbery (sixty-three percent reporting, n = 685), which is followed closely by burglary (fifty-nine percent reporting, n = 4643), and is lowest for assault (fifty-three percent reporting, n = 1097). These average probabilities also suggest that nonwhites are more likely than whites to report burglaries and assaults, but slightly less likely to report robberies. Middle and upper-income victims are more likely than the poor to report robberies and burglaries, but somewhat less likely to report assaults.

The extent to which aggregate characteristics affect reporting will be discussed separately for each of the three crimes analyzed. For robbery, the most consistently significant variables that affect reporting are those variables related to seriousness, that is, the amount of loss and the presence of a weapon (see table 4.2). However, the race of the victim significantly affects reporting in the overall equation and approaches significance in the income equations. This suggests that, *ceteris paribus*, whites report incidents of robbery more frequently

Table 4.1 Average Probability of Victims Reporting Crime by Crime Type and Race and Income Groups (Ns are given in parentheses)

TYPE OF CRIME	ROBBERY	BURGLARY	ASSAULT
Overall percent reporting	.63	.59	.53
	(685)	(4643)	(1097)
Percent White reporting	.63	.58	.52
	(498)	(3925)	(963)
Percent Nonwhite reporting	.61	.63	.58
	(187)	(718)	(134)
Percent lower income reporting	.58	.54	.55
	(222)	(1482)	(346)
Percent mid-upper income reporting	.65	.62	.52
	(463)	(3161)	(751)

Table 4.2 Maximum Likelihood Logistic Regression Coefficients for Robbery Equations

Variables	OVERALL (N = 685)	BLACK (N = 187)	WHITE (N = 498)	LOW INCOME (N = 222)	MIDDLE-UPPER INCOME (N = 463)
	B	B	B	B	B
Percent Nonwhite	.24	.43*	.10	.26	.26
Gini	- .54	- 2.10	.01	- .83	- .08
Race	.34**	—	—	.41*	.31*
Crime Rate	.14	3.89	- .77	- .132	.79
Income Level	.02	- .00	.03	—	—
Amount of Loss	.20**	.23**	.18**	.19**	.20**
Weapon	.42**	.24	.50**	.28*	.49**
Intercept	4.35	4.47	4.54	4.55	4.25

*Coefficient is at least 1.5 times its standard error
**Coefficient is at least 2 times its standard error

than do nonwhites, but this does not seem to be due to aggregate-level "threat" conditions as measured here. Income inequality is consistently non significant in these equations, and in fact, is most often in the opposite direction (negative) of that predicted. The effect of percent nonwhite, although consistently positive, never quite reaches significance. However, contrary to the predictions of conflict theory, the effect of the percent nonwhite on reporting is strongest for blacks. Although a comparison of the difference between this coefficient in the white and black equations was not significant ($z = 1.44$), this finding is certainly noteworthy.

The results for the burglary equations are fairly similar (see table 4.3). The only consistently significant effect on the reporting of burglary is the amount of loss. In addition, income significantly affects reporting in the overall equation. Once again, the coefficient for income inequality, although approaching significance in the overall, white and low income equations, is in the opposite direction from the predictions, suggesting that income equality, rather than inequality, increases reporting. The effects of percent nonwhite were again consistently positive, approaching significance in the overall equation and attaining significance in the lower income equation. This suggests that although a large percentage of nonwhites may tend to increase the reporting of burglary, it has the strongest effect among the poor, regardless of the victim's race.[7]

For assault, it was found again that the majority of variables related to reporting are the control variables: whether medical attention

Table 4.3 Maximum Likelihood Logistic Regression Coefficients for Burglary and Assault Equations

	BURGLARY EQUATIONS				
	OVERALL (N = 4643)	BLACK (N = 718)	WHITE (N = 3925)	LOW INCOME (N = 1482)	MIDDLE-UPPER INCOME (N = 3161)
Variables	B	B	B	B	B
Percent Nonwhite	.14*	.17	.11	.28**	.00
Gini	- .55*	- .02	- .61*	- .79*	- .34
Race	.07	—	—	.10	.03
Crime Rate	- .52	- .17	- .61	.06	- .81
Income Level	.03**	.07*	.03**	—	—
Amount of Loss	.34**	.30**	.34**	.29**	.36**
Intercept	3.98	3.90	4.04	4.17	3.99

	ASSAULT EQUATIONS				
	OVERALL (N = 1097)	BLACK (N = 134)	WHITE (N = 963)	LOW INCOME (N = 346)	MIDDLE-UPPER INCOME (N = 751)
Variables	B	B	B	B	B
Percent Nonwhite	- .00	- .73**	.58**	.04	- .08
Gini	.22	1.65	- .31	.39	.40
Race	- .00	—	—	- .04	- .01
Crime Rate	- 3.44**	- 1.18	- 3.46**	- 2.57*	- 3.87**
Income Level	- .03	.02	- .03**	—	—
Weapon	.22**	.82**	.15**	.21*	.23**
Medical Attention	.46**	.68**	.43**	.65**	.36**
Educational Level	.03**	.01	.04**	- .01	.05**
Intercept	4.88	4.39	4.99	5.01	4.69

*Coefficient is at least 1.5 times its standard error
**Coefficient is at least 2 times its standard error

was needed, the presence of a weapon, the crime rate, and the respondent's education level (see table 4.3). In the overall equation, and the income equations, in fact, these are the only significant variables. However, in examining the racial equations it was found that the percent nonwhite significantly affects the reporting of assault for both whites and blacks, but in opposite directions. For whites, as conflict theory hypothesizes, percent nonwhite positively affects the reporting of assault. But, for blacks, the percent nonwhite negatively affects the reporting of assault. Thus, even though blacks tend to report assault more frequently than whites, as the percentage of nonwhites in their neighborhood increases, reporting decreases. In neighborhoods with higher percentages of nonwhites, blacks call on the police less, either because they have found the police to be nonresponsive (benign-neglect theory), or because assault is defined less as a crime to be dealt with by the criminal justice system. In contrast, white victims, in neighborhoods with higher percentages of nonwhites, call on the police more, presumably as a means of social control. This finding is clearly in line with conflict theory.[8]

Conclusions

It has been argued in this chapter that one of the plausible mechanisms through which variables representing "power threats" may affect crime control (in terms of official counts of crime, arrest rates, and/or police force size and expenditures) is the differential reporting of crime. That is, it has been argued that as the percent nonwhite and income inequality in neighborhoods increased, whites and middle and upper-income groups may be more likely to deal formally with offenders through the reporting of crime. The results of these analyses, however, give only partial support to this argument. No support was found for the hypothesis that income inequality increases the reporting of crime, or for the hypothesis that it especially increases the reporting of crime for the middle and upper-income group. In fact, for the property crimes (robbery and burglary) the effect of income inequality on reporting is negative, with only one exception. One possible explanation for the ineffectiveness of the income inequality variable in these equations lies within the level of analysis. It may be that at the neighborhood level, income is fairly homogeneous and the small amount of income inequality within the neighborhood is considerably less important than inequality between neighborhoods. That is, the issue of income inequality may be more important when middle or upper-class neighborhoods are surrounded by lower-class neighborhoods. Unfortunately, measures of income inequality *between* neighborhoods are not available in this data set.

The effect of percent nonwhite is somewhat more promising, although mixed. The strongest support for an effect on the reporting of crime is in the assault equations. Here, as conflict theory would predict, there is a clear positive effect for whites only, with the effect being negative for blacks. Percent nonwhite was also found to affect the reporting of lower-class burglary victims, but this was regardless of the race of the victim, suggesting that the percentage of nonwhites in the neighborhood may affect the reporting of blacks as well as whites in poor neighborhoods. Thus, if percent of nonwhites is threatening, it is most threatening not to whites, but to the poor in general. Percent nonwhite also approaches significance for black robbery victims. Again, this is not what would be expected from a conflict perspective. This equation was examined further to determine if race, income, and percent nonwhite all interact in their effect on reporting by including an interaction term of income and percent nonwhite in the black equation. The results of this equation suggest that in fact it is middle and upper-income blacks who are most threatened (i.e., most likely to report) by increases in nonwhites. When this interaction term was added to the black equation, it was found to be positive and significant ($b = .59$, s.e. $= .30$, $t = 1.97$).

This paper has suggested that for conflict theory to make a convincing argument, studies that relate variables to crime control need to explicitly propose and examine the realistic processes through which these variables operate, keeping in mind the very real concerns and fears of nonwhites and the poor with regard to crime. One mechanism in line with conflict theory that could explain previous relationships is the differential reporting of crime. The data suggest that high percentages of nonwhites in neighborhoods may lead to a racial bias in reporting some crimes (assault) to the police, which may ultimately lead to some racial bias within the criminal justice system.

One explanation of this finding may lie in the expectations or perceptions of victims in terms of police response. That is, blacks in nonwhite neighborhoods may expect that police will discount their complaints while whites in nonwhite neighborhoods may believe that the police will view their complaints as legitimate. Smith's (1986) findings on actual police behavior suggests that there are empirical grounds for these hypothesized perceptions. Smith's results show that the probability of the police filing a formal report of a victimization were in part determined by an interaction of the victim's race and the racial composition of the neighborhood. Although police were equally likely to file a report for white and black victims in racially mixed neighborhoods, they were less likely to file reports of black victims than reports of white victims in predominantly black neighborhoods.

Similarly, Liska and Chamlin (1984) discuss their findings of a negative relationship between percent nonwhite and the arrest rate for nonwhites in terms of benign neglect.

> [N]on-white victims may be less prone to report it to the police, and when they do report it, they frequently may be unable to legitimate their complaint as a crime and to pressure police to allocate resources to resolve it. (p. 385)

Although the findings here for assault suggest that this may in part be true, they also suggest that the threat hypothesis is relevant. As the percent nonwhite increases, nonwhites are less likely to report (creating a negative relationship), but at the same time whites are more likely to report (creating a positive relationship). But, as percent nonwhite increases, there will of course be more nonwhites, making the overall relationship negative. However, this overall negative relationship, suggestive of processes of benign neglect, hides the other process that is occurring at the same time, and that process is in line with the threat hypothesis.

In contrast to the findings for assault, however, the results for property crimes suggest that it is the poor, in general, and middle and upper-income blacks—not elites as they have generally been defined —who are most likely to bring about crime control through reporting. It seems that conflict theory must attempt to incorporate these findings in studies of crime control if this perspective is to develop and help explain social dynamics in the latter part of the twentieth century in the United States.

Minority Group Threat, Social Context, and Policing

Pamela Irving Jackson

Now classic studies of the police have detailed development of police norms and culture, focusing on police solidarity, secrecy, isolation, low esteem for the profession, and a tacit acceptance of violence administered to maintain respect for law enforcement personnel (Westley 1970; Skolnick 1967). Ignored until recently have been public expectations of the police as social control agents and the relationship of these expectations to the sociocultural contexts of rural-urban location, region, and decade. Also evading serious scrutiny until recently is the social control response to varying levels of minority group threat, a perception based on the subordinate group's size, visibility, and resources.

During the last three decades, however, there has been a rapid accumulation of evidence delineating the role of the police as a coercive, punitive response to significant threats of change in the existing balance of power. This chapter assesses that evidence, detailing the influence of minority threat and sociohistorical context on public support for policing and on public definitions of the police-community relationship.

Minority Group Threat

In *Toward a Theory of Minority Group Relations*, Blalock (1967) made a concerted effort to lay the theoretical foundation for systematic empirical investigation of social processes involving unequal groups. His propositions worked toward a precise depiction of the implications of static and changing levels of numerical and resource inequality between groups. The core of Blalock's argument was that as each group struggles toward dominance or to maintain a favored position, its success depends on its level of resources (including its size), its degree of cohesiveness, and the extent to which competing groups are fractionated. Resources—both financial and political—are invoked as needed to prevent competing groups from moving forward.

Blalock noted that the majority's resistance to minority efforts to improve its position should increase exponentially with increases in minority size or resources until the minority group reaches numerical majority or has accumulated sufficient resources to assure its dominance. At that point, such protection efforts slack off dramatically.

Scholars following Blalock have investigated the extent to which mechanisms of the state—especially policing and incarceration—are mobilized to preserve existing power balances, seeking evidence of Blalock's threat curve. Two decades of research on the police led eventually to the development of an elaborate model linking racial and economic inequality in urban centers to municipal fiscal commitment to policing (cf. Jackson 1989). The new theoretical model presumed minority group threat in spheres related to policing to be derived from both a fear of crime and fear of a loss of dominance on the part of the majority group. A minority group's size, combined with the high levels of poverty and inequality in urban centers, contributes to objectively higher urban crime rates through processes described by social disorganization theory (Shaw and McKay 1942), subcultural theory (Miller 1958), and conflict theory (cf. Quinney 1970).

In addition, however, these conditions give rise to the fear of crime—a political phenomenon linked more to racial and ethnic heterogeneity and social change than to crime itself (cf. Heinz et al. 1983). Fear of crime is one social response to the visibility of a culturally dissimilar minority group (cf. Garofolo 1979; Liska, Lawrence, and Benson 1981; Liska, Lawrence and Sanchirico 1982; Liska and Baccaglini 1983). The fact that public perceptions of the threat of crime are associated with the presence of a structurally disadvantaged group (cf. Turk 1969; Lizotte and Bordua 1980; Liska, Chamlin and Reed 1985) helps to explain the positive influence of percent nonwhite and of income inequality on arrest rates (cf. Liska and Chamlin 1984; Liska, Chamlin, and Reed 1984:389). Similarly, segregation may reduce the pressure on authorities to police minority populations, since segregation reduces interracial crime, the phenomenon most likely to result in pressure on crime control authorities. Fear of crime, coupled with a fear of a loss of dominance, provides fertile ground for mobilization of policing resources.

Dominant group cohesiveness. Efforts to test Blalock's propositions regarding minority group threat dovetailed historically with the 1970's groundswell of interest in conflict theory. No doubt the convergence of these foci of investigation contributed to the early language of these tests, which described a single dominant group or ruling class and its efforts to use the police to protect its advantages. This simple bifurcation between a dominant and subordinate group, one using the mechanisms of the state, the other its victim, is now outmoded. Instead, work in this area recognizes that multiple groups pressure authorities at differing levels of the crime control system to protect their economic situation and to preserve a way of life.

For example, since those groups in closest geographic and economic proximity to poor, minority populations, are most vulnerable to street crime, they may press for mobilization of police resources. More affluent groups, on the other hand, particularly those who are members of the prevailing demographic and cultural group, may exert their influence on lawmakers to retain a legal code protective of their economic privileges (Liska and Chamlin 1984). Economic interests, ethnic antagonism, and cultural identity are the new terms in the current debate. The new discussion has set aside the simplistic initial formulation of a struggle between dominant and subordinate group interests in favor of an investigation of the implications of minority group threat, fear of crime, social disorganization, and competition for sociopolitical dominance on the allocation of social control resources.

Policing

Policing, incarceration in prison or mental institutions, lynching, and implementation of the death penalty are social control mechanisms providing varying levels of coercion and punishment. Since they are invoked by the state in response to perceived deviance, imposition of these penalties is influenced by changes in public opinion and concern. Attitudes toward deviance and public tolerance of heterogeneity and change vary by time and location, both demarcators of social context to be discussed below. They affect policing as well as other forms of social control through the influence of politics.

Fiscal commitment to policing. Two aspects of police budget determination permit politics to enter the police funding process. First, existing formulas do not provide determination of the deterrant capabilities of specific patterns and levels of deployment. The hazard and workload formulas in use for decades (cf. O. W. Wilson 1941, 1972; Larson 1972) estimate optimal police force size and geographic location patterns. But they do not provide information on apprehension rates or public response time. As a result, intuition and experience are still the best guides in this area. Since ninety percent of the typical municipal police budget is allocated to employee salaries and fringe benefits, and almost half of the total police budget is devoted to the patrol force, funding discretion in this area is significant. The second basis for political involvement in the funding process is that city appropriations provide the bulk of the police budget. While the need for policing (in terms of a community's crime rate, population size, and density) as well as a community's ability to appropriate funds for policing (on the basis of its revenues and poverty levels) are important in funding determination, there is still considerable room for political influences—including perceptions of minority group threat, and existing systems of stratification and power—to play a role in determination of the overall allocations.

Early models of public fiscal commitment to policing were based on rational choice theory, and included as predictors of police expenditures measures of city size, intergovernmental revenues, metropolitan political fragmentation, and fiscal capacity (cf. Brazer 1959; Weicher 1970). Economists went so far as to argue that the size of the minority population in a city influenced the community's "taste" for policing, but they developed police resource determination models still based primarily on the assumption of a reciprocal relationship between crime and police strength. The assumption was that higher crime rates trigger a mobilization of police resources which in turn lead to reductions in the crime rate (cf. Becker 1968). Increasingly, researchers modeled both community characteristics and the crime-resources relationship in two-stage least squares regression equations (cf. McPheters and Stronge 1974; Greenwood and Wadycki 1973).

In the 1980s, however, developments in theory and methodology led to a reevaluation of these models. The inconsistency of results in this area, despite the highly sophisticated models, was not ignored by proponents of the newly popular labeling theory (cf. Lemert 1951; Becker 1963; Schur 1972; Gove 1975). Their focus on the impact of race, ethnicity, and social class on social reactions to deviance highlighted the potential significance of the fact that these elements were left out of the early police resource models. In addition, more sophisticated longitudinal modeling techniques, employed to assess the degree of reciprocity in the crime-police strength relationship, found no short or long-term evidence supporting the reciprocity assumption (cf. Greenberg et al. 1983; Loftin and McDowall 1982). At that point, police resource determination was seen to involve a much more complicated theory of collective response to crime. Characteristics and processes of the social system—stratification, power arrangements, and conflict, for example—were seen to influence police strength directly, not solely through their influence on the crime rate (cf. Loftin and McDowall 1982:399).

Police-community relations in historical and current perspectives. Sidney Harring (1983) views police historically as a "component of the state's power," important to the state in its role as mediator of the class struggle. An element in "the state's monopoly on the use of legitimate violence and coercion," police developed as one of the depersonalized mechanisms required by the capitalist society to regulate behavior by rational-legal forms (Harring 1983:8; Spitzer 1981). Bureaucratization, technological innovation, and professionalization of the police were elements of the rationalization process characteristic of all social institutions, and required to legitimize coercive control (Harring 1983:256). Harring (1983:258) goes on to point out that although nonviolent institutions such as the welfare system have reduced the need for overt police intervention in the class struggle, policing still provides the coercive core of the capitalist welfare state complex, always potentially available for the violent repression that was characteristic of their strikebreaking role in U.S. cities as late as the 1930s.

Johnson (1979), in describing the impact of crime on the development of the police in the United States from 1800 to 1887, notes that many of their patterns, especially those relating to their use of physical force, evolved from the need to establish authority on the streets, creating the "practical solutions" necessary to implement the "theoretical promise" of public order in a tumultuous and violent era. In Johnson's (1979:10) words:

> Individual patrolmen struggled with their own difficulties. Since no governmental agency had effectively mediated the spontaneous disputes of urban residents prior to the emergence of a preventive police, few citizens knew what to expect or respect in their new protectors.

This self-taught professionalism, Johnson later argues (1979:187), "reduced police sensitivity to the excesses possible in policies based on violence...." The introduction of civil service standards to policing "left police matters [even] more completely in the hands of the police (Johnson 1979:186)."

Recent evidence in the United States suggests that issues of class and physical force have not diminished in police-community relations. However, their parameters have been influenced by the evolution of clear, yet shifting, public expectations for policing, expectations that were themselves influenced by the 1960s era of minority entitlement.

Minority threat and social control. Scholarship during the last three decades has underscored the role of the municipal police in regulating threats posed by minority populations when their challenge to the prevailing culture appears overwhelming—as in the United States during the years after the riots of the 1960s and the early 1970s' immigration of Hispanics into U.S. cities. Police provided an intergroup buffer and ensured preservation of traditional values and patterns of dominance. Funds were appropriated to bolster police force size and equipment where minority threat appeared greatest, a judgment influenced at least in part by the proportion minority in the community. Federal funding by the Law Enforcement Assistance Administration (LEAA) stimulated capital expenditures by municipalities during the early 1970s; the level of these expenditures was influenced by the relative size of a city's black population (cf. Jackson and Carroll 1981; Jackson 1986).

Public conceptions of the role of police officers in U.S. cities in recent decades have varied directly with the degree of ethnic antagonism. During periods of tense intergroup relations, police were expected to control crime and restore order, using the level of force necessary to establish control. As antagonism subsided, public expectations for policing became less conflict centered. Police were called upon to be community relations officers, to avoid physical force whenever possible, and to refrain from deadly force (cf. Jackson 1989).

Social Context

Social context acts as a prism altering perceptions of the degree of minority group threat. Even after crime rates and other city characteristics as well as revenues are controlled, clear differences can be discerned in the influence of minority group threat on public fiscal commitment to policing in large versus small cities, in cities of the

South and West versus those of the Northeastern and North Central regions, and according to the degree of temporal proximity to racial strife.

City size. Traffic control and other service-related problems require greater police expenditures in large than in small cities. Such obvious differences have been well documented (cf. Brazer 1959; Weicher 1970; Rubinstein 1973), as have the higher crime rates of large cities (cf. Harries 1974; Pyle 1976). However, less obvious differences between the two groups of cities may also be important in determining the context of social life. For example, the anonymity and heterogeneity of large cities, as well as their reduced social cohesion and lower levels of informal surveillance (cf. Fischer 1984:139-41; Liska et al. 1981; Wirth 1938) may increase fear of crime (beyond what would be expected given the likelihood of crime, cf. Fischer 1984:108) as well as perceptions of minority group threat. These characteristics of city life also make policing more difficult (cf. Ogburn 1935; Pyle 1976; Harries 1974; Wolfgang 1968; Blau and Blau 1982; Mayhew and Levinger 1976; Jacobs 1982). Although in large cities competing demands for city services may reduce the level of fiscal commitment to policing, it appears that the social context of large cities intensifies the effect of minority size on public financing for policing (cf. Jackson 1986).

Recent work has demonstrated that in cities of fifty thousand or more, where anonymity and weak informal social controls may exacerbate both the fear of crime and the degree of threat represented by a minority group, the relative size of the black population had a greater impact on police expenditures than in smaller cities, even after the city's total crime rate, revenues, population size, density, and interracial inequality were controlled. (These variables have increasingly been included in studies of police force size and expenditures (cf. Brazer 1959; Becker 1968; Weicher 1970; Greenwood and Waycki 1973; Jacobs 1979; Jackson and Carroll 1981; Liska et al. 1981; Loftin and McDowell 1981; Greenberg et al. 1983).) Furthermore, in 1971, just after the riots, the impact of percent black on capital police expenditures in large cities was curvilinear, forming a threat curve portraying higher expenditures with progressively larger proportions of blacks in the population, and a drop-off in expenditures for capital police items where blacks outnumber whites (cf. Jackson 1986).

Region. There are several noteworthy differences among regions in the United States with potential implications for policing. First, crime rates show consistent regional variation, with the highest rates of crime overall in cities of the South and Southwest (Brantingham and Brantingham 1984; Pyle 1976; Harries 1971, 1974; Kowalski et al. 1980). The stability of these variations over time has been the subject of a long debate as to its subcultural or sociodemographic sources (cf. Gastil 1971; Hackney 1969; Loftin and Hill 1974). Secondly, across the regions there are observable variations in lifestyle as well as in affluence, both of which influence the ease and profit of crime (cf. Reppetto 1974; Boggs 1965; Cohen and Felson 1979; Mansfield, Gould, and Namenwirth 1974; Jackson 1984). In addition, regional variations in culture (cf. Zelinsky 1973), in climate, and in the range of economic opportunities for legitimate success might influence the likelihood of crime. Thirdly, and most importantly for the present discussion, are regional differences in the size of urban minority populations and in racial and ethnic stratification systems, in that they form a backdrop for minority police relations and influence public tolerance for a minority's numerical and economic growth.

There are several empirical examples of the influence of regional context on the relationship between minority size and social control resource levels. The long history of hostile black-white relations in the South has been found to be evidenced in the strength and form of the impact of percent black on 1971 capital police expenditures in that region (Jackson 1986). This relationship formed a more pronounced threat curve in the South than in other regions even after other socioeconomic characteristics of cities were controlled. In addition, minority threat models, developed to explain 1971 police expenditures for salaries and operations, retained more of their explanatory power in the South than in the other subpopulations even in 1978, a relatively quiescent period of race relations (Jackson 1989).

A threat curve also depicted the 1971 relationship between percent Hispanic and capital police expenditures in Western and Southern cities (cf. Jackson 1985), reflecting the history of Anglo-Hispanic tensions in the region. The importance of this history did not decline during the 1970s; by 1978 the Hispanic-police salaries and operations relationship was also curvilinear. However, in Northern and North Central cities, even at the end of a decade of national growth in Hispanic population groups, their relative size did not influence the level of urban police expenditures. Thus, regional context, as a sociohistorical construct, filtered non-Hispanics' perceptions of the minority group, influencing the degree of threat triggered by the group (cf. Jackson 1985).

Temporal proximity to racial strife. The influence of minority group threat on social control resources should, of course, be greatest in those historical periods closest to major intergroup conflict. Over twenty years ago, Silver (1967) summarized the historical record of police-community relations by noting that police-minority hostility varies with majority group concern over the dangerous class. Demonstrative political activity by blacks in the 1960s and by Hispanics soon after, as well as the riots of the same period, sparked sufficient public concern for the United States to mount its first federal effort to assist municipal authorities in bolstering the size and conflict preparation of their police forces. This federal war on crime may have reinforced hostile police-community relations where they existed and stimulated their development in other cities (cf. Feagin and Hahn 1973; Button 1978; Jackson and Carroll 1981; Jackson 1985, 1986). In fact, it has been argued that the political solidarity and activity of black and Hispanic ethnic groups in the 1960s and 1970s may have had as many costs as benefits in terms of their civil rights (Jackson 1989:9).

By the end of the 1970s, large-scale minority-majority conflicts had subsided. In fact, in 1973 the Community Relations Service, an organization within the federal bureau of justice charged with the resolution of community racial conflicts, found its staff cut by two-thirds, and its funding sliced in half. These slashes signaled federal recognition of the easing of racial tensions. The agency began to focus more on interracial crisis resolution than on prevention, and on minorities other than blacks. In addition, the Law Enforcement Assistance Administration's annual report began to show no listing for expenditures for civil disorders and riot control.

It is not a surprise, then, that in the late 1970s the impact of minority group size on policing expenditures differed from the pattern early in the decade and closer to the strife-filled 1960s. By 1978 the threat curve found in cities of fifty thousand or more in 1971 was not apparent, and percent black no longer had a statistically significant impact on capital police expenditures (Jackson 1985, 1986, 1989). The dissolution of the threat curve is not surprising in light of the other evidence suggesting that by 1972 the Nixon administration had set aside its fears of large-scale black rioting, focusing its attention instead on other minorities and concerns (cf. Button 1978:151). In fact, for capital expenditures, even in the South, the explanatory deficits for the minority threat models in 1978 (compared to the 1971 linear prediction levels) were clear and consistent. The decline in federal support for law and order in the face of reductions in interracial tension may be responsible for the greater variability among cities in the determinants of capital police spending at the end of the decade.

Public Conceptions of Policing in U.S. Cities

The impact of minority group threat on police-community relations along with the contextual variations noted above were also reflected in municipal newspapers from 1970 to 1980 (cf. Jackson 1989). Clearly demonstrated was the competition during the federal war on crime (in the early 1970s) between officers and the community for control of police procedures and standards of behavior. Police brutality toward citizens, racial and ethnic biases in police hiring and promotions, mobilization of police resources, and minority-majority control over the police were the subject of discussion in city newspapers. Emphasis on the law-and-order approach to the control of crime, and the struggle by sizable minority groups for some involvement in or control over police policy and operations, were also evident.

By the late 1970s, after the federal retreat on this issue, a new image of police as community relations officers emerged in public discussion. Some easing of interracial tensions was reflected in police-related newspaper reporting. For large industrial cities especially, the decade was a period of gradual movement away from municipal reliance on the police and on the law-and-order approach to the reduction of crime. As blacks grew in relative population size in these cities, achieving or approaching numerical majority, citizen demands for police accountability and fiscal cutbacks constrained the municipal police agenda. Citizens assumed greater control over police policymaking. Curbs were placed on police use of deadly force and new codes of ethics specified severe sanctions for excessive use of force by police officers. Public expectations for policing scaled back permissible violence and emphasized police accountability. Police layoffs and reductions in the police budget also signaled declines in public faith in the ability and power of the police to fight crime.

Police and Minority Group Threat in the 1990s

By the end of the 1970s U.S. urban populations had begun to carve out a new role for their police, one which recognized the limits inherent to the police function. As municipal social programs—many of which had been federally funded—were cut back, more than one

local public figure articulated the understanding that social programs, not the police, control crime.

From this beginning, a new emphasis on community policing, as
opposed to incident-oriented policing, emerged in the literature on
police (Wilson and Kelling 1989; Skolnick and Bayley 1986). But before
urban populations have had a chance to fully develop these notions of
community policing, they may be moving—out of fear and for lack of
affordable and effective alternatives—to an official law enforcement
response to two new "crime problems," gangs and drugs, that will be as
unresponsive to police intervention as was the racial unrest of the late
1960s. Since these problems are most intense in minority communities,
they will fuel public perceptions of a minority group threat as well as a
fear of crime.

Gangs. In both the national and local press, for example, police
are now conceptualized as a major element in strategies to control the
problem of urban gangs—whose violence and persistence suggest the
development of a new breed of the transitory youth gang that has historically been a part of the transitional zones of U.S. cities.

The alienation of youth in marginal racial, ethnic, and socioeconomic status positions continues to foster the formation of youth
gangs. But gang members' traditional stepping-stone into the more
conventional world of adulthood and its associated economic and
social privileges and obligations crumbled with the deindustrializa-
tion of the U.S. economy. Jobs in the manufacturing and industrial
sectors, Hagedorn and Macon (1988) point out, have traditionally provided that step and help to account for the historically transitory
nature of urban gangs in the U.S. In Hagedorn and Macon's view, the
current tendency of urban officials is to ignore the existence and persistence of gangs in their cities until a violent incident makes it necessary to acknowledge their presence, and then to view them as a problem of law enforcement. This can only exacerbate the situation, they
argue, leaving the problems of lack of legitimate opportunity in the
mainstream economy to fester, and perpetuating the social isolation
of urban minority communities. Gangs may be the only social connection for their members even as they move into adulthood.

Police will be unable to stem the development or significantly
thwart the activity of the 1980s urban gangs. They have emerged out
of the urban minority underclass experience, which can be remedi-
ated only by federally coordinated labor market policies and job training programs (cf. Wilson, 1987). In the absence of such efforts, police
can only engage in skirmishes with individual gangs, winning occa-

sional battles, but unable to prevent escalation of the war as the urban underclass becomes increasingly isolated.

Drugs. Law enforcement has also figured prominently in recent municipal and federal initiatives in the "War on Drugs." To the U.S. public, pushers are conceptualized as Hispanic in origin (given the Latin American drug connection) or as black urban dwellers (gang members, perhaps). Cracking down on their apprehension, evicting them from public housing, and introducing military-like discipline to their prison confinement situations are the strategies currently receiving the most public discussion. While these approaches may have some measure of success in their own right, they will not stem the tide of illegal drug use in the United States. Yet public expectations have again begun to structure a major role for municipal police officers in confronting and scaling down a problem whose roots and solutions are essentially beyond the scope of their control.

As municipalities proceed with the war on drugs and struggle with the violence of rival gangs, the nation may respond by providing funding to augment city law enforcement initiatives in these areas, arming and training municipal police departments in order to suppress these threats to domestic stability, much as was done after the racial unrest of the 1960s. Research indicates that its focus on matters unrelated to the central grievances that led to the disorders may have guaranteed the ineffectiveness of the early 1970s' response to the riots, and reinforced the hostility that was already evident in police-minority community relationships. Policy makers should heed these lessons of the past in shaping programs for the future. Otherwise, urban police may again be enmeshed in struggles that are beyond their their scope of resolution and out of their range of expertise. That would undo what social progress has been made in moving toward more realistic expectations for policing.

Summary and Conclusions

The role of the police as a coercive, punitive response to threats to destabilization of the existing sociopolitical system has received serious scrutiny during the last three decades. The need to contain urban masses, defined as troublemaking and threatening, triggered creation of the police in the seventeenth century and has stimulated repeated cycles of their mobilization since then. However, the first federal effort to stimulate readiness of municipal forces was in response to the urban racial unrest of the 1960s.

In retrospect, this federal effort may well be seen as a failure, and one that fostered greater levels of intergroup hostility. While it encouraged cities to react to urban upheavals with a law-and-order response, the federal government (under both fiscal and political pressure) quickly backed away from its financial commitments in this area. Initially encouraged by the federal initiative, however, municipal governments used federal resources and their own to respond to minority group threats with police mobilization at levels reflecting sociocultural conditions that varied with city size and region. Traditions of intergroup hostility carved in history and culture, perceptions of minority group threat triggered by civil rights gains and recent unrest, and the fear of crime all converged in shaping police-community relations after the riots of the 1960s.

In the end, though, a redefined police role did emerge as one of the legacies of the 1960s' protests for minority entitlements. During the 1970s, new public expectations were developed for police behavior, expectations that were more limited in scope, but carried with them considerably greater prescriptions for police-minority relationships. Before these expectations are fully institutionalized in police procedure and policy, however, current national urban crime problems threaten in the 1990s to involve the still largely white municipal police forces once again in unfruitful and hostile encounters with citizens in minority communities.

6

Social Structure and Crime Control Revisited: The Declining Significance of Intergroup Threat

Mitchell B. Chamlin and Allen E. Liska

The conflict perspective conceptualizes crime control as an instrument of dominant and powerful groups to control those actions and groups which threaten their interests. Turk (1969), for example, argues that culturally dissimilar groups are perceived by authorities as threats to the social and political order and that crime control can be understood as an instrument for controlling them. Drawing on the conflict perspective, considerable macroresearch examines the effects of intergroup threat, as reflected in the racial and economic composition of cities, on the capacity for crime control (police size and/or expenditures). In general, these studies (Jacobs 1979; Liska et al. 1981; Jackson and Carroll 1981; Greenberg et al. 1985; Jackson 1985, 1988; Chamlin 1989) show that the racial and economic composition of cities substantially affects policing resources and that the effects are most pronounced for the period just after the civil disorders of the 1960s (Liska et al. 1981; Jackson and Carroll 1981) and tend to decline thereafter (Greenberg et al. 1985; Chamlin 1989).

Recently Liska and Chamlin (1984) have extended this work to the actual volume of crime control (arrest rates). Their analyses focus on the effects of three variables (percentage of nonwhites, racial residential segregation, and economic inequality) on crime-specific (property and personal) and race-specific (white and nonwhite) arrest rates. Consistent with the policing literature, they report that these three variables significantly affect 1972 arrest rates. The present investigation attempts to replicate these findings for the succeeding decade. Specifically, we seek to determine whether or not Liska and Chamlin's 1972 results reflect period effects (i.e., the heightened perception of intergroup threat immediately following the civil disorders of the 1960s) or more enduring social relationships.

Percentage of Nonwhites

Liska and Chamlin (1984) identify three distinct theoretical hypotheses that link the percentage of nonwhites to arrest rates. The first (power) hypothesis focuses on the effect of the percentage of nonwhites on total arrest rates. According to Liska and Chamlin, conflict theory assumes that nonwhites experience a substantially higher arrest rate than whites because, relative to whites, they are less able to resist and because authorities share common stereotypes linking them to crime. Therefore, as the percentage of nonwhites increases, the total arrest rate of a city increases. Consistent with this view, they report that the percentage of nonwhites directly affects total arrest rates for property and personal offenses in 1972.

The second (threat) and third (benign-neglect) hypotheses focus on the contextual effects of the percentage of nonwhites on arrest rates. The threat hypothesis suggests that a high percentage of nonwhites produces an emergent property, "perceived threat of crime," which increases arrest rates through increasing pressure on police to control crime. The benign-neglect hypothesis suggests that the percentage of nonwhites affects arrest rates by constraining the racial composition of crime. For nonwhites, the proportion of in-group to out-group interaction in everything from marriage to crime increases (Blau 1977); so, as the percentage of nonwhites increases, the ratio of intraracial to interracial crimes increases for nonwhite offenders and decreases for white offenders. Especially for nonwhite offenders intraracial crime may carry a lower arrest rate than interracial crime does. Intraracial crime may be viewed by both victims and police as more of a personal and family problem than a matter requiring official intervention. Nonwhite victims may be less prone to report it to the police; and when they do report it, they frequently may be unable to legitimate their complaint as a crime and to pressure police to allocate resources to resolve it. Hence, Liska and Chamlin (1984:385) conclude that the percentage of nonwhites may negatively affect the nonwhite arrest rate. For white offenders, because intraracial crime involves high as well as equal status victims, the implications of the ratio of intraracial to interracial crime on arrest rates is not so clear. In support of the benign-neglect hypothesis but contrary to the threat hypothesis, Liska and Chamlin find that the percentage of nonwhites negatively affects nonwhite arrest rates for property and personal offenses.

Segregation

Drawing on the theoretical work of Blauner (1972) and Spitzer (1975), Liska and Chamlin argue that racial residential segregation should negatively affect arrest rates, especially nonwhites. According to Liska and Chamlin, the threat and benign-neglect hypothesis yield identical predictions concerning the relationship between segregation and arrest rates, although assuming different causal processes. The threat hypothesis contends that by reducing the threat of crime perceived by authorities, the segregation of nonwhites reduces the pressure on police to control crime, thereby decreasing the arrest rate, especially that of nonwhites. The benign-neglect hypothesis suggests that by increasing the ratio of intraracial to interracial crime for nonwhite offenders, the segregation of nonwhites decreases the pressure on police to control crime, thereby decreasing the arrest rate, especially that of nonwhites. Liska and Chamlin (1984) find that segregation negatively affects total property and personal arrest rates as well as those disaggregated by race.

Economic Inequality

Based on the economic conflict perspective, Liska and Chamlin argue that the greater the economic inequality, the greater the level of crime control, including arrests. In brief, economic conflict theorists (Chambliss and Seidman 1982; Jacobs 1979) argue that economic stratification or inequality accentuates economic conflict, which in turn increases the level of threat perceived by the dominant class; and the greater the conflict, economic stratification, and perceived threat, the greater the disposition of the dominant class to use coercion to maintain a social order favorable to its interests. Hence, as the level of economic inequality increases, so too should the arrest rate, especially for property offenses. In support of the economic conflict perspective, Liska and Chamlin report that economic inequality affects nonwhite property and personal arrest rates, and white property arrest rates.

In sum, Liska and Chamlin's (1984) research extends the earlier work on the capacity for crime control (policing resources) by demonstrating that the racial and economic composition of cities substantially affects the actual volume of crime control (arrest rates). The present investigation seeks to determine whether or not these findings are indicative of ongoing social processes or reflect the heightened perceptions of intergroup conflict that emerged from the urban unrest of the mid-1960s.

Methods

The sample and variables used in the proceeding analyses are virtually identical to those used by Liska and Chamlin. The sample is part of a larger sample of 109 cities, originally selected because their residential segregation levels have been calculated since 1940. Arrest data are available for ninety-seven cities.[1]

Crime control. The volume of crime control is measured by arrest rates (ratio of arrests to population) for both property (robbery, larceny, burglary, and auto theft) and personal (homicide, aggravated assault, and rape) index crimes. Studying general arrest categories minimizes inconsistencies in classification among departments (McClearly et al. 1982).

Capacity for crime control. Rational-choice theory (Becker 1968) suggests that an increase in the capacity for crime control should result in an increase in the actual volume of crime control; therefore, capacity is included. It is measured by the number of police employees per capita (Federal Bureau of Investigation, 1982). Civilian clerical employees are included in the measure because they free uniformed personnel for the immediate task of crime control.

Racial/economic composition. The percentage of nonwhites is taken from the census. Racial residential segregation is measured by the dissimilarity index, which describes the extent to which the racial composition of city blocks reflects the racial composition of the city as a whole (Choldin 1985).[2] Income inequality is measured by the Gini index of economic concentration, which expresses the average difference in income between all pairs of individuals in a city relative to the average income of that city (Blau 1977).

Control variables. Population size (in counts of one thousand), the percentage of poor people (measured as the percentage of families below the "poverty line"), and reported crime rates are included as control variables. Urbanism theory (Fischer 1976) suggests that a large population is associated with reliance on formal means of social control; a traditional Marxist perspective (Bonger 1916) suggests that the poor are least able to resist arrest; and rational-choice theory (Becker 1968) implies that reported crime rates positively affect arrest rates. Since theory and research also suggest that these variables are related to the dimensions of racial and economic composi-

tion examined here, their omission from the analyses may bias estimates of the effects of these dimensions on arrest rates.

Analytic procedures. Regression analysis is used to estimate the
direct effect of the causal variables on arrest rates.[3] Because of the
time lag involved in budget decisions, police size is measured two years
later (1982) than the other causal variables (1980). The 1982 budget
reflects decisions made sometime in late 1981, which can only be
based on information (reported crime rates) for 1980 or before. To
maintain the logical temporal order between police size and arrest
rates, the latter are also measured in 1982.

Results

Following Liska and Chamlin (1984) the analyses proceed as follows. Because conflict theory suggests that the income inequality effect is contingent on the type of crime (personal or property), the
equations are estimated separately for property and personal arrest
rates. First, the property and personal arrest rate equations are estimated; and second to isolate the contextual from the aggregate effect
of the percentage of nonwhites, these equations are estimated separately for whites and nonwhites.

Total arrests. The mean arrest rate ranges from a low of 1.4 per
one thousand whites for personal offenses (with a standard deviation
of 1.1) to a high of 17.4 per one thousand nonwhites for property
offenses (with a standard deviation of 6.6). Clearly, there is considerable variation in the chances of being arrested across crime categories, races, and cities.
Although high zero-order correlations between the causal variables do not in and of themselves indicate multicollinearity, the zero-
order correlation between the percentage of families below the poverty level and the percentage of nonwhites (r = .75) is large enough to
warrant concern. To assess the extent to which collinearity among the
exogenous variables affects the parameter estimates, collinearity
diagnostics are used. Experiments by Belsley, Kuh, and Welsch (1980)
reveal that a condition index threshold of thirty is indicative of potentially harmful collinearity and that a variance-decomposition proportion threshold of 0.5 should be used to identify dependencies among
the predictor variables. None of the condition indices for any of the
specifications exceeds thirty, indicating that collinearity is not a prob-

lem.[4]

Table 6.1 presents the OLS estimates of the property and personnel arrest rate equations. The first and second columns present the standardized and unstandardized coefficients for property arrest rates, and the third and fourth columns present those for personal arrest rates. The results are clear. They reveal that the racial and economic composition of cities has a consistently smaller effect on total arrest rates in 1982 than it did in 1972.

To review, Liska and Chamlin (1984) report that income inequality, segregation, and the percentage of nonwhites significantly affect property and personal arrest rates in 1972; but they have no appreciable effect on property and personal arrest rates in 1982. Of the social and racial composition dimensions, only the percentage of families below the poverty level significantly affects total arrest rates, and the reported crime rate and police size remain significant predictors of total arrest rates. Consistent with Liska and Chamlin, the reported crime rate positively affects both property and personal arrest rates; but, contrary to their research, police size positively affects the personal arrest rate.

Racial subsamples. As noted above, Liska and Chamlin (1984) estimate separate equations for white and nonwhite arrest rates to isolate the contextual from the aggregate effect of the percentage of

Table 6.1 Estimates of Arrest Rate Equations

| | PROPERTY | | PERSONAL | |
	Beta	B	Beta	B
Population	- .027	- .001	- .092	- .001
Police size	.187	.704	.248	.473**
Percent poor	- .300	- .183*	.060	.018
Crime rate	.572	.082***	.558	.259***
Income inequality	.170	17.897	.126	6.713
Segregation	.126	.047	.063	.012
Percent Nonwhite	.122	.023	- .019	- .002
Constant		- 9.278		- 4.751*
Adjusted R^2	.37		.48	

*p < .05
**p < .01
***p < .001

nonwhites and to facilitate interpreting the effect of the percentage of nonwhites on the total arrest rates. Although the present analyses indicate that the percentage of nonwhites has no effect on the total property and personal arrest rates, it is quite possible that it may affect white arrests, nonwhite arrest rates, or both. That is to say, strong countervailing social processes (positive power effects and negative benign-neglect effects) that are reflected in race-specific arrest rates may yield insignificant parameter estimates when total arrest rates are not decomposed by race.

The conflict perspective identifies two likely contextual effects for the percentage of nonwhites. The threat hypothesis suggests that it should be positive, the benign-neglect hypothesis suggests that it should be negative, and both hypotheses suggest that the effect, positive or negative, should be stronger for nonwhites than whites. The parameter estimates for 1972 (Liska and Chamlin 1984) strongly support the benign-neglect hypothesis, showing that the effect of the percentage of nonwhites is negative and strongest for nonwhite arrests, regardless of crime category. The parameter estimates for the 1982 equations are also very supportive of the benign-neglect hypothesis, showing that the effect of the percentage of nonwhites is negative and strong for both white and nonwhite arrests, regardless of crime category (see tables 6.2 and 6.3). Indeed, for nonwhite arrests the parameter estimates are very similar for 1972 and 1982. The betas are

Table 6.2 Estimates of White Arrest Rate Equations

	PROPERTY		PERSONAL	
	Beta	B	Beta	B
Population	.089	.003	- .020	- .001
Police size	.012	.045	.238	.297*
Percent poor	- .022	- .012*	.234	.047
Crime rate	.505	.067***	.546	.166***
Income inequality	.144	14.124	.092	3.211
Segregation	- .039	- .014	- .025	- .003
Percent Nonwhite	- .286	- .050*	- .300	- .018*
Constant		- 3.23		- 1.735
Adjusted R^2	.22		.37	

*p < .05
**p < .01
***p < .001

Table 6.3 Estimates of Nonwhite Arrest Rate Equations

| | PROPERTY | | PERSONAL | |
	Beta	B	Beta	B
Population	- .109	- .004	- .158	- .004
Police size	.140	1 .063	.306	.832***
Percent poor	- .225	- .275	- .059	- .026
Crime rate	.373	.107***	.585	.389***
Income inequality	- .021	- 4.373	.121	9.218
Segregation	.133	.100	.110	.030
Percent Nonwhite	- .364	- .138**	- .326	- .044*
Constant		8.023		- 5.148*
Adjusted R²	.29		.30	

*p < .05
**p < .01
***p < .001

remarkably similar. For property arrests the beta = - .38 for 1972 and
- .36 for 1982, and for personal arrests the beta = - .41 for 1972 and
- .33 for 1982, suggesting that the effect of the percentage of nonwhites relative to that of other variables is exactly the same over the
decade. However, the Bs drop from 1972 to 1982 (table 6.4),
suggesting that the absolute effect of the percentage of nonwhites on
nonwhite arrests, while still substantial in 1982, decreased over the
decade. For white arrests the opposite is true. For both property and
personal arrest rates the percent nonwhite Bs and betas are small and
statistically insignificant in 1972 but substantial and statistically
significant in 1982, suggesting that both the relative and absolute
effects of the percentage of nonwhites on white arrests increased over
the decade.

Support for the conflict perspective, however, is limited to the
effects of the percentage of nonwhites. Income inequality has no effect
on race-specific arrest rates regardless of the crime category in 1982,
while Liska and Chamlin (1984) find that it affects white and
nonwhite property crime arrest rates in 1972. Similarly, racial
residential segregation has small and inconsistent effects across race-
specific equations in 1982, while Liska and Chamlin find that it
moderately affects white and nonwhite property and personal arrest
rates in 1972.

Consistent with the results for 1972, the reported crime rate positively affects both the property and personal arrest rates for both

Table 6.4 Summary of Conflict Variables on Arrest Rates by Crime Type, Race, and Year

White Arrest Rates*

	PROPERTY				PERSONAL			
	1972		1982		1972		1982	
	Beta	B	Beta	B	Beta	B	Beta	B
Income inequality	.31	26.700	.14	14.100	.16	2.400	.09	3.200
Segregation	- .25	- .074	- .03	- .014	- .39	- .020	- .02	- .003
Percent Nonwhite	.00	.000	- .28	- .050	- .07	- .002	- .30	- .018

Nonwhite Arrest Rates*

	PROPERTY				PERSONAL			
	1972		1982		1972		1982	
	Beta	B	Beta	B	Beta	B	Beta	B
Income inequality	.24	105.200	- .02	- 4.300	.23	20.100	.12	9.200
Segregation	- .21	- .326	.13	.100	- .24	- .073	- .11	.030
Percent Nonwhite	- .38	- .375	- .36	- .138	- .41	- .081	- .33	- .044

*All equations also include population, police size, percent poor, and crime rates.

whites and nonwhites in 1982. Finally, the effects of the percentage of poor, population size, and police size are generally statistically insignificant and inconsistent in 1972 and remain so in 1982.

In short, while the analyses of the racial subsamples provide strong evidence of a benign neglect effect in both 1972 and 1982, the overall impression of these findings is that social processes identified by the conflict perspective affect the volume of crime control less in the early 1980s than in the early 1970s.

Discussion

Based on the conflict perspective, considerable research has examined the effects of racial and economic composition on policing resources. Recently, Liska and Chamlin (1984) have extended this work to the actual volume of crime control, demonstrating that the percentage of nonwhites, racial residential segregation, and economic inequality substantially affect crime-specific and race-specific arrest rates in 1972. The present investigation finds mixed evidence of these effects in 1982.

The partial failure of this study to replicate Liska and Chamlin's (1984) findings regarding the threat effects of segregation and economic inequality suggests that their findings in part reflect historical period effects. Liska et al. (1981) report that the percentage of non-whites and segregation have small and inconsistent effects on police size prior to the 1970s but strong effects during the 1970s. They conclude that the civil rights activities and the urban riots of the middle and late 1960s intensified interracial conflict and thereby associated threat with racial and economic structures during the 1970s. Similarly, Piven and Cloward (1971, 1987) argue that welfare programs (which they view as a vehicle for social control) were expanded during the 1960s and 1970s to quell the rash of civil disorders and were contracted when political stability was restored. It is our contention that the relationship between racial segregation and economic inequality and arrest rates may, too, have been accentuated by the events and intergroup conflict of the 1960s and 1970s.

While the percentage of nonwhites may also be associated with threat, especially during the late 1960s and 1970s, the threat effect may be obscured by a stronger benign-neglect effect, which is evident in both 1972 and 1982. As the percentage of nonwhites increase, non-whites constitute an increasing proportion of crime victims. Lacking political and economic clout, nonwhite victims may be unable to legitimate their complaints as crimes and to pressure police to allocate resources to resolve them. While this may well explain the negative relationship between the percentage of nonwhites and the nonwhite arrest rate, it cannot explain the negative relationship between the percentage of nonwhites and the white arrest rate, especially for personal crimes which tend to be intraracial. It may be that a high percentage of nonwhites, and thus a high percentage of nonwhite victims, produces a context or climate of neglect whereby both nonwhite and white victims experience difficulty in legitimating their complaints as crimes and in mobilizing the police.

Extralegal Influences on Imprisonment: Explaining the Direct Effects of Socioeconomic Variables

James Inverarity

In his 1902 speech to the inmates of the Cook County jail, Clarence Darrow observed,

> First and last, people are sent to jail because they are poor. . . . There are more people who go to jail in hard times than in good times—few people, comparatively, go to jail except when they are hard up. (Darrow 1957; 8-9).

Darrow's observation closely coincides with the central conclusions of recent research on the determinants of imprisonment rates: holding crime constant, imprisonment varies with poor people and hard times.

The basis of social and economic influences on imprisonment rates is discretion. For example, of the 91,000 larceny convictions in the United States in 1986, only about forty percent resulted in prison terms (Langan 1989). The legal system routinely treats unemployment of offenders as a risk factor in deciding pretrial release and post-conviction probation. For example, Hagan's case study of an urban court reveals that "in cases with individual victims . . . the independent variable that most consistently predicts bail, adjudication, and sentencing decisions is the employment status of the accused" (1982: 1010). Larceny and other offenses lying in the middle range of severity have the greatest variability in sentencing outcomes and the highest risk of racial or class discrimination (cf. Unnever and Hembroff 1988: 56).

The labor market, thus, may directly affect the imprisonment rates. Figure 7.1 schematically portrays the relationship between postwar U.S. cycles of unemployment and imprisonment. This graph plots the standardized variables (z-scores), showing annual standard deviations of each variable from its mean (set at zero).

The trends do not behave uniformly throughout the postwar period. All three trends rose above their means after 1975, partly reflecting the impact of the baby boom on unemployment, crime, and imprisonment. From 1948 to 1972 the crime rate gradually increased, then sharply accelerated in the 1970s. In contrast, imprisonment and unemployment follow parallel cycles. For example, both unemployment and imprisonment rates began declining in 1961 and reached record lows in 1969. This decline occurred despite an accelerating crime rate during this period. Multivariate analyses confirm the impression given by this graph: unemployment appears directly linked to imprisonment.[1]

Dissecting the relationship between race and imprisonment proves to be more complicated. Young black males in the U.S. run the highest risk of imprisonment, at present twenty-five times the national average. "About eight percent, or one out of every twelve, is in jail or prison on any given day" (Blumstein 1988:232). While black risk of imprisonment may reflect greater involvement of young black males in crime, considerable interstate variation in racial disparity remains once crime is controlled (Bridges and Crutchfield 1988).

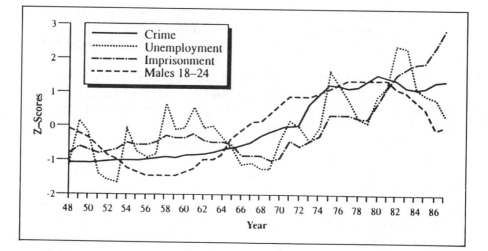

Figure 7-1 Imprisonment, unemployment, crimes, and males 18-24 per population in standardized scores (1948-1987)

Most empirical studies focus on either race or unemployment, but they usually draw upon a common set of theoretical frameworks. Relationships among these theoretical frameworks may best be understood by distinguishing theories of action from theories of structure (cf. Giddens 1982; Humphries and Greenberg 1981). Action theories explain prison admissions as the result of decisionmakers choosing crime control policies that advance their interests. *Rational choice, power elite, and state managerial* theories share a common focus on decision processes, but differ in who they identify as the key actors. *Structural theories*, in contrast, try to explain imprisonment rates by focusing on processes beyond the understanding and control of decisionmakers. We will focus here specifically on the structural theories that use labor market variation to explain variation in imprisonment.

Each of these theoretical frameworks assigns a distinct role to and provides a different interpretation of how the social threats posed by unemployment and race influence imprisonment apart from crime. The alternative explanations of social threat are the primary concern of this discussion. This chapter outlines these perspectives, evaluates their current empirical status, and details their current agendas for future research.

Action Theories of Imprisonment

Rational Public Choice Explanation of Imprisonment

The rational public choice explanation of imprisonment views crime and punishment as market phenomena. Market participants are rational decisionmakers capable of calculating advantage when given full information about the alternative choices. Criminals are rational decisionmakers who respond, among other things, to the costs of imprisonment (Wilson 1975:197-9). Race and unemployment correlate with imprisonment only indirectly because of their relationships with crime rates. Equally, rational law enforcement agents adjust the levels of imprisonment to levels of crime. In democracies this crime control response comes about primarily through a political process in which the rational voters' aggregate demand for sanctions varies with their victimization by criminals. Interaction among rational criminals, victims, politicians, and administrators produce a long-term equilibrium that allocates resources efficiently.

On the surface this perspective appears to account for some recent trends in crime and punishment. A sharp increase of urban crime in the mid-1960s became a campaign issue in local and national elections. For example, presidential candidate Ronald Regan argued:

> If you want to know why crime proliferates in this nation, don't look at the statistics on income and wealth; look at statistics on arrest, prosecutions, convictions, and prison population. These data show that the failure of the criminal justice system and the impediments of court trials that seek to discover if the police made some error in the gathering of hard evidence are behind the crime rate. (1976 speech quoted by Finckenauer 1978:23).

Public opinion polls seemed also to indicate an increase in popular demand for locking up more criminals for longer terms. By 1975, the new conservative ideology supported by a beleaguered, victimized population appeared to have reversed the decline in the rate of imprisonment.

Despite the apparent correspondence of the rational public choice model to recent trends in imprisonment, closer inspection of its underlying premises reveals the superficiality of this explanation. In thinking about crime, people evidence very little rational calculation. Although crime rates affect the fear of crime (Liska et al. 1982), victimization does not explain fear. If fear of crime were rational, crime victims would express more fear than those untouched. This is especially true considering the extent of repeat victimization. Mass media influence crime anxieties more than either personal or peer experiences of victimization (Scheingold 1984:64; Liska and Baccaglini 1990).

Furthermore, little relationship seems to exist between anxiety about crime and preference for increasing imprisonment. This general lack of correlation arises from peculiar variations in anxiety by age, sex, race, and region. Women, for example, suffer higher crime anxiety, but tend to be less punitive than men. Blacks experience higher victimization risks, but are less inclined than whites to increase imprisonment levels. Rural whites favor tougher sentencing than urban whites, even though rural areas experience less crime. Actors responding rationally to their objective circumstances seem to be a rare species (Taylor et al. 1979).

The relationship between political rhetoric and public sentiment, thus, is more complicated than it appears. Some research suggests that policymakers overestimate the conservatism of public sentiment (Riley and Rose 1980; Cullen et al. 1985; Gottfredson et al. 1988). Even where public opinion is conservative, the connection with policy is unclear. For example, variation in public opinion about the death penalty has no relationship to the actual number of executions

(Zimring and Hawkins 1986:135).

Similarly, presidential campaign promises of criminal justice reform are normally unfulfilled because the president possesses little constitutional authority over crime control (Epstein 1977:63-71). The largest federal crime control initiative, the Law Enforcement Assistance Administration created in 1968, conflicted with state prerogatives over criminal justice policy and never accomplished the envisioned reforms in crime control (Feeley and Sarat 1980). At the state level, legislation attempting to make prison terms more certain and longer may have little actual impact on a legal system. Judges and prosecutors routinely nullify reforms that interfere with standard practice.[2] Fiscal constraints and commands from the federal judiciary to meet minimum standards of humane confinement serve as further countervailing forces to changing standards (Taggert 1989).

While the growth of prison populations in the 1980s coincides with sentencing reform legislation, multivariate studies fail to find net effects of such reforms on either prison admission rates or racial composition (Carroll and Cornell 1985; Link and Shover 1986; Inverarity and Tedrow 1990). Overall, despite its surface plausibility, rational public-choice theory awaits systematic empirical support.

Power Elite (Conflict) Theories

Besides the rational-choice theory, the action orientation includes two major alternative formulations that differ in how they weigh the roles of insiders and outsiders in forming social control policy. *Power elite formulations* locate the relevant actors outside the institutions of social control, most often as owners and controllers of economic resources. The second, *managerial elite*, position assigns priority in explaining policy to state managers within the criminal justice system. This position views policymakers as motivated by vested interests in crime control organizations and as capable of resisting external pressures to change fundamentally existing organizations. Like rational public-choice theories, conflict theories are instrumentalist theories, viewing crime control as one of several weapons intentionally used by actors to advance their interests; elite theories essentially differ from rational public-choice theory in viewing imprisonment as responsive to a small group sharing certain vested interests and monopolizing resources.

The term "conflict perspective" often denotes a version of action theory that explains rates of imprisonment by the intervention of power elites. The power base of these elites lies outside legal institutions, which they influence by direct participation or indirect manipulation (campaign contributions, sponsorship of think tanks, networks of association). One of the more precisely stated empirical applications of conflict theory to the explanation of imprisonment rates is Jacobs' (1978) analysis of interstate variations in risk of imprisonment. Jacobs postulates "criminal statutes are created and enforced according to the wishes of those with power" (1978:515). Jacobs breaks the common circularity in such arguments (the "powerful" actors being identified by the outcome of the legal change) by measuring concentration of political power with interstate variation in the Gini index of income inequality: "Where economic resources are distributed more unequally, economic elites ought to be better able to achieve their aims, i.e., the criminal codes will be administered in a way that pleases monied elites" (1978:516). Furthermore, because economic elites may be particularly threatened by property crime, a significant correlation should exist between income inequality and the risk of imprisonment for property but not for violent offenses.[3]

Other evidence for the power-elite explanation of imprisonment rates is mixed. For example, Balbus (1973) studied felony sentencing by the criminal courts facing acute threats. While soaring unemployment or extreme inequality may indirectly threaten power elites, the urban riots of 1965-1968 posed a clear and direct threat that should theoretically increase imprisonment rates: "As the contradictions of capitalism become more apparent and the control system more unsuccessful, the methods of coercion become similarly more explicit and more desperate" (Platt 1974:389). Balbus found that although during riots police exercised extraordinary levels of coercion and made large numbers of unfounded arrests, the courts did not similarly jettison standard procedure. Indeed, there appears to be an *"inverse relationship between the magnitude of the revolts and the severity of the court sanctions* imposed on participants" (1973:250; emphasis in original). The risk of imprisonment for a felony arrest paradoxically decreased during a riot, in part because the courts adhered to due process standards to preserve legitimacy.

Given such inconsistent evidence, the most productive research strategy may be to specify the general circumstances under which the conflict model holds.[4] For example, we might seek to understand under what kinds of economic systems the norms of due process effectively constrain power-elite manipulation of legal coercion (cf. Thompson 1975) Alternatively, we might explore more directly the linkages between economic elites and criminal justice policymakers.[5]

Managerial Elite Theories

In 1972, Commissioner of the Massachusetts Department of Youth Services Jerome Miller unilaterally shut down the juvenile training schools (Coates et al. 1978). This dramatic episode of decarceration epitomizes a second version of action theory that focuses on administrators as independent decisionmakers. Indeed, Rutherford rejects the role of such variables as unemployment in explaining imprisonment because such explanations are "deterministic." One should instead "regard prison populations as primarily the consequence of policy choices and practice" (1984:47). Prison growth is an organizational imperative, providing administrators with career opportunities and imbuing the organization with legitimacy.

Rutherford's formulation of the managerial control theory fails to weigh competing alternative explanations of imprisonment rates or to suggest ways of measuring variation in organizational expansiveness. In a multivariate analysis of California prison admissions and releases from 1851 to 1970, Berk et al. (1983) do find evidence of administrators' efforts to maintain predictable levels of custodial populations over time.

The theoretical bases of such findings have been elaborated in recent theories of the state (Skocpol and Amenta 1986), which suggest that state managers shape policy independently of both elite preferences and structural forces. Block (1977) portrays state policy as the outcome of a three-way conflict among capitalists, workers, and "managers of the state apparatus." Only the latter have a sustained and systematic understanding of particular state policies, such as corrections. In working to protect their vested interests, state managers attempt to implement effective policy and to maintain their own organization. Similarly, Balbus (1973) identifies "organizational maintenance" as one mechanism of limiting criminal courts in prosecuting urban rioters. Given a short-term fixed capacity for incarceration, managers resist unpredictable increases in the institutionalized populations.

One important variant of managerial theories is the fiscal crisis thesis: declines in incarcerated populations result from cost-cutting efforts of state managers faced with fiscal constraints (Scull 1977, 1982). Although the past two decades of rising imprisonment rates combined with chronic fiscal crises appear counter to this theory, it is better supported by trends in imprisonment relative to the increase in crime rates (Inverarity and Grattet 1989:357). Further evidence for the thesis may be found in the apparent substitution of violent offenders for nonviolent offenders in prison admissions (Sherman and Hawkins 1981), and interstate variations in the relationship between crime rates and imprisonment rates (Michalowski and Pearson 1990: 71).

Managerial elite formulations concentrate on intraorganizational constraints on social control. The full implications of this perspective for explaining the covariation of imprisonment and unemployment remains undeveloped. Dickson (1968) suggests that social control agencies faced with budgetary declines during economic recessions may respond by increasing their scope of operations. This line of reasoning suggests that the correlation between imprisonment and unemployment is spurious; economic recession stimulates expansion of institutional commitments by crime control agencies seeking to maintain their resources. Testing such an argument requires elusive evidence about the (unconscious) processes of decision making. Its present significance lies in the alternative interpretation it provides of macrolevel relationships used to support other explanations.

Structural Theories of Imprisonment: Labor Market Explanation

In contrast to action theories, structural theories do not try to explain how imprisonment rates are manipulated by motivated and capable elites. Indeed, for structural theories individual and collective actors are best understood as carriers or transmitters of forces over which they seldom exercise understanding or control. The choices made by such actors are, at best, highly circumscribed by structural constraints, which constitute the proper focus of investigation.

One influential formulation of this position in the study of imprisonment is Rusche and Kirchheimer's (1939) work, *Punishment and Social Structure.* Central to their neo-Marxist approach is a distinction between manifest functions of imprisonment (deterrence, incapacitation, retribution, rehabilitation) and its latent functions. While the rationales of imprisonment stand as significant in their own right, the latent functions of punishment explain more of the variation in its forms and frequency. Thus, they argue, we must study "the intensity of penal practices as they are determined by social forces, above all by economic and then fiscal forces" (1939:5). Rusche and Kirchheimer's study revealed that transitions between modes of production coincide historically with the origins of new modes of punishment. Recent research has continued to follow some variant of their premise that the mode of production shapes the form of law. This orientation treats as secondary and derivative cultural and political variations, while assigning priority to two major independent variables: business cycles and labor markets.

Business Cycle Variation

Several studies using a variety of econometric methods have found a direct influence of the business cycle on imprisonment. The initial studies of such trends in the U.S. (Jankovic 1977) and Canada (Greenberg 1977) detected a direct effect of unemployment on imprisonment, but used few control variables. Later research discovered that in postwar England and Wales unemployment rates significantly affect imprisonment rates, holding constant age composition, crime, and conviction rates (Box and Hale 1985; Hale 1989; Sabol 1989). Similarly, Italian prison admission rates from 1896 to 1965 follow more closely the business cycle than they do crime rate fluctuations (Melossi 1985). In France during two periods (1920 to 1938 and 1952 to 1985) unemployment affected imprisonment rates net of crime rate and age composition (Laffargue and Godefroy 1989). The same result appears in analyses of the U.S. imprisonment rate for both national aggregate (Inverarity and McCarthy 1988) and interstate data (Inverarity and Tedrow 1990). Thus, with fair consistency, research reveals that with crime held constant, imprisonment rates vary closely with the business cycles.

Research on business cycles generally analyzes highly aggregated data that tend to obscure the historical and comparative variations central to Rusche and Kirchheimer's analysis. Some of this research, however, suggests that unemployment's effect on imprisonment varies with the type of labor market. For instance, unemployment affects imprisonment only for blacks (Myers and Sabol 1987), and unemployment in the competitive sector more strongly influences imprisonment rates than unemployment in the monopoly sector (Inverarity and McCarthy 1988). Similarly, although some correlation appears between unemployment and imprisonment in prewar Poland, the postwar period reveals no such relationship; the major fluctuations in imprisonment rates appear to result from government amnesties unrelated to economic conditions (Greenberg 1980). Similarly, variation in unemployment in the Netherlands appears unrelated to prison admissions (deHaan 1990). Such exceptions call for rethinking the role of labor markets.

Variation in Labor Markets

One direction for such rethinking is to study the relationship between imprisonment and types of labor market. To illustrate this approach, the following discussion contrasts regional and historical variation in the following three types of labor market: plantation, competitive capitalist, and monopoly capitalist. The federal system of the U.S. created wider regional variation in state policies than exists within most other industrial societies (Heidenheimer et al. 1983). As a result, the connections between the type of labor market and the form of punishment may appear much more transparent in this nation-state.

The plantation system retarded the development of imprisonment, much in the same way it retarded the development of state welfare programs (cf. Quadagno 1988). In the first, competitive stage of capitalism, the prison was invented and diffused (Lea 1979). The second, monopoly stage of capitalism bred alternatives to incarceration, most significantly probation and juvenile justice. Even these basic connections between economy and punishment help explain several odd regional and racial variations in U.S. imprisonment rates.

Social control in plantation modes of production. In the plantation mode of cotton production that developed in the South, a class of planters who owned large tracts of land extracted surplus value from agricultural workers. The relations between these two classes were conditioned by the nature of the production process. Cotton required extensive hand labor, particularly in the spring planting and late fall picking seasons. Because picking could not be done mechanically and had to occur immediately after the crop ripened, planters sought to maintain a reliable work force throughout the year. Slavery had been, from this standpoint, an optimal mode of labor management; indeed, the slow economic recovery of the South after the Civil War may have been due primarily to the difference in modes of labor control (Ransom and Sutch 1977:47). The principal institutional replacement for slave labor became the annual sharecropping contract, reinforced by constraints on mobility, both legal (vagrancy and antilabor enticement legislation) and informal (lynching and other forms of terrorism).

Plantation systems typically administer crime control informally and locally (Cohen 1976). In the antebellum period, the Southern penitentiary was virtually reserved for serious white offenders, while slaves were disciplined by their owners (Adamson 1983; Guttman 1975:5–41; Petchesky 1981). After the Civil War, crime control remained largely a local matter. To maintain their labor supply, planters diverted tenants in trouble away from the legal system.

Employers either provided jailed tenants with money to pay fines and hire lawyers or engaged directly in plea bargaining and political influence (Davis et al. 1941:234). This paternalistic system parallels that of rural England in previous centuries (Hay 1975). This system was not, however, universal; considerable mobility occurred among the tenant farmers, albeit primarily within the local labor markets (Wright 1986). In addition, a pool of migratory day laborers added to the instability of local controls.

In response to the new labor markets and acute state fiscal crises after the Civil War, a new Southern prison system evolved characterized by (1) disproportionate incarceration of young black males, primarily for minor property offenses (Ayers 1984:199), and (2) extensive use of the convict lease system, in which states rented convict labor power to private enterprise. For the most part, such labor was employed in railroad construction, mining, and other industries that faced severe shortages of chear unskilled labor (Shelden 1981).

Prisons and factories: Innovations in social control accompanying competitive capitalism. Capitalism begins logically and historically with the free market exchange of labor power for wages. Unlike the plantation, factory's demand for labor varies not with the regularity of the seasons, but with fluctuations of the business cycle. Mobility of workers is important to the efficient investment of capital. These distinct requirements for the labor force generated corresponding changes in the demands for social control.

The elective affinity between the penitentiary and competitive capital has been subject to much theoretical speculation. The penitentiary was an institutional innovation that provided effective social control in an environment in which relationships between the classes were impersonal, temporary, and large-scale (Rothman 1971). In early, competitive capitalism, the *laissez-faire* state neither limited hours, established health and safety standards, nor imposed minimum-wage levels. Workers and their families bore the cost of unemployment, disability, and accidental death.

Competitive capital resists state subsidy of these costs of labor market participation. Competitive capital favors coercion over welfare state policies. Racial differences facilitate such policy choices: "When a particular racial group does the most menial work for the lowest wages, the relief system cooperates by reducing the amount of aid to that group or by closing off the posssibility of any aid whatsoever" (Piven and Cloward 1971:133). Unlike precapitalist legal coercion, which is administered locally by the dominant class, the state takes over legal coercion, freeing the capitalist from the burdens of social control. Thus the emergence of competitive capital was facilitated by the criminalization of traditional modes of economic gain (Linebaugh 1976). Similarly, criminal laws regulating migration serve to provide a cheap and docile labor force critical for labor-intensive enterprise (Burawoy 1976). When legitimate opportunities in the labor force shrink during recessions, the state expands the use of confinement. Imprisonment, unlike welfare, maintains a competitive labor market by stigmatizing alternative but illicit forms of economic enterprise.

Emergence of monopoly capital and new forms of social control. By 1900 in several industries small firms in competitive markets were displaced by large firms in monopolistic markets. Simultaneously, labor was becoming increasingly organized. The concentration of capital and unionization of workers produced a form of *monopoly capitalism* that supported new forms of social control (Humphries and Greenberg 1981).

First, monopoly capital is, on the average, less hostile to state welfare programs. Both plantation and competitive capital resisted welfare programs because such policies reduce the competitiveness of labor markets. Southern congressmen actively impeded the growth of the welfare state because they feared federal control over benefits would disrupt labor arrangements (Quadagno 1988). Because workers in the monopoly sector earn higher wages and benefits and are more insulated from job competition, minimal state subsidies are less likely to undermine monopoly sector work incentives. Furthermore, firms in the monopoly sector find it easier to pass along to the consumer the burden of taxation.

As monopoly capital became politically dominant around 1900, the state began to intervene increasingly in the economy. This domination culminated in New Deal legislation that substantially expanded the federal role in welfare and financed a shift in state priorities toward noninstitutional forms of social control (Lerman 1982). Crime control reforms, such as probation, indeterminate sentencing, and juvenile justice became increasingly diffused.[6]

While the plantation mode of production has been all but extinct since the 1960s, competitive and monopoly capital coexist in a dual economy and contemporary capitalism is a complex mixture of both elements. Dual economy and labor market segmentation research has, with some difficulty, sought to delineate these variations (Hodson and Kaufman 1982).

The simplest characterization divides labor markets into two sectors. Competitive-sector industries involve small-scale production by nonunion workers earning low wages for irregular employment that has low productivity. Such workers are disproportionately young, female, and minority. Currently, the competitive capital sector includes agriculture, retail sales, the garmet industry, and repair shops. Monopoly forms of capital consist of large-scale firms that are capital- rather than labor-intensive. Such firms have higher productivity, capital-labor ratios, profits, and unionization. Examples of such enterprises currently include steel, automobile, appliance, and electrical equipment manufacturing and transportation.

Labor market segmentation research finds that unemployment has different consequences for workers depending upon their industry. Monopoly-sector workers (e.g., autoworkers) are more likely to experience temporary layoffs than competitive-sector workers (e.g., retail clerks) who more often face outright discharge (Schervish 1983). Competitive-sector workers are more marginal in job security and bargaining power. Some evidence suggests a greater responsiveness of imprisonment rates to surges in the competitive-sector unemployment rate (Inverarity and McCarthy 1988) or labor force participation (Colvin 1990).

During economic downturns, imprisonment, then, substantially reduces the number of surplus workers who are provided with neither work nor welfare. The unskilled, uneducated and unemployed—who constitute most of the prison population—are not an attractive source of labor power for most firms. They may appear more trouble than they are worth, even employed below the minimum wage. Prison admission, therefore, becomes a method of containing and constraining this surplus population. Overall, the 533,309 state prison inmates in 1987 amount to less than half of one percent of the civilian labor force; were they added to the ranks of the unemployed, they would have increased the unemployment rate only from 6.6 percent to seven percent. For the black population, the impact is more substantial. Some 254,700 black males entered state prisons. Had these offenders been placed on probation, they would (in the worst-case scenario) have joined the 721,000 unemployed black males aged sixteen to forty-four. Their addition would have increased the number of black unemployed males by as much as thirty-five percent. In a credential society, a prison record may serve in the labor market to demarcate a subclass of undersirable laborers. Imprisonment rates expand with the size of this surplus population.

The alternative channels for surplus labor (welfare, military induction) are less viable options for both fiscal and ideological reasons. Welfare programs are directed to the respectable working class in the form of unemployment insurance, worker compensation, and old-age insurance. For the underclass, job training programs, general assistance, and AFDC are sporadically funded and politically contested.

Conclusions

Eighty years ago Clarence Darrow pointed out that the propensity to incarcerate the surplus population varied with economic conditions. Current research has elaborated this theme by examining variations in the imprisonment rates of the unemployed and minorities. Studies of race and unemployment tend to be conducted separately and their theoretical foundations remain unarticulated and fragmented.

This chapter has spelled out four types of explanation for the connection between the variation in surplus and incarcerated populations. *Rational public choice theory* traces changes in imprisonment rates to changes in crime rates, which stimulate a mass political constituency for expanding crime control. *Power elite theories* link changes in imprisonment more narrowly to threats posed by a surplus population to a dominant elite. *Managerial elite theories* imply that prisons expand in response to initiatives of criminal justice officials facing threats from recessionary economic pressures on their budgets. In contrast to these action theories, *structural theories* point to a symbiotic relationship between competitive labor markets and incarceration.

Several of these theories share a generic social threat proposition: size, increase, or concentration of the underclass increases the level of social control independently of the crime rate. They differ in the contingencies they impose on this relationship: action theories point primarily to the distribution of resources available to actors, while structural theories seek to specify the conditions that shape options and preferences.

Both action and structural orientations have a long history of development in sociology. Conversion or dissolution of these perspectives appears unlikely. Sometimes attempts to accomplish the latter are made on methodological grounds. For example, Elster (1984:28) argues that the structural explanations typically concocted by sociologists lack any specification of the mechanism by which the social institution accomplishes its purported function. In contrast, the action theories specify an intervening process that can in principle be directly investigated. While as a practical matter such direct investigation is difficult, the hypothetical bases of social policy is at least intelligible. The same cannot be said for structural accounts that ignore or discount the intervening process; their silence invites doubts about the validity of structural explanations.

The causal connections between unemployment and imprisonment have been stated in a very casual fashion. Jankovic wrote simply that "imprisonment can be used to regulate the size of the surplus labor force.... Two main components of the state's effort to support, and thus control, the surplus population are the social welfare system and the criminal justice system" (1977:20). He did not elaborate what function "control" serves nor explicate the nature of the trade-off between prison and welfare (cf. Garland 1985; Inverarity and Grattet 1989).

While specifying the intervening process would, as Elster argues, substantiate the causal connection, it is not the only way to do so. The preferred methods of testing for structural theories is to control for extraneous variables and to refine the components of the variables. Thus, the research agenda for specifying the structural relationship between unemployment and imprisonment entails introducing controls for age composition (which may influence both unemployment and imprisonment) and elaborating the types of labor markets in which prison admissions respond to unemployment rates. Both intervening variables and control variables serve to test for spuriousness, but they do so at different theoretical levels.

Choice between action and structural theories cannot be made on methodological grounds. They provide two vantage points on the process of social control. At the level of decisionmakers, action theories specify what goes through the minds of judges and parole boards in deciding to admit or release an offender. The unemployment rate may influence the perception of job opportunities and thus the risk of recidivism; regardless of the individual's job history, the prevailing economic conditions will condition expectations (Greenberg 1977). Sentencing decisions may be guided by a belief that unemployment causes crime (Box 1987).

At a different level, structural theorists may ask what system function is being performed by such judicial decision making. From a structural perspective, the action theorist describes how sentencing is done, not why it is done in a particular fashion. This issue becomes salient when we compare sentencing in different modes of production. Structures shape options.

While research will not soon resolve this debate, it is important that the issues become better articulated. These theoretical perspectives, if only unconsciously, shape the questions we ask and the ways we seek answers. Understanding imprisonment requires explicit consideration of a plurality of theories.

Part III

Beneficent Controls

8

The Mental Health and Criminal Justice Systems: Complementary Forms of Coercive Control

Thomas M. Arvanites

Today, insanity is recognized as a medical problem. This, however, has not always been the case. Until the eighteenth century, the insane were defined as witches, and the problem was considered a religious one. By the late eighteenth century, insanity began to be transformed from a religious to a medical problem. The first public mental asylum opened in the United States in 1773, and within the next one hundred years seventy-three mental hospitals were constructed. Insanity and commitment determinations were made by the local magistrate. Prior to the development of the mental asylum, the mentally ill were treated as paupers and confined in almshouses and, in the case of the violently mentally ill, imprisoned and punished as criminals.

The emergence of psychiatry was the dominant force in defining insanity as a medical problem. The Association of Medical Superintendents of American Institutions for the Insane was formed in 1844. The association began publication of the *American Journal of Psychiatry* which reported remarkable success rates in the psychiatric treatment of the insane. This enabled the association to legitimize psychiatry as a medical specialty and to "justify the exclusion of others without formal training in this specialty" (Grob 1970:312). The hospitalization of the mentally ill became the dominant response to the problem and continued to increase until 1955 when the number of people hospitalized reached an all-time high of 558,922 patients (Morrissey 1982).

Most involuntary mental hospitalizations were done through a civil commitment that was justified under the state's *parens patriae* power. This rationale refers to the state's sovereign guardianship over persons unable to care for themselves. The manifest function of this broad paternalistic power was to provide care and treatment to the mentally ill. The realities of state mental hospitalization, however, stood in stark contrast to the benevolent intent. Despite the fact that the patients were hospitalized for treatment, it was often nonexistent or dreadfully inadequate. The constitutional right to treatment was not established until more than two centuries after the first asylum emerged. Two landmark cases in establishing the right to treatment were *Rouse v. Cameron* (1966) and *Wyatt v. Stickney* (1971). In the first case, the court recognized the statutory right to treatment. In the latter case, the constitutional right to treatment was established. The federal district court judge ruled that "to deprive a citizen of his/her right to liberty upon the altruistic theory that confinement is for humane therapeutic reasons and then fail to provide adequate treatment, violates the very fundamentals of due process" (p. 785).

The involuntary hospitalization of individuals without adequate treatment clearly reveals the latent function of the mental hospital. Throughout its history, the mental health system has served more than a therapeutic function. Since its emergence, it has functioned to encourage conformity among the population. Early psychiatrists, like penologists, viewed proper behavior in terms of "respect for authority and tradition and acceptance of one's station in life" (Rothman 1971:154). The work of Szasz (1970) and Kittrie (1971) illustrates quite vividly the coercive, controlling nature of the mental hospital.

While the criminal justice system is limited to responding to behavior that has violated the law, the mental health system "recognizes no such boundaries" (Szasz 1970:62). As with imprisonment, the involuntary hospitalization of "threatening"individuals not only segregates them from the community, but also identifies and reinforces the parameters of behavior that social control agents find socially acceptable. Throughout its history the mental hospital has sequestered lower-class individuals who suffer from a wide range of physical, social, or mental ills and who are viewed as threatening or irritating. The modern mental hospital has been described as a "multi-purpose institution: a hospital, a jail, a poorhouse, and an old peoples' home" (Kittrie 1971:65). The mental health and criminal justice systems have been described as the "states' twin coercive control powers" (Kaplan 1978).

Within the past two decades, the study of the relationship between the two systems of control has emerged. A current question in the study of these coercive control mechanisms is the extent to which they compete or function together. A recent development that led to this question was state mental hospital deinstitutionalization, which significantly reduced the use of the mental hospital as a means of controlling certain forms of deviant behavior. This chapter suggests that the two mechanisms are increasingly functioning interdependently to confine some individuals.

Much of the debate on the interaction between these two coercive control bureaucracies has focused on the broad theoretical explanations of the interrelationship. This is probably due to the fact that two major, yet very different, sociological perspectives could be used to explain it. The structural-functionalists would suggest that the interaction between the two systems fulfill some requisite need that cannot be fulfilled by either system independently. Conflict theorists could predict the same relationship, suggesting that it increases the elite's control over subordinate classes. What is lacking in most of the literature, however, is the clear explication of what mechanisms exist that permit the interaction and how it occurs.

The legal system in the United States provides the structural opportunity for the mental health and criminal justice systems to operate interdependently to control individuals defined as threatening by social control agents. By law, the criminal justice system is prohibited from convicting defendants incompetent to stand trial and from punishing those who are insane and who were not responsible for their actions. Determinations of "Incompetency to Stand Trial" (IST), and adjudications of "Not Guilty by Reason of Insanity" (NGRI) or "Guilty But Mentally Ill" (GBMI) are viable mechanisms for the two systems to work together to control individuals defined as mentally ill and criminal.

The purpose here is twofold. First, using the case of commitments for Incompetency to Stand Trial (IST), this chapter delineates one of the links between the mental health and criminal justice systems that enables them to work together to control certain individuals. The IST commitment was selected for several reasons. First, commitments for IST or evaluations of competency represent the single largest category (fifty-eight percent) of mentally disordered offenders (Steadman et al. 1988). Second, the issue may be raised by the state. Finally, a commitment to a mental hospital for IST evaluation may be secured after an arrest for an offense as minor as criminal trespass or disorderly conduct.

If the two control mechanisms are interdependent, then it is plausible to assume that a major change in one mechanism should result in changes in the other. The second task of this chapter is to determine whether this is indeed the case. This will be done by examining the empirical literature for evidence that a policy shift in the mental health system (e.g., state mental hospital deinstitutionalization) has resulted in the increasing use of the criminal justice system in controlling the mentally ill. This new processing is referred to as the criminalization of the mentally ill. This can occur through (1) arrest and incarceration, or (2) through an arrest and a criminal commitment (IST, NGRI, GBMI) to a mental hospital.

Incompetency to Stand Trial: Treatment and Control

The competency to stand trial doctrine provides the best opportunity for the mental health system to work "hand in hand" with the criminal justice system to control segments of the population. Competency to stand trial is a legal consideration. It refers to whether the defendant has a rational and factual understanding of the nature and consequences of the proceedings against him or her and the present ability to consult with their lawyer with a reasonable degree of rational understanding (*Dusky v. U.S.* 1960). Raising the issue is relatively easy. In *Pate v. Robinson* (1966) the Supreme Court ruled that a hearing should be conducted if a "*bona fide*" doubt exists as to the competency of the defendant. There are, however, no "fixed or immutable signs which invariably indicate the need to determine fitness to proceed" (*Drope v. Missouri* 1975:172).

If the court decides that a competency hearing is necessary, it usually appoints a psychiatrist or psychologist to examine the defendant. It has been reported that hospitalization for a competency evaluation is unnecessary in all but a small fraction of the cases (Roesch and Golding 1980), and that it is reasonable to complete an evaluation in several days or weeks (Burt and Norris 1972). In most jurisdictions, however, the defendant is committed to a state or county mental health facility for the evaluation. Inpatient evaluations take longer to complete, typically ranging from thirty to eight days. Thus, simply raising the issue virtually guarantees an involuntary mental hospitalization. Upon completion of the evaluation the defendant is returned to court for a competency hearing. The hearings tend to be perfunctory and brief. In a study of competency hearings in New York, Steadman (1979) reported that they lasted an average of ten minutes and that thirty-five percent lasted less than three minutes.

While the presence of mental illness is a necessary condition for incompetence, the "medical judgement of mental illness does not control the essentially legal question of competency" (*Swisher v. U.S. 1965:731*). Despite this decision, the empirical evidence clearly reveals the decision is heavily influenced by medical factors. Steadman (1979) reported that in cases where the psychiatrist found the defendant incompetent, the judge concurred ninety-two percent of the time. This reliance on psychiatric opinion for determining the defendant's competency has been referred to as the application of psychiatry to legal issues for legal ends (Pollack 1974).

In most jurisdictions an IST determination results in an automatic commitment to a maximum-security state mental hospital. When the length of hospitalization is examined, the coercive nature of IST commitments becomes even more apparent. It has been suggested that six months is sufficient to restore competency in most cases since this is the length of time normally required to treat patients committed civilly (Group for the Advancement of Psychiatry 1974; Roesch and Golding 1980; Wininick 1983). An examination of the data reveals that the actual length of hospitalization is considerably longer. Steadman (1979) reports that unindicted defendants in New York State averaged fifty-nine weeks while indicted defendants averaged slightly more than two years. Felony defendants in North Carolina averaged 2.8 years (Roesch and Golding 1980).

If the defendant's competency is restored, the defendant is returned to court for disposition of criminal charges. Thus, in treating the defendant, the psychiatric profession assists the criminal justice system by preparing the individual for criminal sanctions. While the constitutional right to refuse treatment has been granted to civil mental patients and to offenders incarcerated in jail or prison, this right has not been extended to ISTs. The justification for the imposition of treatment is generally based on the state's right to bring to trial individuals accused of violating the law.

If the medical expert concludes that the restoration of competency is unlikely, the mental health system may assist the criminal justice system through the civil commitment process. Psychiatric testimony from the competency hearing will be introduced in the civil commitment hearing as evidence of mental illness, and the arrest record is often cited as evidence of dangerousness. In many jurisdictions, civil commitment does not terminate the criminal court's control over the individual. In most jurisdictions, criminal charges remain outstanding (Roesch and Golding 1980). This often results in criminal detainers being filed against such patients that often result in confinement in a maximum security mental hospital or in secure wards. These patients generally receive fewer privileges than other civil patients, and release is subject to approval by both the mental hospital and by the court. Several jurisdictions permit the refiling of criminal charges that were previously dismissed (Winick 1983).

Brief Overview of State Mental Hospital Deinstitutionalization

If the mental health and criminal justice systems operate interdependently, then a change in one system should result in a change in the other. During the past three decades there has been a major policy shift in the care of the mentally ill in the United States. A series of treatment, legal, and economic initiatives has resulted in an increased emphasis on community mental health care. This policy is generally described as deinstitutionalization.

The deinstitutionalization movement consisted of three distinct components. The first, emerging in the middle to late 1950s, was the introduction of psychotropic medications. The widespread use of these medications proved effective in treating many of the mentally ill who previously would have been institutionalized. This shift in care from the large state facilities to community-based mental centers (CMHC) was assisted by the federal government through reimbursements to CMHCs. These initiatives, directed primarily at preventing and reducing the length of hospitalization, were matched with a readiness to (re)admit patients whose condition had deteriorated (Morrissey 1982).

It did not require much "deterioration" to effect a hospitalization. Commitment standards were vague and liberal. The standard generally applied was "mentally ill and in need of treatment." For example, the civil commitment code in Massachusetts in 1965 permitted the involuntary hospitalization of individuals so deficient in "judgement or emotional control" that they were likely to conduct themselves in a manner that "clearly violates the established conventions of the community" (Kittrie 1971:68). Thus, as long as commitment statutes remained lenient, this aspect of deinstitutionalization had little impact on the coercive control function of the mental hospital.

The second component, which began in the mid-1960s and continued through the early 1970s, involved tightening the civil commitment standards and increasing the patient's legal rights. Since the commitments were civil, not criminal, and were intended to treat and not punish, courts traditionally "ruled that the full range of due process safeguards were not required" (Shah 1981:222). Through a series of court cases, the federal courts increasingly began to reject the civil versus criminal distinction as a basis for denying due process and equal protection. In *Heryford v. Parker* (1968), the Supreme Court ruled that a distinction between criminal and civil proceedings was not valid for the denial of due process during involuntary commitment proceedings. As a result, a series of subsequent cases successfully challenged the traditional civil commitment process.

The landmark case in the rights of the mentally ill to resist involuntary hospitalization was *Lessard v. Schmidt* (1972). This federal district court ruled that the substantive standard for involuntary civil commitment was "dangerous to self or others." Further, the court granted a full range of procedural safeguards: the right to timely notice or reason for detention, the right to counsel, the right to a probable cause hearing within forty-eight hours, the right against self-incrimination, and an increased standard of proof (beyond a reasonable doubt). A total of forty-six states have civil commitment statutes requiring a finding of dangerousness and including these procedural safeguards (Shah 1981).

Changes in the fiscal policies of the mental health system represented the third and final component. Scull (1977) suggested that the shift from treating the mentally ill in large state facilities to community mental health centers (CMHCs) might have been motivated as much by fiscal concerns as treatment issues of patient rights. Studies of expenditures on the mental health system indicate that funds were not diverted from large state facilities to CMHCs; they were simply cut back. Teplin (1984) reports that when adjusted for inflation, federal support for the mental health system actually declined after 1975. Kiesler (1983) reports that federal funds were cut twenty-five percent in 1981 alone. An examination of state and county expenditures for mental hospitals reveals that state and local governments did not increase their funds to cover reductions in federal spending. Between 1979 and 1983 spending actually decreased two percent after adjusting for inflation (NIMH 1983, 1986).

Deinstitutionalization has had a significant effect on the frequency and nature of hospitalizations. Although there is some evidence that the rate of inpatient care episodes remained constant or even increased over the past twenty years (Kiesler 1982), there have been significant changes in other aspects of hospitalization. Between 1970 and 1987 the number of residents in state and county mental hospitals decreased sixty-eight percent, from 337,619 to 107,531 (NIMH 1983, 1989). The admission rate per 100,000 adults declined thirty-two percent between 1973 and 1983 (NIMH 1986). During the same period the average length of a hospitalization declined from 421 days to 189 days (Kiesler 1982). Clearly one of the results of deinstitutionalization is an increased number of mentally ill individuals in the community with fewer psychiatric beds and less fiscal resources necessary to treat them.

It has been suggested that there is a limit to a community's tolerance of deviant behavior. The increased presence of the mentally ill may, at best, be viewed as unpleasant or annoying. Since the mentally ill are often viewed as dangerous (Steadman and Cocozza 1978), their presence in the community may be unacceptable. If commitment statutes and/or the availability of beds restrict the use of the mental health system in responding to the real or perceived threat presented by the mentally ill, social control agents may invoke the criminal justice system. The following section examines the empirical literature for evidence that the criminal justice system is increasingly being used to confine the mentally ill.

Criminalization of the Mentally Ill

Just as insanity was redefined from a religious problem to a medical problem in the late eighteenth century, a variety of "deviant" behaviors were redefined from criminal problems to medical or social problems during this century. At the turn of the century, juveniles were removed from the adult court, leading to the birth of the juvenile court. Through a series of "legislative and judicial actions, psychopaths and alcoholics were removed from the jurisdiction of the courts" (Kittrie 1971:33). Drug addiction has been medicalized, then criminalized, and is once again becoming medicalized (Conrad and Schneider 1980).

This divestment of criminal law has been described as the growth of the therapeutic state (Kittrie 1971). The therapeutic state is based on the premise that deviants are socially maladjusted or psychologically abnormal, and that these pathologies can be identified and treated. The treatment, whether voluntary or involuntary and regardless of effectiveness, has been an effective form of coercive control.

Recently, however, the legal and fiscal components of deinstitutionalization have restricted the use of the mental hospital as a mechanism to control the mentally ill. It has been suggested that the criminal justice system will increasingly be used to control socially unacceptable behavior by the types of individuals traditionally confined by the mental health system. The criminalization of the mentally ill can occur through arrest and incarceration or through a criminal commitment to a mental hospital.

Arresting the Mentally Ill

When the presence or the behavior of the mentally ill becomes intolerable, the police are naturally the first to respond. Since many of the mentally ill are too disordered to remain in the community but cannot be hospitalized, either because they do not meet the new commitment statutes or because there are no beds available for them, the police may resort to an arrest. The use of arrest as an alternative was made explicit in a Philadelphia police commissioner's directive which stated in part:

> Persons who are unruly or disorganized but who do not present a danger to themselves or others may not be taken into custody under the provisions of the Mental Health Act of 1976. Individuals who make unreasonable noise, use obscene language or gestures... or create a physically offensive action may be charged with disorderly conduct. (Bonovitz and Guy 1979:1045)

There is some evidence that suggests that the mentally ill are being arrested more often since deinstitutionalization. Studying the criminal histories of two samples of mental patients in New York State, Melick et al. (1979) report that the percentage of patients with prior arrests increased from thirty-two percent to forty percent between 1968 and 1975. Not only were more mental patients arrested, but the number of times they were arrested also increased. Cocozza et al. (1978) report that among these mental patients annual arrest rates per thousand increased from 73.5 to 98.5 (+ 34%). During the same time, the increase among the general population was eighteen percent (from 27.5 to 32.5).

A recent study of 2,179 civilly committed patients from five states reported the same pattern. Between 1968 and 1978 the percentage of civilly committed patients with prior arrests increased from 29.8 to 45.6 percent (Arvanities, 1990). Again, the number of times these patients were arrested also increased. The average number of prior arrests increased from 5.7 to 7.6.

While these studies use aggregate-level data, studies of police-citizen interactions report consistent findings. Teplin (1984) reported that the probability of being arrested was much greater among those persons who appeared mentally disordered (46.7 percent) than among individuals who did not (27.9 percent). More importantly, this pattern did not change when controlling for the nature of the offense that precipitated the police response. Others have reported that police may very well arrest the individual because it "is less time consuming and ensures the persons' removal from the community." (Lamb and Grant 1982:20)

In a study of police officers' decisions to arrest or seek hospitalization for individuals appearing mentally ill, Monahan et al. (1979) report that in most cases the individuals entering either system were described as clearly inappropriate for referral into the other system. They conclude that there is "little evidence that the seriously mentally disturbed are being criminalized by placement in jails as alternatives to civil commitment" (p. 517). This may be valid for the seriously mentally ill, but the same conclusion should not be drawn about the non-seriously mentally ill. They are the ones with the greatest risk of arrest because they do not meet the new commitment criteria or because bed space is not available for them. The "seriously mentally disturbed" individuals to whom Monahan et al. refer are the first to be (re)admitted and the last to be discharged. The authors do, however, report that almost one-third of the individuals arrested met the criteria for civil commitment.

A critical question is why are the arrest rates increasing? One hypothesis suggests that arrests for "fictional" offenses such as disorderly conduct or disturbing the peace will replace civil commitment as a means of institutionalizing the nondangerous mentally ill who no longer can be civilly committed. If this is occurring, it is plausible to predict that the mentally ill should increasingly be arrested for minor offenses. This would suggest that the "net" of control of the criminal justice system is expanding to include the nondangerous mentally ill previously dealt with by the mental health system. A second hypothesis, however, suggests that without appropriate treatment, the condition of some of the mentally ill will deteriorate to the point where their behavior does in fact become criminal. Thus, it is reasonable to predict that the seriousness of the crimes for which they are arrested will increase or at least remain stable.

The results of research on the types of criminal activity for which the mentally ill are being arrested are inconsistent. As will be dis-

cussed in a later section, several studies report that criminal commit-
tes to mental hospitals are increasingly being arrested for less serious
offenses. Other studies, however, report increases in the seriousness
of the criminal acts for which the mentally ill are arrested. Steadman
et al. (1978) reported that while the arrest rate for minor offenders
increased fifty-one percent (from 20.3 to 31.5 per one thousand)
between 1968 and 1975, the arrest rate for violent offenses increased
114% (from 5.6 to 12.0 per one thousand). Among the general population the opposite trend was evident. The increase in arrest rates for
minor offenses (ninety-six percent) far exceed the increase in arrest
rates for violent offenses (fifty-seven percent).

A similar increase was reported by Arvanites (1990). The percentage of civil patients with a history of an arrest for a violent crime increased from 11.6 percent in 1968 to 23.6 percent in 1978. Further, the
percentage of patients with a history of an arrest for a crime against a
person increased almost twofold (17.0 to 33.7 percent).

These two studies suggest that the increasing arrest rates are not
occurring simply because arrests are replacing hospitalization as a
means of confining the nondangerous mentally ill. The increases in the
seriousness of the crimes for which the mentally ill are being arrested
is more consistent with the hypothesis that there are more mentally ill
offenders in the community. In other words, there is more crime by
the mentally ill. Thus, the increasing arrest rates suggest an appropriate response by the criminal justice system rather than an expansion of their coercive control power. Once the individual has been
arrested, the criminalization may continue through incarceration or
criminal commitment to a mental hospital.

Incarcerating the Mentally Ill

Once arrested, the mentally ill may be institutionalized within the
criminal justice system or within the mental health system through a
criminal commitment. The obvious prediction of the criminalization
hypothesis is that there will be an increase in the number and percentage of mentally ill individuals in jail and prison. While there have been
numerous cross-sectional studies describing the mental conditions of
inmates, there is an astonishing lack of longitudinal studies that are
necessary to determine whether the mental health characteristics of
jail and prison inmates have changed.

As the mental hospital population steadily declined and the
prison population steadily increased there was speculation that deinstitutionalization was a major contributor to the increasing prison

populations. The suggestion that prison and mental health populations are inversely related is not new. Penrose (1939) reported as "a
general rule of prison, if prison services are extensive, the asylum population is relatively small, and the reverse tends to be true." Research
spanning forty years and three continents reports negative correlations between prison and mental health populations (Penrose 1939;
Biles and Mulligan 1973; and Steadman et al. 1984). These negative
correlations do not adequately address the premise that persons previously hospitalized are now being transferred to prisons. This can
only be determined through longitudinal studies to ascertain if the
composition of the prison populations has changed.

To date, the work of Steadman et al. (1984) has been the best
investigation of the extent to which deinstitutionalization has resulted in the imprisonment of the mentally ill. Between 1968 and 1978
the population of state mental hospitals nationwide decreased from
399,000 to 147,000 (– 63 percent) while the population of state prisons
increased from 168,000 to 277,000 (+ 65 percent). Further, the correlation between the annual resident census of state mental hospitals
and state prisons was an astonishing – .87. While the overall correlation is certainly consistent with the criminalization hypothesis, the
changes in the mental histories, as measured by prior hospitalizations, were not. Two samples of prison admittees (approximately
1,950 each) were randomly selected from six states. Between 1968
and 1978 the percentage of inmates with prior mental hospitalizations increased from 7.9 to 10.6 percent.

Although this overall increase is consistent with the criminalization of the mentally ill, several factors temper its support. First, the
percentage of inmates with previous hospitalizations decreased in as
many states as it increased. The overall increase was simply due to the
fact that the increase in three states was great enough to offset the
decreases in the other states. While the increase (2.7 percent) was
statistically significant, the fact remains that only 10.6 percent of the
1978 prison population had a prior mental hospitalization.

More significantly, Steadman et al. compared the actual number
of 1978 prison admittees with prior hospitalizations with the number
that would have been expected if the percentage of 1968 admissions
with prior hospitalizations had remained constant. This comparison
revealed that in three states the number of 1978 admittees with prior
hospitalizations was less than expected. They conclude that there is
little evidence that state mental hospital deinstitutionalization was a
significant factor in the increase in prison population. They suggest
that the 125 percent increase in the FBI Index of Offenses during the
time of their study, longer prison sentences, and increased use of

determinate sentencing were greater contributors to the increase in prison populations.

The police officer's decision to hospitalize rather than arrest the seriously mentally ill person, and the relatively small increase in the percentage of prison admittees with prior mental hospitalization clearly do not support the premise that the mentally ill are being transferred to the state prison system. The alternative form of confinement is in city or county jails or prisons. Since it is the nondangerour mentally ill who are the most affected by state mental hospital deinstitutionalization, it is reasonable to predict that their criminality will be less serious. Thus, if they "act out" it will most likely be in terms of minor offenses that result in incarceration at the local level. Between 1978 and 1986 the number of jail inmates increased from 156,783 to 274,444 (seventy-five percent). Again, deinstitutionalization has been identified as a contributing factor. The fact that few 1978 state prison admittees (10.9 percent) have prior hospitalizations while most (55.5 percent) of the 1978 hospital admittees have previous arrests (Steadman et al. 1984) is consistent with the claim that more of the mentally ill are being jailed.

The extent to which there have been increases in the number of mentally disordered offenders in jail is critical to the criminalization hypothesis. There are a number of cross-sectional studies which report that approximately five percent to eight percent of jail inmates are psychotic (Swank and Winer 1976; Lamb and Grant 1982). There is some evidence that the rate of mental illness among jail populations has increased (Pogrebin and Regoli 1985). Most of these claims are based on estimates or comparisons between different studies rather than longitudinal research.

Bonovitz and Guy (1979) investigated the number of psychiatric consultations and the number of admissions to the psychiatric unit of the Philadelphia County Prison System prior and subsequent to the Pennsylvania Mental Health Act of 1976 which prohibited the civil commitment of the nondangerous mentally ill. During the time period six to twelve months after the act became effective the number of consultations per month increased, on average, fifty-eight percent. The increase in admissions to the psychiatric unit was even more dramatic. Average monthly admissions increased from 43.5 to 74.5 (+ 71 percent).

Also examined were the demographic, diagnostic classification and criminal activity of the individuals admitted to the psychiatric unit. The pre- and post-cohorts did not differ significantly in age, race, education level, or employment status. Approximately three quarters of each cohort were diagnosed as suffering from schizophernia. Inmates admitted to the psychiatric unit after revisions in the commitment statutes were less likely to have a record of a violent offense (forty versus seventy-four percent) and more likely to have been arrested for a minor offense such as trespassing or disorderly conduct (twenty-five versus nine percent). These findings suggest that the criminal justice system is expanding to confine the mentally ill previously dealt with by the mental health system.

If the criminal justice system is expanding to confine a portion of the mentally ill previously committed involuntarily, it is most likely occurring at the local level through jails and county prisons. These institutions are the "frontline" defenses against socially unacceptable behavior. While the increased presence of the mentally ill in jail is consistent with this permise, some have argued that it is due more to better recognition of the mentally ill than a real increase in their numbers. The simple fact is that there are not enough good, quality longitudinal studies pre- and post-deinstitutionalization. This is primarily because of the nature of the jail system. There were over thirty-five hundred jails in the country with an average daily census of 290,300 in 1987. They are overcrowded, and inmates move into and out of them so quickly that the data necessary to adequately test this component of the criminalization hypothesis are virtually impossible to collect.

Criminal Commitments

It seems unlikely that an overburdened criminal justice system would be willing to confine the mentally ill in its already overcrowded facilities. In reality, it may have a vested interest in facilitating a transfer to the mental health system. In order to gain treatment for those who present serious management problems, relieve overcrowding, and save money, local officials may be anxious to transfer the mentally ill to the state. An additional factor is the relatively common belief that it is the state's deinstitutionalization policy that is ultimately responsible for the increased number of the mentally ill in the community. Thus it is quite possible that the criminal justice system will initially "absorb" some of the mentally ill and then transfer them to the mental health system through criminal commitments.

During the past two decades several studies have suggested that criminal commitments to mental hospitals have increased. As discussed earlier, the most common and simplest commitments to obtain are those for an evaluation to determine competence to stand trial and continued hospitalization if found incompetent. In 1969 California passed the Laterman-Petris-Short (LPS) Act tightening the civil commitment criteria. Abramson (1972) reported that the number of

IST commitments in San Mateo County increased from sixteen to thirty-three between 1968 and 1970. In Los Angeles County the IST commitments increased from twenty in 1969 to sixty in 1970 (GAP 1974). It should be noted that although these numbers are small, they are from only two of California's fifty-seven counties.

Studies in other states report similar findings. Dickey (1980) reported that the number of commitments for IST increased forty-two percent following a revision of the civil commitment statutes in Wisconsin. More important, however, were the changes in the nature of the criminal activity for which the defendants were arrested. Between 1976 and 1977 the percentage of defendants charged only with a misdemeanor increased from twenty-eight to forty-two percent. Further, in twenty-five percent of the cases, the only charge filed was disorderly conduct.

Hawaii experienced increases in the number of criminal commitments following the revision of its civil commitment statutes. Gudeman (1981) reported that between 1976 and 1980 criminal commitments increased from .6 to 8 percent of all state mental hospital admissions. Again, there was a significant decrease in the seriousness of the criminal activity for which these individuals were arrested. The percentage of criminal commitments carrying at least one felony charge declined from ninety percent in 1976 to thirty percent in 1980.

Geller and Lister (1978) reported that the ratio of criminal to civil commitments increased in Massachusetts from .076 in 1966 to .821 in 1975. Among those committed for an evaluation of competency, thirty percent were arrested for disturbing the peace only. In cases where the authors were able to obtain disposition data, they reported that seventy-two percent of the defendants had the criminal charges against them dropped upon returning to court. This clearly suggests that the real reason for the arrest may have been to secure a mental hospitalization rather than a conviction. Studies in New York State report mixed results. Melick et al. (1979) report the ratio of criminal to civil admissions did not significantly change between 1967 and 1977. Between 1975 and 1982, however, criminal commitments increased from 4.7 to 7.4 percent of all admissions (New York State Office of Mental Health 1983).

These increases in the criminal commitments, both in raw numbers and as a percentage of all admissions, are frequently cited as a shift in the control of the mentally ill, especially the nondangerous, from the mental health system exclusively to the criminal justice system. More important than the increase in the number is the evidence that the seriousness of the criminal activity is decreasing. This suggests that it is not simply more criminal behavior by the mentally ill that is causing the increase in criminal commitments, but rather that the criminal commitments are expanding to include individuals previously dealt with by the mental health system. This is consistent with the premise that criminal commitments are being used in lieu of civil commitments. Criminal commitments may be a relatively easy way for the state to secure an involuntary hospitalization.

While these studies are consistent with the criminalization hypothesis they are far from conclusive. Despite the fact that these studies attribute the documented changes to deinstitutionalization, none of the studies have investigated whether the changes were associated with the *rate* of deinstitutionalization. If the observed changes are the result of deinstitutionalization then they should vary with its rate. These studies were limited to a single jurisdiction or hospital and did not include any measure of deinstitutionalization.

The first multi-jurisdictional study examined the relationship between increases in the number of IST commitments and the rate of deinstitutionalization. Arvanites (1988) reported that IST commitments increased twenty percent in California, Massachusetts, and New York between 1968 and 1978. More importantly, this increase was positively and significantly related to the rate of deinstitutionalization. Also examined were the correlations between the increase in the number of ISTs and the increase in the number of prison admissions and population. These were examined to investigate whether the increase in ISTs was the result of the IST commitment being used as a relief valve for the overcrowded prison system. These correlations were weaker, and none were statistically significant. Thus, the increase in ISTs should not be attributed to prison overcrowding, but rather to deinstitutionalization.

Contrary to prior research which reported that IST commitments are increasingly being used to hospitalize a less serious offender, the above study reported a small, statistically nonsignificant increase in the percentage of defendants charged with a violent offense (thirty-four verses forty-two percent) and a small decrease in the prevalence of minor offenses (twenty-two versus seventeen percent). This suggests that deinstitutionalization may have resulted in increases in IST commitments, but not in the way generally accepted. Rather than the IST commitment expanding to include a new type of individual—the mentally ill traditionally dealt with by the mental health system—these data suggest that there has been no change in the criminal characteristics of the persons found IST after deinstitutionalization.

While the above study failed to document significant changes in the seriousness of the offenses for which the ISTs were arrested, significant changes in the racial characteristics have been reported. In a study of ISTs from five states, Arvanites (1989) reported that between 1968 and 1978 nonwhite defendants increased from 34.0 to 51.4 percent of all ISTs. This increase (51.2 percent) far exceeded the overall increase in the percentage of the population accounted for by nonwhites over the age of sixteen (14.1 percent). Subsequently analyses have investigated the correlation between the increase in nonwhite ISTs and the rate of deinstitutionalization and changes in prison admissions. Whereas the overall increase in ISTs was more closely related to deinstitutionalization, the increase in nonwhite ISTs is more closely associated with prison admissions ($r = .78$, $p = .06$) than with deinstitutionalization ($r = .64$, $p = .106$). While Monahan et al. (1979) report that nonwhites are arrested more frequently than whites, the correlation between the increase in nonwhite IST defendants and prison admissions suggests that the IST commitment may be used as an alternative method of confining nonwhites.

A recent study, however, has questioned the reports of increasing criminal commitments. Steadman et al. (1988) reported that overall the rate of mentally disordered offenders admitted to state and county mental health facilities remained relatively consistent between 1967 and 1980. It must be noted, however, that while the rate of criminal commitments may remain stable, the overall rate of hospitalizations is decreasing. Thus, criminal commitments are comprising a greater share of all hospitalizations.

Conclusion

It has been suggested that one of the key elements of social control in modern societies is the clear distinction among the different types of deviance and the subsequent assignment of each to the appropriate social control agents (Scull 1977). The mental health and criminal justice systems, society's two control bureaucracies, are responsible for the problem populations whose presence in society is often viewed as intolerable: the mentally ill and the criminal. For the most part, the "mad" and the "bad" represent two distinct populations managed separately by each system. There is, however, a considerable volume of unconventional and/or threatening behavior that does not fit neatly into one and only one of these categories. As a result, depending on societal or organizational factors (such as public opinion or cell or bed space), these behaviors may be alternatively managed by either or both control mechanisms. Further, changing definitions of crime and illness may result in this behavior being controlled by one system at one time and by the other at another time.

The premise that the mental health and criminal justice systems are functionally interdependent suggests that a major change in one system should have some impact on the other. The deinstitutionalization movement over the past three decades has had a significant impact on the use of the mental health system in responding to the problems posed by the mentally ill. The obvious prediction is that the criminal justice system will expand to confine some portion of those individuals labeled mentally ill, who, for whatever reason, are no longer subject to control by the mental health system. A variety of opportunity structures linking the two systems enables them to complement each other in controlling socially unacceptable behavior.

There is little doubt that increased numbers of individuals are experiencing both forms of social control. Increasing numbers of mental patients have longer arrest histories and more inmates have increased histories of mental hospitalizations. Further, there is evidence that there is increased interaction between the two systems. Criminal commitments to mental institutions are increasing, both in raw number and as a percentage of all admissions. The key question is whether this is due to the criminalization of the mentally ill, other factors (such as increases in the population and crime rates), or some combination. While the research is supportive of the criminalization hypothesis, it is not conclusive.

The research does indicate that the criminal justice system can and is used to facilitate a mental hospitalization. An arrest for a crime as minor as disturbing the peace can result in an involuntary hospitalization for an evaluation of incompetency, commitment for treatment to restore competency, or a civil commitment in lieu of criminal prosecution. Alternatively, the mental health system complements the criminal justice system in controlling "problem populations" by confining those individuals not convicted of a criminal offense (e.g., defendants found incompetent to stand trial or found not guilty by reason of insanity).

In addition, the mental health system assists the criminal justice system in the prosecution of the individual. This occurs most often through the issue of competency to stand trial. The psychiatric profession plays a major role in determining if the defendant is legally competent, and, if not, it is the mental health system that prepares the defendant for criminal sanctions through treatment for restoration of competency. Although not discussed in this chapter, additional links between the two systems include psychiatric testimony concerning the defendant's criminal responsibility at the time of the alleged act; and the newest link, the guilty but mentally ill verdict that results in a prison sentence preceded by a hospitalization for treatment.

These linkages allow the social control agents to shuttle some individuals between the two systems, clearly increasing society's coercive control capacity. While this may benefit the social control bureaucracies, this type of processing has a distinct set of consequences for the individuals involved. Again, it should be noted that these individuals increasingly are nonwhite. These individuals often receive the worst of both worlds; they are treated against their will, often housed with violent individuals regardless of their own propensity towards violence, and their release is subject to approval by both the mental health and criminal justice systems. Finally, they carry the double stigma of "mentally ill" *and* "criminal."

9

Intergroup Threat and Social Control: Welfare Expansion among States during the 1960s and 1970s

Mitchell B. Chamlin

This chapter is concerned with welfare expansion among states. Most research, based on the mass insurgency (Piven and Cloward 1971) and developmental theses (Wilensky 1975; Gronbjerg 1977), examines the effects of social structure on welfare expansion (Winegarden 1973; Betz, 1974; Albritton 1979a; Isaac and Kelly 1981; Schram and Turbett 1983; Hicks and Swank 1983). This research, also rooted in these perspectives, examines the effects of changes in social structure on welfare expansion during the 1960s and 1970s.

Mass Insurgency and Welfare

Piven and Cloward (1971) maintain that welfare programs serve to placate potentially rebellious underclasses and to ensure that the economy has a sufficient supply of labor. Specifically, they contend that welfare programs are established and/or expanded to quell civil disorder brought on by mass unemployment. When political stability and economic vitality are restored, eligibility requirements are stiffened and relief programs are dismantled, thereby providing employers with a ready pool of low-wage workers. For example, Piven and Cloward (1971:46-80) argue that the economic hardships of the Great Depression did not, in and of themselves, lead to the expansion of relief programs in the 1930s. Rather, it was the severity and pervasiveness of riots and protests, and the anticipation of further labor unrest, that finally brought a response from federal and local officials. However, as political and economic stability were reestablished in the

1940s, and the demand for cheap labor increased, relief programs began to contract.

Recent examinations of the Piven and Cloward thesis have focused on the influence of racial insurgency on the growth of welfare recipient rates during the 1960s. Specifically, Piven and Cloward (1971) contend that the modernization of southern agriculture and the consequent decrease in demand for unskilled labor led to the migration of poor blacks to the urban North. Black rioting in urban areas (brought on in part by the inability of northern industries to absorb the increased supply of labor), coupled with the Democratic party's desire to maintain, and possibly increase, the size of the black vote in upcoming elections, produced a relaxation of federal and state eligibility requirements for receiving welfare transfers. In short, the abrupt increase in the size of the welfare population during the latter half of the 1960s is viewed as a response to the threat to political stability caused by a rash of civil disorders in the mid-1960s.

In sum, welfare programs are conceptualized as vehicles for the maintenance of political and economic stability which respond to the level of threat to the extant social order. Clearly, Piven and Cloward do not focus on the effects of the current level of threat on current levels of welfare programs. Rather, they seek to explain relatively abrupt changes in the size of welfare apparatuses in terms of episodic occurrences of disruptive behavior within macrosocial units. Hence, the specification of change becomes critical to the evaluation of the Piven and Cloward thesis.

Developmental Theory and Welfare

The develomental perspective (Wilensky and Lebeaux 1965; Wilensky 1975; Gronbjerg 1977) suggests that benevolent institutions arise to ameliorate economic dislocations that emerge from the continual maturation of modern industrial society. Employing revenues secured from general increases in affluence and discretionary income that accompany the growth of capitalist economies, the state provides pecuniary resources to combat a variety of social ills, including poverty.

From this vantage point, welfare programs are expected to expand and contract in response to changes in the demand for, and the capacity to provide, welfare services. For example, a number of urban theorists (Guest 1977; Ganz and O'Brien 1973; Karsarda 1978; Wilson 1987) point to changes in the economic structure of central cities that contribute to an increase in demand for amelioratory services. Specifically, they demonstrate that during the previous two decades many cities have simultaneously experienced growth in demand for a highly educated labor force to work in administrative and professional occupations and a decline in demand for unskilled labor force to work in manufacturing and retail occupations. Unfortunately, this change in the economic opportunity structure of cities occurred at a time when an increasing percentage of the resident labor force possessed poor educational backgrounds and minimal job skills. The consequent mismatch between employment opportunities and occupational skills led to an increased demand for amelioratory programs, including welfare. In short, it seems reasonable to conclude that changes in the economic structure of macrosocial units are likely to affect the demand for, as well as the capacity to provide, welfare services. Hence, a failure to control for changes in the levels of need and capacity is likely to underestimate the influence of developmental processes on changes in the size of the welfare population.

The Empirical Literature

The publication of Piven and Cloward's *Regulating the Poor* (1971) has generated a growing body of research that has sought to critically evaluate the relative efficacy of the mass insurgency and developmental explanations for changes in the level of welfare services. Support for these two theoretical perspectives has been mixed. Some studies tend to support the mass insurgency thesis (Isaac and Kelly 1981; Schram and Turbett 1983; Hicks and Swank 1983; Jennings 1983), while others do not (Betz 1974; Albritton 1979a; Isaac and Kelly 1981). Similarly, some studies tend to support the developmental perspective (Hicks and Swank 1983; Jennings 1983; Winegarden 1973), while others do not (Betz 1974; Albritton 1979a; Isaac and Kelly 1981; Schram and Turbett 1983). These inconsistencies in the findings have produced a rather heated debate concerning the methodological (e.g., the proper unit of analysis) and substantive (e.g., the proper specification of the models) decisions that affect the examination of the macrosocial determinants of welfare services (cf. Betz 1974; Albritton 1979b; Piven and Cloward 1979; Jennings 1983).

I, too, have serious reservations about the extant research. Specifically, it is my contention that many of these studies fail to adequately control for changes in the level of the exogenous and endogenous variables specified in the models. The problem is twofold. Some studies use measures of change that fail to remove the effects of the initial level of the variable of interest from the measure of change, while others fail to control for the influence of change at all.

A number of studies utilize gain scores (the difference between measures of a variable at two points in time) to estimate the change (growth) in the size of the welfare population and/or of welfare expenditures over time. For example, Winegarden (1973), in an evaluation of the developmental perspective, measures the change in the Aid to Families with Dependent Children (AFDC) population as the ratio of the AFDC recipient rate in the first quarter of 1971 to the rate observed two years earlier. Betz (1974) compares the percentage increase in state and local welfare expenditures in twenty-three and twenty non riot cities from 1960 to 1969. Similarly, Albritton (1979a) uses the percentage increase in AFDC caseloads to examine the relationship between riots and welfare expansion, while Schram and Turbett (1983) measure welfare expansion as the net difference in the number of families receiving AFDC per thousand poor families (from 1965 to 1968 and from 1969 to 1972).

However, as Borhnstedt (1969) notes, gain scores and the initial level of a variable are not statistically independent of one another. Rather, in the absence of perfect measurement, gain scores tend to be negatively correlated with the initial level of the variable. Hence, Borhnstedt concludes that gain scores should not be used to estimate the change of a variable over time.

Reservations concerning the extant literature are not confined to questions about the manner in which welfare expansion and contraction are measured. A number of studies of welfare growth among states and/or localities fail to adequately consider the effects of changes in the level of the developmental perspective variables. For example, Isaac and Kelly (1981), in an analysis of the growth in welfare expenditures among cities between 1960 and 1970, use static measures of poverty and total government expenditures (less expenditures for welfare) to control for the predictions of the developmental perspective. Isaac and Kelly (1981) find that the developmental variables (measured in 1960) have little impact on the change in welfare expenditures. Schram and Turbett (1983), using states as the unit of analysis, fail to consider the effects of changes in development variables on the growth of AFDC families. Their measures of need and capacity are simply averages. Unemployment is averaged for 1960, 1965, and 1970, while the remaining developmental variables are averaged for 1960 and 1970. They also find that developmental variables have relatively little impact on the change in welfare practices (i.e., AFDC caseloads).

In contrast, Abritton (1979a) and Betz (1974) do explicitly consider the effects of changes of structural variables (e.g., nonwhite population, population size) on changes in welfare services. However, they measure the change as gain scores (percentage increases) and thereby fail to remove the effects of the initial values of these variables from their estimates of change.

Lastly, Winegarden's (1973) research suffers from both types of defects. Specifically he measures two developmental variables at a single point in time and a third as a gain score (ratio change).

In sum, I believe that much of the research concerning variations in welfare programs is problematic. It either fails to account for changes in the levels of need and capacity or uses inappropriate measures of change in developmental and welfare variables. This research seeks to address these two deficiencies. Specifically, the proceeding analyses examine the effects of structural change, as well as the effects of racial insurgency, on changes in the level of AFDC recipient rates among states during the 1960s and the 1970s.

Procedures

The sample consists of the fifty states. I use states as the unit of analysis because previous research indicates that the focus of this study, the AFDC program, is best thought of as a state-level program that operates within the constraints established by the federal government (Gronbjerg 1977; Schram and Turbett 1983; Jennings 1983).

Dependent variables. The analyses focus on the change in the AFDC recipient rate per thousand population (from 1960 to 1970 and 1970 to 1980) rather than changes in other welfare programs. There are several reasons for this choice. In contrast to public assistance expenditures for the blind, aged, or disabled, AFDC payments support those individuals (i.e., the potentially employable) who are most likely to pose a threat to the social order and are the most susceptible to the discretionary actions of federal and state governments. Moreover, during the 1960s the AFDC program experienced the greatest change (growth) of all major relief services. By 1970 approximately seventy percent of all public assistance recipients garnered income from the AFDC program (Piven and Cloward 1971; Gronbjerg 1977). In short, as others have argued (Schram and Turbett 1983; Jennings 1983), the AFDC measures are best suited for the purpose of analyzing changes in the welfare population during the previous two decades.

Developmental variables. Changes in per capita revenues, the percentage of unemployed workers, and the percentage of families below the poverty level are included to control for the predictions derived from developmental approaches to welfare expansion. Changes in per capita revenues are used to approximate changes in the capacity of states to supply AFDC benefits. Changes in the percentage of families below the poverty level are used to estimate changes in the level of need across states. Following previous research (Isaac and Kelly 1981; Jennings 1983; Hicks and Swank 1983), changes in the percentage of unemployed workers are used as a rough estimate of the lack of convergence between job opportunities and labor force skills.

Racial insurgency. The number of riots and the change in the rate of black elected officials from 1970 to 1980 are included to estimate the level of racial insurgency during the 1960s and 1970s, respectively. Following previous research (Jennings 1983), a cumulative count of the number of riots (1964 to 1968) is used to estimate the degree of racial insurgency across states during the 1960s. This research focuses on the amount of rioting between 1964 to 1968, because it was during these years that states experienced the most frequent and intense civil disorders.

Clearly, in the 1970s states did not experience the type of racial insurgency (riots) that Piven and Cloward identify as precipitating welfare expansion.[1] Nonetheless, there is reason to believe that less extreme forms of racial insurgency may have also led to an expansion of the welfare population. Specifically, I contend that black political mobilization may have led to increases in the size of the welfare population because such behavior may have been perceived as threatening to whites and authorities. For example, Kinder and Sears (1981) conclude, upon the analysis of voting behavior among whites in the 1969 and 1973 Los Angeles mayoralty elections between Yorty and Bradley (a black candidate), that blacks are perceived to be a symbolic threat to the extant social order. Specifically, whites tend to fear that black officials may disproportionately allocate the municipal government's resources to blacks. Similarly, Henry (1987), upon the analysis of factors influencing the outcome of the 1982 California gubernatorial contest between Bradley and Deukmejian, concludes that fear of blacks was the major factor in Bradley's defeat. Hence, it seems reasonable to contend that black elected officials, regardless of whether or not they are actually more willing to redistribute wealth to the disadvantaged or merely pose a symbolic threat to whites, may be perceived by authorities as representing a significant threat to the ongoing political order. The change in the number of black elected officials per 100,000 blacks is used to measure change in racial insurgency during the 1970s.

The percentage of blacks. The change in the percentage of blacks is included to control for Blalock's (1967) power-threat thesis. In brief, Blalock contends that increases in the relative population size of blacks enhances the capacity of blacks to secure more social services, while simultaneously increasing the perception of threat to a white majority. Consistent with this thesis, a number of recent studies of crime control indicate that the percentage of blacks and/or nonwhites positively affect the level of policing resources (Liska et al. 1981; Jackson and Carroll 1981; Greenberg et al. 1985), the rate of arrest (Liska and Chamlin 1984), and the certainty of arrest (Liska et al. 1985). Hence, I anticipate that changes in the percentage of blacks will also be positively related to changes in preventive control (i.e., the welfare population).

Southern location. Historically, the South has evidenced a propensity to provide considerably less public and private monies to combat poverty than other regions of the country. Racial discrimination (against blacks), as well as a more pervasive disregard for the poor, appears to motivate the actions of southerners (Schiller 1973; Chamlin 1987). Therefore, I anticipate that independent of changes in the level of need, capacity, or threat, southern location will negatively affect changes in the welfare population. The South is measured as a dummy variable, where 1 = South and 0 = non-South.

Sources. Revenues, the percentage of families below the poverty level, the percentage of unemployed workers, and the percentage of blacks were ascertained from the *County and City Data Book.* The number of AFDC recipients and the number of black elected officials were obtained from the *Statistical Abstracts.* The number of riots was coded from the *New York Times Index.*

The Measurement of Change

Following Bursik and Webb (1982), residual-change scores are used to estimate the changes in the level of the variables (excluding riots, southern location) during the 1960s and 1970s. Specifically, the level of a variable at time t is regressed on its level at time t_{-10}. The equation is then used to predict the level for each state at time t. This predicted value is subtracted from the observed level at time t, yielding a residual-change score.[2]

The residual-change score has two properties which recommend its use for the purpose at hand. First, as Bohrnstedt (1969) demonstrates, residual-change scores are statistically independent of the initial levels of a variable. Therefore, they represent the change in the variable level that is not expected on the basis of the initial level alone. This is an important advantage from the viewpoint of the Piven and Cloward and developmental perspectives. In contrast, gain scores do not remove the effect of the initial level of a variable on a subsequent level of that same variable. Rather, they tend to be negatively correlated with the initial level of the variable. Second, since all the states are used to estimate the regression equation which predicts the levels at time t, the predicted scores are automatically adjusted for changes that other states have undergone during the same ten-year period. Thus, residual-change scores remove the effects on ongoing processes of change common to all the states and capture the level of unexpected changes in the variables of interest. Residual-change scores appear to be better suited than gain scores for the task of evaluating the Piven and Cloward and developmental explanations for welfare expansion.

Results

Although high zero-order correlations between predictor variables do not in and of themselves indicate that multicollinearity is present (Hanushek and Jackson 1977:90), the zero-order correlations between the change in the percentage of blacks from 1960 to 1970 and the number of riots ($r = .64$) is large enough to warrant concerns about this issue. To assess the extent to which collinearity among the exogenous variables affects the parameter estimates, collinearity diagnostics (Belsley et al. 1980) are examined. Experiments conducted by Belsley et al. (1980) reveal that a conditions index threshold of thirty is indicative of potentially harmful collinearity and a variance-decomposition proportion of 0.5 should be used to identify dependencies among the predictor variables. None of the condition index numbers (associated with either equation) exceeded fifteen, indicating that multicollinearity is not a problem.

Table 9.1 presents the results of the OLS regression estimates of the effects of the predictor variables on changes in AFDC recipient

Table 9.1 Regression Estimates for Changes in AFDC Recipient Rates

	AFDC RECIPIENT RATE 1960–1970		AFDC RECIPIENT RATE 1970–1980	
	Beta	B	Beta	B
Revenue	– .055	– 1.369	.281	22.408**
Poverty	.249	2.052*	– .253	– .344
Percent unemployed	.131	1.985	.395	3.844**
South	.093	2.292	– .260	– 6.732*
Percent black	.292	2.293*	.418	4.617***
Riots	.401	.984**		
Black officials			.232	.140*
Constant		– 4.758		4.127
R^2	.46		.45	

*p < .05
**p < .01
***p < .001

rates. The first and second columns report the standardized and metric coefficients for the change in AFDC recipient rates during the 1960s, while the third and fourth columns report those for the change in AFDC recipient rates during the 1970s. The results are clear. Variables derived from the racial insurgency threat and the developmental perspectives have a substantial impact on changes in the level of AFDC recipient rates during the previous two decades.

Consider the findings for the 1960 to 1970 equation. Almost fifty percent of the variance in the change of AFDC recipient rates among states is explained by the measures of ecological change and the number of riots. Consistent with the developmental perspective, an increase in the percentage of families below the poverty level (B = .249, p < .05) promotes welfare expansion. In support of the racial insurgency threat theses, the change in the percentage of blacks (B = .292, p < .05) and the cumulative number of riots (B = .401, p < .01) are signigficant predictors of the change of AFDC recipient rates.[3] In short, it appears that the growth in AFDC recipient rates among states during the 1960s can be attributed to increases in the level of need as well as increases in the level of threat to the social and political order.

The effects of changes in levels of need, capacity, and threat on the change in the level of AFDC recipient rates between 1970 and 1980 also provide support for the developmental and racial insurgency threat theses. As anticipated by the developmental perspective, the change in the percentage of unemployed workers (B = .395, p < .01) and the change in per capita revenues (B = .281, p < .01) are significant predictors of the change in AFDC recipient rates. Moreover, independent of the changes in the levels of need or capacity, the change in the percentage of blacks (B = .418, p < .01) and the change in the rate of black elected officials (B = .232, p < .05) are significant predictors of the change of AFDC recipient rates.

Although southern location had no appreciable effect on changes in the welfare population during the 1960s, southern location (B = .260, p< .05) moderately affects the change in the welfare population during the 1970s. Specifically, southern states, regardless of changes in the levels of need, capacity, or threat, are less likely to provide welfare services for their citizens.

Supplementary Analyses

The present investigation provides support for *both* the mass insurgency and developmental perspectives, while most of the previous cross-sectional and panel analyses (Betz 1974; Albritton 1979a; Isaac and Kelly 1981; Schram and Turbett 1983) do not. It is possible, however, that these inconsistencies reflect differences other than the use of the residual-change scores to measure the dependent and predictor variables. In an effort to address this issue, I reanalysed the data, using alternative analytical techniques.

First, following Isaac and Kelly (1981), I regressed static measures of the AFDC recipient rates on static measures of the predictor variables as well as a lagged measure of the AFDC recipient rates. Specifically, the AFDC recipient rate in 1970 is regressed on the full set of predictor variables and the AFDC recipient rate (1960 values); and the AFDC recipient rate in 1980 is regressed on the full set of predictor variables and the AFDC recipient rate (1970 values). Table 9.2 contains the unstandardized and standardized parameter estimates for each of these specifications. The results are clear. In each of the equations, the lagged AFDC recipient rate is the single best predictor of the current AFDC recipient rate. In comparison, the effects of variables derived from the mass insurgency and developmental perspectives are negligible. Within the 1970 equation, the only other variable that significantly affects the AFDC recipient rate is the cumulative count of riots (B = .373, p < .01). Within the 1980 equation, the percentage of blacks is the remaining significant predictor (B = .508, p < .01) of the AFDC recipient rate. The developmental variables have no appreciable effect on the AFDC recipient rate in either decade.

Table 9.2 Regression Estimates for Lagged Dependent Variable Equations For Determinants of Decade Changes in AFDC Recipient Rates

	AFDC RECIPIENT RATE 1970		AFDC RECIPIENT RATE 1980	
	Beta	B	Beta	B
AFDC recipient rate	.715	1.324***	.631	.729***
Revenue	.160	35.750	.080	2.474
Poverty	.008	.074	- .259	- .792
Percent unemployed	.131	1.985	- .122	- 1.566
South	.124	3.664	- .312	- 10.710
Percent black	.302	.403	.508	.879***
Riots	.373	1.098**		
Black officials			.071	.151
Constant		11.382		21.574**
R^2	.60		.58	

*p < .05
**p < .01
***p < .001

Second, I replaced the residual-change scores with gain (difference) scores and reestimated the equations. Inspection of the model residuals and the statistic "Cook's D" (Cook and Weisberg 1982) for the 1960 to 1970 change equation indicates that one state (Alaska) has a disproportionate influence on the parameter estimates. Therefore, I present the analysis of the change in AFDC recipient rates from 1960 to 1970 excluding Alaska.[4] Generally, the multivariate analyses provide weak support for the mass insurgency threat and developmental explanations for changes in the level of the welfare population, especially for the changes that occurred during the 1970s.

Consider the 1960s change (gain) in the level of AFDC recipient rates. Consistent with the initial results, the cumulative frequency of riots positively affects (B = .481, p < .001) the change in the AFDC recipient rate. However, there are two notable differences from the residual-change equations. Specifically, the change in poverty no longer affects and southern location positively affects (B = .406, p < .05) the change in the AFDC recipient rate during the 1960s.

The choice of the method used to measure change has an even greater affect on the findings for the 1970s. The use of gain scores does

Table 9.3 Regression Estimates for Changes in AFDC Recipient Rates: Gain Scores

	AFDC RECIPIENT RATE 1960–1970		AFDC RECIPIENT RATE 1970–1980	
	Beta	B	Beta	B
Revenue	.254	43.668	.172	5.004
Poverty	.567	.300	– .025	– .122
Percent unemployed	.108	1.502	.488	4.374**
South	.406	9.965*	– .218	– 5.859
Percent black	.025	.151	.218	2.509
Riots	.481	1.179**		
Black officials			.067	.040
Constant		9.493		– 8.596*
R^2	.44		.33	

*p < .05
**p < .01
***p < .001

not substantially alter the effect of the change in the level of poverty (B = .448, p < .01) on the change in the AFDC recipient rate during the 1970s. However, the two measures of change in interracial threat (change in the percentage of blacks and change in the rate of black officials), change in the level of revenue, and regional location no longer significantly affect the change in the AFDC recipient rate.

Taken together, these supplemental analyses suggest that measurement decisions have a non trivial impact on the evaluation of hypotheses derived from the mass insurgency and developmental perspectives. Consistent with past research (Betz 1974; Albritton 1979a; Isaac and Kelly 1981), the use of static measures of the exogenous variables and gain (difference) scores substantially underestimates the effects of the predictor variables, especially those derived from the developmental perspective.

Conclusions

The central thesis of this study is that much of the extant research that seeks to examine the relative efficacy of the mass insurgency and developmental perspectives as explanations for the growth of welfare programs during the 1960s is suspect. It either fails to consider changes in the levels of demand for, and the capacity to provide, welfare services (Isaac and Kelly 1981; Schram and Turbett 1983) or relies on inappropriate measures (gain scores) of change in the level of the exogenous and endogenous variables (Winegarden 1973; Albritton 1979a; Betz 1974; Schram and Turbett 1983). This research, in an attempt to address these deficiencies, uses residual-change scores to examine the effects of changes in the levels of need, capacity, and threat on changes in AFDC recipient rates during the 1960s and 1970s.

In brief, the findings provide support for both the Piven and Cloward and developmental explanations for changes in the level of the welfare population. To review, the change in the AFDC recipient rate from 1960 to 1970 is directly related to the change in need (poverty), the change in the racial composition of states (the percentage of blacks), and the onset of racial insurgency (riots). Similarly, the change in the AFDC recipient rate from 1970 to 1980 is directly related to the change in the demand for labor (the percentage of unemployment), the change in capacity (revenues), the change in racial insurgency (the percentage of elected black officials), the change in the racial composition of states (the percentage of blacks), and region (South). Taken together, these results indicate that states respond to changes in the economic structure, as well as to the level of threat to the political order.

These findings, as well as those provided by the supplementary analyses, also buttress the contention that the inability of previous studies to find substantial relationships between developmental and welfare variables (e.g., Isaac and Kelly 1981; Schram and Turbett 1983) or between the racial composition of macrosocial units and welfare variables (Albritton 1979a; Betz 1974) may reflect methodological deficiencies rather than the absence of actual relationships.

Lastly, this study complements a growing body of research, also rooted in the conflict perspective, which focuses on the macrosocial determinants of the capacity to provide crime control (i.e., policing resources). Specifically, a number of recent analyses of the capacity to provide crime control reveal that black political mobilization (Jackson and Carroll 1981), as well as the relative population size of racial minorities (Jackson 1989; Greenberg et al. 1985; Jackson and Carroll 1981), especially the race-related riots of the 1960s (Liska et al. 1981), have a substantial impact on the police force size and/or expenditures. Consistent with this literature, the present investigation also indicates that interracial threat (i.e., black political mobilization, the relative population size of blacks) directly affects the size of the welfare population.

The implications of these findings are clear. In brief, it may prove useful to specify models that explicitly consider the theoretical linkages among intergroup threat, preventive control (welfare transfers), and crime control strategies. Two possible linkages come immediately to mind. First, political units that provide relatively high levels of preventive control may have less of a need for more intrusive means of social control (i.e., does the level of welfare transfers mediate the effects of intergroup threat on policing resources or arrest rates?). Second, political units may respond to intergroup threat by increasing the size of both preventive and crime control bureaucracies (i.e., do the welfare and the criminal justice systems serve as complementary, rather than alternative, responses to an increase in intergroup threat?). A resolution of these questions may lead to a more general theory of social control.

10

Conclusion: Developing Theoretical Issues

Allen E. Liska

The Problem

The subject matter of this book is the social organization of deviance and crime control. Studies of control organizations, institutions, programs, and policies have mushroomed since the 1960s. Using the individual as the unit of analysis, most studies examine how various control activities, such as arresting, prosecuting, and sentencing, are affected by the legal, psychological, and social characteristics of people and their behavior. Because these microlevel studies are reasonably well organized and synthesized and constitute a clearly defined literature, they are not the subject of this book.

Using collectivities—organizations and communities—as the unit of analysis, some studies examine how deviance and crime control patterns are affected by social structure. Most of this research takes the form of historical case studies; most of it focuses on only one organization or program of either the criminal justice, mental health, or welfare systems; most of these studies are isolated from each other; and their implications for a general macrotheory of deviance and crime control are not fully exploited. They are the subject of this book.

A substantial proportion of these studies can be organized around the threat hypothesis of the conflict perspective. The hypothesis asserts that the greater the number of acts and people threatening to the interests of the powerful, the greater the level of crime control. Perhaps the major problems with the hypothesis are that of definition clarity and theoretical linkages. Concerning the former, the major concepts such as "the powerful," "interest," and "threat," are neither clearly defined nor measured independently of what they are supposed to explain, frequently yielding tautological propositions.

Because the critical causal variables are not well defined theoretically and operationally, and are not clearly linked to each other in the form of propositions or a causal model, the relevant research literature is also not well defined and integrated. Consequently, studies are categorized by substantive forms of control (lynching, imprisonment, arrests, hospitalization, welfare), rather than by theoretical propositions. Conflict theory and the threat hypothesis in particular are employed to loosely guide research and to interpret findings; and explanatory variables are selected because they are easily measured or generally amenable to a conflict interpretation. Conceptual integration across these substantive areas and a tightening of theoretical and epistemic linkages are clearly needed.

Focus and Contribution of this Book

The goal of this book is threefold: one, to use the threat hypothesis to organize and interrelate seemingly diverse literatures on deviance and crime control; two, to use new data to resolve puzzles and crucial issues in these literatures; and, three, to use these literatures to develop and expand the threat hypothesis.

As a working strategy, this book categorizes patterns of deviance and crime control by the level of force: fatal controls, including the use of deadly force and lynching; coercive controls (the criminal justice system), including crime reporting, police size, arrest and prison admission rates; and beneficent controls, including the welfare and the mental health systems. Each of the book chapters takes a step further in using the threat hypothesis to understand a form of social control and in using a form of social control to test and elaborate the threat hypothesis.

Fatal Control

Fatal control refers to those forms of social control where the threatening population is killed—the most extreme form of social control. This book examines two forms of fatal control: lynchings and police homicide of citizens.

In chapter 2 of this book, "Toward a Threat Model of Southern Black Lynchings," Tolnay and Beck review and elaborate the threat hypothesis in respect to lynching during the Reconstruction and post-Reconstruction South. While the hypothesis asserts that during that era whites perceived themselves as under siege and perceived blacks as threatening the traditional social order, they argue that the hypothesis does not clarify whether the threat was predominantly political or economic and which class of whites was most threatened. While it is difficult to isolate these two types of threat, Tolnay and Beck argue that blacks were primarily a political threat during Reconstruction, but after that period their political power was controlled through disenfranchisement and other functionally similar institutions. Concerning the class of whites who were most threatened, Marxists argue that in the Reconstruction and post-Reconstruction periods the elite were the most threatened, whereas split market theorists, such as Bonacich (1975), argue that poor whites, especially during hard economic times, were the most threatened. Tolnay and Beck suggest that both were threatened under different social conditions. Blacks were perceived to be an economic and a status threat by poor whites, particularly during hard economic times.

Their major contribution is that of elaborating the threat hypothesis. Whereas the traditional hypothesis specifies simply that black concentration leads to threat which in turn leads to lynching, they specify that black concentration leads to three types of threat (political, economic, and status), which are differentially experienced by different social classes. Whether or not any one type of threat leads to lynching depends on the availability and effectiveness of other forms of social control.

Considerable research on homicide by police has been conducted (Fyfe 1982); however, only a few macrostudies bear on the conflict perspective or specifically on the threat hypothesis. Liska and Yu explicate and test the social (threat) processes that underlie the effect of the percentage of nonwhites on the overall police homicide rate. An aggregate effect assumes that because nonwhites are more threatening than whites, nonwhites are killed by police at a higher rate than whites; therefore, an increase in the percentage of nonwhites increases the overall police homicide rate. A contextual effect assumes that nonwhite offender crime and the day-to-day visibility of nonwhites create a general climate of threat, which influences interaction between police and whites as well as between police and nonwhites; therefore, as the percentage of nonwhites increases, the police homicide of both whites and nonwhites increases. Disaggregated by race, the analysis strongly supports the contextual threat hypothesis, which entails two related processes. One process associates a climate of threat with the presence and day-to-day visibility of nonwhites, and the other associates a climate of threat with a high rate of nonwhite offender crime. The analysis suggests that nonwhite offender crime does not mediate the effect of the percentage of nonwhites on the

police homicide rate of whites or nonwhites but that threat as perceived by the police is associated with just the presence and day-to-
day visibility of nonwhites.

Police homicide may reflect emotional responses to street situations in which police feel threatened and have little time to calculate
alternative courses of action. Because cultural beliefs in the United
States link nonwhites to street violence and crime, police may feel particularly threatened in neighborhoods and cities where the percentage of nonwhites is relatively high.

Coercive Controls: Criminal Justice System

Physical controls refer both to the activities of social control
agents (arrests and imprisonment) and to the infrastructures of the
crime control bureaucracies (police size and prison size) that support
these activities. This book examines the impact of threat at various
stages of the criminal justice process from crime reporting to imprisonment.

Barbara Warner's chapter, "The Reporting of Crime: A Missing
Link in Conflict Theory," both critiques conflict theory for neglecting
the microprocesses, particularly crime reporting, that underlie
macro effects, and tests the threat hypothesis as an explanation of
crime reporting. While the hypothesis locates the sources of threat to
political and economic elites in macrosocial structures such as income inequality, she argues that it does not explain how or why these
structures are perceived to be threatening to elites and how the perceived threat is translated into criminal justice policies, programs,
and activities. She further argues that the criminal justice system is
mobilized through the reporting of crime and that the vast majority of
crime reports are citizen initiated. Hence, if we are to understand how
income inequality and racial composition affect arrest, prosecution,
or sentencing rates, we must first understand how they affect crime
reporting. Crime reporting is, thus, the missing link in conflict theory.

According to conflict theory, elites, authorities, and majority
groups—who have the most to lose—are the most threatened; thus,
they should have the highest level of crime reporting. Using the
national victimization survey data, Warner reports that the racial and
economic characteristics of neighborhoods affect reporting but not as
predicted by traditional conflict theory. That is, controlling for the
neighborhood crime rate and the seriousness of the crime, the racial
composition of neighborhoods affects the reporting of property crime
more for nonwhites than for whites and more for low-income people
than for high-income people. This suggests that crime and the symbols

of crime are not that threatening to the upper class and majorities who can avoid them, even if they live in the same general area. The poor and minorities, who have little to lose, are most threatened and most sensitive to the signs and symbols of crime. Interestingly, it is the nonwhite middle class—who because of racial discrimination reside in the high-crime neighborhoods—that is the most likely to report crime.

Assault as a personal crime is different. Warner reports that the percentage of nonwhites has a negative effect on reporting which is strongest for nonwhites. She argues that as the percentage of non-whites increases the percentage of nonwhite offenders increase, thereby increasing the percentage of crime that is intraracial for nonwhites and interracial for whites. Intraracial crime between minorities is not reported. It is not that it is neglected by police (though it might be) it is just not reported, perhaps because minorities feel that it will be neglected by police or feel uncomfortable reporting it to police.

To a large extent the volume of crime control is limited by the processing or carrying capacity of the police department, which is a direct function of its size (i.e., numbers and expenditures per capita).

In chapter 5 "Minority Group Threat, Social Context, and Policing," Pamela Jackson traces the minority threat hypothesis from the conflict approach of the 1960s, particularly the work of Blalock (1967), and specifically examines the functional form of the relationship between minority group size and police size. She reports that the relationship is curvilinear with its shape and strength contingent on time and place. From zero to ten percent black, police expenditures decrease; from that point to about forty-five percent they accentuate; and from that point they decrease. Jackson argues that blacks are not perceived as threatening until they reach a certain percentage of the population. From that point the perceived threat accelerates until blacks become the majority and assume political power, and at that point a large black population is perceived, not as a threat, but as a resource to local black authorities.

Further, she locates the threat hypothesis in a sociohistorical context. She reports that it is stronger in the South, where blacks traditionally have been more of a political threat, than in the non-South. It is stronger in the 1970s, the period of racial confrontation, than in the 1980s. It is stronger for large cities, which rely on formal social control, than in small cities. And it is stronger for capital expenditures, for which federal funds were allocated, than for salary expenditures. She supports the above quantitative analysis with a content analysis of newspapers in the early and late 1970s, which document the struggle between the police and urban minorities in large cities.

She concludes by noting that as majority-minority conflict has declined in the 1980s, police size has also declined. Recently, however, police are being used to control another perceived threat, this time from urban gangs and drugs. She predicts that the urban gang and drug threat, which is also associated with race, may again lead to another expansion in police size in the 1990s.

Liska and Chamlin extend the work on police size to the study of actual crime control activities, such as arrests. Using 1972 data, Liska and Chamlin (1984) initially reported that an increase in the percentage of nonwhites, while not affecting the arrest rate of whites, strongly decreases the arrest rate of nonwhites. In chapter 6 of this book, "Social Structure and Crime Control Revisited: The Declining Significance of Intergroup Threat," Chamlin and Liska find even more support for the benign-neglect hypothesis in the negative effects of the percentage of nonwhites on the arrest rates of both whites and nonwhites for 1982.

Two related processes may be operating. Because the percentage of nonwhites affects the 1972 arrest rates of only nonwhites, Liska and Chamlin first emphasized that it is intraracial crime among nonwhites that fails to mobilize the police. They argued that this occurs because as the percentage of nonwhites increases, the victims of nonwhite offenders also tend to be nonwhite and nonwhite victims are less able to define their misfortunes and victimizations as crimes deserving of police attention. Crimes between nonwhites may be treated more as personal than legal problems by police. Because the percentage of nonwhites affects the 1982 arrest rates of both whites and nonwhites, Chamlin and Liska now emphasize that nonwhite victims, independently of the race of the offender, fail to mobilize the police. Additionally, the fact that so much crime, especially personal crime, is intraracial implies that the percentage of nonwhites probably affects the ability of white—as well as nonwhite—victims to mobilize the police. A high percentage of nonwhites may lead to a general climate of police neglect.

Conflict theorists explain the development of prisons during the seventeenth, eighteenth, and nineteenth centuries as a strategy of authorities to control the urban masses of immigrants and migrants and to manage the labor supply. Rusche and Kirchheimer (1939) explicitly argue that during times of economic depression prisons absorb the unemployed and during times of prosperity they provide a ready supply of labor. Developing this theme, contemporary research focuses on the relationship between unemployment rates and imprisonment rates.

In chapter 7 of this book, "Extralegal Influences on Imprisonment Rates," James Inverarity argues that most of this research is hindered by the fact that few studies theoretically explicate or empirically test the intervening social processes between unemployment, race, and imprisonment. In developing the theoretical underpinnings for these relationships, he distinguishes between two broad types of explanations: action and structural.

Conceptualizing the intervening social process in terms of choices made by more or less rational decisionmakers, action theories argue that unemployment is threatening to the interest of some decisionmakers and that imprisonment is a solution to the unemployment problem. Inverarity discusses and criticizes three action theories: rational choice, conflict (elite), and managerial theory. In rational-choice theory, crime policy, including the rate of imprisonment, is conceptualized as a macro-outcome of the micro decisions of policymakers, which in turn reflect collective sentiments as expressed in elections. In conflict theory, elites are thought to intervene in the criminal justice process and to influence the outcomes, including imprisonment, in order to advance their own interests. Managerial theory argues that the managers of the criminal justice system manipulate it in order to maximize their own interests, not the interests of elites.

Structural theories conceive of imprisonment in terms of forces that individual actors "neither understand nor control." Inverarity discusses two types of forces: business cycles and modes of production. He focuses on several modes of production: the plantation system of the South, competitive capitalism, and monopoly capitalism. He argues that in the Old South blacks were controlled not through imprisonment but through the informal relationships of the plantation. A black in trouble with the law was taken care of informally by the master of the plantation; the prison system of the Old South was used to control deviant whites. With the breakdown of the plantation system and the development of competitive capitalism, a new system of control was needed to maintain competitive wages, to provide incentives to work, and to deal with those who performed no useful role during downturns of the business cycle. The prison system played this role. In monopoly capitalism the costs of production can be passed on to the consumer; therefore, higher wages can provide an incentive to work and welfare can be used to ease the pains associated with downturns in the business cycle. Imprisonment is no longer needed.

Generally, he argues that the meaning of race and unemployment depends on the mode of production, which varies over time and region. In the plantation system of the Old South, unemployment did not literally exist for blacks; therefore, blacks were not imprisoned. In competitive capitalism, unemployment does exist, is threatening, and is controlled by imprisonment; therefore, a positive relationship exists between unemployment and imprisonment. In monopoly capitalism, while unemployment exists, it is not threatening; therefore, while imprisonment exists (a residual of competitive capitalism), it is not related to unemployment. Hence, to understand the relationship between unemployment and imprisonment rates, we must examine the relationship within systems of economic production.

Beneficent Controls

The emergence of mental asylums in the Western world can also be explained by the threat hypothesis. Historical studies equate the emergence of asylums with the emergence of both urban police and prisons as responses by authorities to the social disorder associated with the large-scale processes of urbanization, industrialization, and capitalism. Other than showing that asylums and prisons emerged during similar time periods in response to similar social conditions, these studies do not show how these two control bureaucracies function together to control threatening populations and acts. Are they independent, competing, or functional alternatives?

The recent contraction of the asylum population and expansion of the prison population provides opportunities for crucial tests of these questions. Many asylums are no longer operating at full capacity, thereby providing space for the overflows from other control bureaucracies, such as prisons (Melick et al. 1979). In chapter 8 of this book, "The Mental Health and Criminal Justice Systems: Complementary Forms of Coercive Control," Thomas Arvanites examines the micro social processes by which the contraction of the mental health system drives the expansion of the criminal justice system. Specifically, he studies how threatening populations that in the past might have been admitted directly into asylums are now first processed into the criminal justice system; some of them then remain in local jails and others through various mechanisms, such as "Incompetent to stand trial," and "Not guilty by reason of insanity," are channeled into asylums.

To examine the first process, Arvanites reviews studies of the arrest and imprisonment of the mentally ill before and after deinstitutionalization. He reports that after deinstitutionalization the arrest rate of the mentally ill and their proportion of the prison and jail populations increased. To examine the second process, Arvanites reviews studies of the rate of criminal commitments to mental hospitals. He reports that after deinstitutionalization criminal commitments increased, both absolutely and as a proportion of total admissions, and he reports that the rate of increase is related to the rate of mental hospital deinstitutionalization. In sum, while far from conclusive, the data suggest that the recent deinstitutionalization of the mentally ill has considerable implications for the criminal justice system.

Within conflict theory, welfare is conceptualized as a form of social control. Piven and Cloward (1971), specifically, have stimulated considerable controversy by arguing that the welfare expansion in the United States during the middle and late 1960s was a response to the urban riots during that period—an attempt to pacify an economically deprived and threatening population.

In chapter 9, "Intergroup Threat and Social Control: Welfare Expansion among States during the 1960s and 1970s," Mitchell Chamlin argues that much of the literature bearing on conflict theory is inconsistent and provides inappropriate tests of the theory. While Piven and Cloward develop their theory to explain periods of rapid welfare expansion, especially during the 1960s and 1970s, most research tries to explain static cross-sectional variation. The few studies that do examine change in welfare operationalize that change in terms of simple difference or gain scores, which have been criticized as negatively related to base year scores.

Using states, Chamlin estimates the effect of changes in various forms of threat, including riots, percent black, percent of unemployed, and the election of black officials, and of changes in need and financial capacity such as poverty and revenue on changes in welfare from 1960 to 1970 and from 1970 to 1980. He calculates change using simple gain scores and residual scores that reflect the variance in present scores that cannot be predicted from past scores. As a point of comparison he also estimates the effects of static levels of these variables on static levels of welfare in 1970 and 1980. The findings confirm his argument. Changes in welfare are better predicted by changes in both threat and need/capacity than static levels of welfare are predicted by static levels of the causal variables; and residual measures of changes in welfare are better predicted by residual measures of changes in the above causal variables than gain measures of welfare are predicted by gain measures of these variables.

Chamlin's work alerts us to two very important points. Cross-sectional variation reflects both the simultaneous effects of present processes and the lag effects of historical processes. It is thus difficult to isolate the effects of present from historical processes on cross-sectional variation; it is sometimes easier to observe the effects of present processes on dynamic (change) variation. Two, sometimes threat is less associated with static levels of community structure, such as percent nonwhite or income inequality, and more associated with changes in it. A change in the percentage of nonwhites from twenty to forty percent may be more threatening to white authorities than a constant level of forty-five percent.

Summary

The threat hypothesis assumes that social control is a response of elites, authorities, and majorities to acts, people, and distributions of people deemed threatening to their interests. Research appears on a variety of substantive topics, ranging from fatal or lethal controls to beneficent controls. Unfortunately, this work is scattered, is not well synthesized, and is organized around substantive forms of control rather than theoretical hypotheses. Researchers studying one form of control (e.g., welfare or lynching) are unfamiliar with theoretically similar work on other forms of control. This book addresses this problem. Through the substantive chapters, this book tries to synthesize work on the threat hypothesis within different areas of social control; and by bringing work in different substantive areas together, it tries to cross-fertilize these areas, making researchers who study one form of control aware of theoretically similar work on other forms of control.

Developing the Threat Hypothesis: The Next Decade of Research

The second major goal of this book is to shift the focus of study from substantive forms of control to theoretical issues that cut across these substantive forms and thereby to develop the threat hypothesis. I organize this section around three types of issues: the big issues, which are more conceptual than empirical; the middle-range issues, which are both conceptual and empirical; and the little issues, which are more empirical than conceptual.

Big Issues

One big issue, which has been discussed repeatedly over the last decade and in various chapters of this book, is that of embedding the threat hypothesis of social control in more general theories of social structure and social process.

By a structural theory I mean a theory that explains action in terms of social forces that people neither understand nor control. These forces are generally conceptualized as patterns of enduring social relationships or as positions in these patterns, such as positions in a capitalist economic system or in a nuclear family.

For the most part threat research implicitly assumes a structural theory. That is, without articulating a theory of structure, it embeds threat in enduring patterns of actions, social relationships (crime, collective movements, riots, unemployment, political unrest and movements), and population distributions (percentage of nonwhites, percentage of urban poor, racial segregation, and economic inequality) that seem to be either threatening in themselves or associated with threatening social actions and relationships. Yet, without an explicit theory of structure we have only a loose collection of causal variables whose relationship to each other is unclear. Some forms of social control are linked to some structural variables and other forms of social control are linked to other structural variables. It is not clear which causal variables affect each other and which of them are conceptually subsumed under others.

To a large extent this is not much of a problem in traditional Marxism. It explicitly assumes that the interest of those who own capital conflict with the interests of those who do not; that capitalists are threatened by poor urban masses and specific forms of action such as riots, crime, and unemployment; and that social control is an effort by capitalists to protect their interests. While perhaps too simple to capture the complexities of contemporary postindustrial societies, it provides a relatively clear conception of social structure in industrial society and embeds the threat hypothesis in that structure.

Starting with Dahrendorf, theorists have assumed various lines of economic, political, social, and racial conflict which crosscut each other. Those threatened include political elites, economic elites, bureaucratic managers, ethnic majorities, and the middle class. They are assumed to fear a loss of economic resources, political position, social status, and physical safety both from specific classes of people (the lower class, ethnic and racial minorities) and from specific actions (crime, unemployment, urban riots, political movements) associated with them. While pluralistic conflict theory broadens traditional Marxism, it yields somewhat of a conceptual disarray. Different studies emphasize different sources of threat to different authorities, managers, majorities, and classes, and emphasize different forms and degrees of social control.

Some of these issues are raised in chapters of this book. In studying lynching, Tolnay and Beck (chapter 2) argue that we must elaborate the threat hypothesis by specifying who perceive blacks as threatening (aristocratic elite or poor whites) and by specifying what exactly is perceived to be threatened (political or social positions). In examining the relationship between racial composition and police homicide of citizens, Liska and Yu (chapter 3) conclude that a high percentage of nonwhites is not only threatening to local politicians (leading to high police expenditures) but that it is also threatening to police on the beat, leading to police homicide of citizens. In examining the relationship between racial composition and crime reporting, Warner (chapter 4) reports that the percentage of nonwhites affects the reporting by blacks, especially middle-class blacks, more than whites and the reporting by the poor more than the rich. Hence, racial composition may be threatening not only to elites, control agents, and majorities but also to minorities.

As a working strategy toward embedding the threat hypothesis in a theory of social structure, researchers might begin by seriously addressing the question: who and what are threatening and who and what are threatened. The former refers to what actions (crime, riots, collective movements, unemployment) and what people (nonwhites, poor, minorities) are threatening. The latter refers to what resources (power, economic position, status) of what social categories (elites, bureaucratic managers, middle class, ethnic majorities) are threatened. These two questions are not independent. Defining what and who are threatening in part defines what and who are threatened.

For the most part threat research also does not embed the threat hypothesis in a general theory of social process. That is, it does not clarify the sequence of events by which threatening acts, people, and distributions of people influence social control. Specifically, it is not at all clear how or why specific acts, people, and distributions of people are perceived to be threatening; and it is not clear how or why a level of perceived threat by some specific majority, managers, or elites leads to a specific form of social control.

For example, a considerable volume of research examines the relationship between racial structures (percent nonwhite and segregation) and economic structures (unemployment rate, percentage below poverty, inequality) and various forms of social control; however, the underlying social processes remain elusive. The problem is not just that the concept of social threat, used to interpret these relationships, is not operationalized; it is also that research is simply not designed to study the underlying social process.

Some research, however, does bear on this issue: research that specifies the conditions upon which social structure or composition effects are contingent; research that specifies the process through which social structure or composition influence forms of social control; and research that isolates the threat effect from other effects.

Regarding the first category, Liska (1981) and Jackson (chapter 5) report that the effect of racial composition (percent nonwhite and segregation) on police size is contingent on time and region. The effect is strongest in the South where blacks historically have been associated with political and economic threat and during the early and mid-1970s when blacks were associated with urban riots. And Inverarity (chapter 7) argues that the effect of the unemployment rate on social control is contingent on the mode of production. It is strongest in competitive capitalist systems where the unemployed are geographically segregated and where their problems associated with economic downturns are not ameliorated by social welfare.

Concerning the second category, Warner (chapter 4) states that we really know very little about the processes by which macro characteristics of social units influence the level and form of social control. She examines one segment of the process: how macro characteristics impinge on the decision to report a crime and thus to mobilize the criminal justice system. Liska and his coauthors also address this general issue. In their earlier work, Liska et al. (1981) report that the effect of racial composition on police size is mediated through the fear of crime and the racial composition of crime, and Liska and Chamlin (1984) report that the percentage of nonwhites influences arrest rates by altering the racial composition of crime. An increase in the percentage of nonwhites increases the percentage of nonwhite victims who are less able than white victims to mobilize the police force. In chapter 6 Chamlin and Liska report that the percentage of nonwhites influences arrest rates by creating a general climate of neglect that decreases the arrests of both nonwhite and white offenders; and in chapter 3 Liska and Yu report that racial composition influences the police homicide of citizens by creating a climate of threat that increases the police use of force against both nonwhites and whites.

Regarding the third category, Liska and Chamlin show that, while a high percentage of nonwhites may be perceived as threatening to whites and even in some cases to nonwhites, a high percentage of nonwhites initiate other social processes that counterbalance the effects of the threat process. Based on 1972 data, Liska and Chamlin (1984) initially argued that the percentage of nonwhites increases the proportion of crime with nonwhite victims who lack the resources to mobilize the police, thereby leading to a low nonwhite arrest rate; and based on 1982 data, they (chapter 6) now argue that a high percentage of nonwhites creates a climate of neglect that leads to low arrest rates for both whites and nonwhites.

In sum, traditionally most social threat research simply has assumed that certain social structures, compositions, and formations are inherently threatening to certain social categories in economic and racially stratified societies, leading to various forms of social control. More recently, some research has tried to specify the social conditions under which these social structures, compositions, and formations are perceived by elites, authorities, and majorities as threatening, to specify the processes by which they lead to perceived threat, and to partition the effects of threat from those of other social processes.

Middle Range Issues

One of the major issues in the study of social control is to specify the interrelationships between forms of social control and the causal processes and structures that underlie these interrelationships. Both conflict and structural-functional theories vaguely address this question. Structural-functionalism assumes that societies need some level of social control, which can be satisfied by different forms of control. As one form satisfies the need, other forms decrease (the functional-equivalent hypothesis). Conflict theory is more ambiguous. On the one hand, it assumes that all forms of control serve the interests of authorities and elites; thus, it implies that if existing forms are effective, other forms do not emerge. On the other hand, it assumes that all forms respond to threats to these interests; thus, it also seems to imply that all forms covary together. While both theories hypothesize some type of relationship between forms of social control, neither theory specifies a causal model that underlies this relationship; that is, neither specifies a causal structure among forms of social control, a causal process by which an increase in one form influences another form, and a causal process by which one, rather than another, form of social control emerges. It is not at all clear whether research supports both theories, either theory, or neither theory.

Consider two areas of research that explicitly examine the functional equivalence hypothesis: the relationship between the criminal justice system (prison population) and the mental health system (mental asylum population), and the relationship between lynchings and legal executions.

Macro research over the last forty years provides mixed support for a relationship between the size of prison and mental asylum populations. Historical studies by Rothman (1971) and Foucault (1965) trace the rise of mental asylums as a new form of social control that complements, if not substitutes, for prisons. Social indicators research, however, provides somewhat mixed support for the functional equivalence hypothesis (Penrose 1938; Biles and Mulligan 1973; Steadman 1979; Grabosky 1980). Drawing on data from eighteen European and six non-European countries, Penrose (1939) concludes that social control systems have evolved from physically controlling people (prisons) to medically treating them. In what is perhaps the first rigorous statistical study of this idea, Biles and Mulligan (1973) report a correlation of –.78 between the 1968 U.S. prison population and the number of hospital beds. Contradicting these studies, Grabosky (1980), in a time series study of the United States from 1930 to 1970, reports a positive correlation (.42) between the size of the prison and mental hospital populations.

These studies have continued to yield inconsistent results, although they have become methodologically sophisticated. Perhaps one of the best is a study by Inverarity and Grattet (1989). Using a time series from 1948 to 1985, they examine the extent to which the unemployment rate (as a threatening population) affects the prison and asylum populations and admission rates, as well as the number of welfare recipients and military personnel per capita; and they examine the extent to which the asylum admission rate and the number of welfare and military personnel per capita affect the prison admission rate. While they report some evidence that unemployment affects all four forms of social control, they report no evidence that the mental asylum admission rate and the number of welfare and military personnel per capita affect the prison admissions rate (the functional-equivalence or trade-off hypothesis).

Since the 1980s, a second strategy has emerged for examining the relationship between the criminal justice and mental health systems. Rather than estimating the statistical relationship between them over time, this strategy examines the mechanisms through which problematic populations move from one system to another. Steadman and associates (Steadman 1979; Melick et al. 1979; Arvanites 1988) argue that because asylums today do not operate at full capacity, they provide space for overflows from other control bureaucracies, such as the criminal justice system. They show how threatening populations that in the past might have been admitted directly into asylums are now first processed into the criminal justice system; some of them remain in local jails and others through various mechanisms, such as Incompetent to stand trial and Not guilty by reason of insanity, are channeled into asylums.

Recent years have witnessed a renewed interest in lynchings in the South from the post-civil War era to the Great Depression. Particular interest has focused on the relationship between illegal lynchings and legal state executions. Two general hypotheses have been advanced. One, lynchings and executions are substitute forms of social control (the trade-off hypothesis). When the criminal justice system is perceived to be ineffective, some citizens turn to various forms of self-help, ranging from buying guns, vigilantism, and lynching; hence, executions and lynchings should be negatively related. Two, both lynchings and executions are responses to conflict and threat. As conflict and threat increase, both lynchings and legal executions should increase; thus, the relationship between them should be positive.

Using time series data sets and recent statistical techniques, some researchers (Phillips 1986, 1987; Massey and Myers 1989; and Beck et al. 1989) have recently addressed this issue. Using a time series of Georgia from 1882 to 1935, Massey and Myers (1989) report that the lynching, legal execution, and incarceration rates of black males are not interdependent. Using a time series of North Carolina from 1889 to 1918, Phillips reports that lynchings and legal executions are positively related from 1889 to about 1903 and are unrelated after that time. He suggests that both were political responses of white authorities to racial threat and conflict during the Reconstructive era. When the conflict and threat were reduced through the political disenfranchisement of blacks around the turn of the century, both lynchings and executions no longer performed a political function; thus, they decreased and ceased to covary. Using an even more detailed and longer time series dataset of both North Carolina and Georgia, Beck, Massey, and Tolnay (1989) report no relationship between lynchings and executions both before and after disenfranchisement for North Carolina and some support for a positive relationship before disenfranchisement for Georgia; additionally, they find that the total amount of lethal sanctioning (lynchings and executions combined) decreased somewhere around the time of political disenfranchisement.

In conclusion, national time series data of imprisonment and mental admission rates and state time series data of lynchings and executions provide little empirical support for the functional-equivalence or trade-off hypothesis. While Steadman and his associates have documented the flows of people between the mental health and the criminal justice systems, the numbers of people involved is really too small to produce a noticeable effect on the overall relationship between the two systems. There does, however, seem to be some empirical support for the hypothesis that some forms of social control respond to the same causal variables and thus covary. Inverarity and Grattet (1989) report that prison and asylum admissions and the number of welfare recipients and military personnel per capita respond to unemployment; and both Phillips (1986 and 1987) and Beck et al. (1989) suggest that lynchings and legal executions respond to political disenfranchisement.

To some extent, the lack of clear and consistent findings may result from the two major research strategies employed. In one strategy researchers examine the flows between social control bureaucracies, particularly between mental asylums and prisons. While interesting research, it may not test the trade-off hypothesis, simply because the flows between control agencies are too small to affect the overall relationship between them. In another strategy, researchers examine the covariation between different forms of social control (e.g., Inverarity and Grattet 1989), sometimes observing the simple covariation between them, sometimes observing the detrended covariation between them, and sometimes observing the covariation between them controlling for other variables. This strategy incorrectly associates the functional-equivalence or trade-off hypothesis with a negative covariation between forms of control.

The theoretical problem, referred to as either the functional-equivalence or trade-off hypothesis, should be addressed within a causal modeling strategy, where covariation between forms of social control is clearly partitioned into causal processes or structures.

One source of covariation between forms of social control is a direct causal effect between them, in which a decrease in one form directly increases another. To a large extent, this occurs through the allocation of finite resources. Many forms of social control depend on finite economic resources; thus, resources expended on one form are not available for others. As prison expenditures increase, mental asylum or welfare expenditures frequently decrease. This hypothesis is advanced by Arvanites (chapter 8) in understanding the flow between mental asylums and prisons. He argues that the 1960s decarceration of mental asylums provided funds to construct prisons and provided physical facilities to control some portion of the jail and prison populations (see figure 10.1, model A).

A second source of covariation is an indirect causal effect through social threat. That is, as one form of social control expands, it reduces social threat, which reduces other forms of social control. This causal

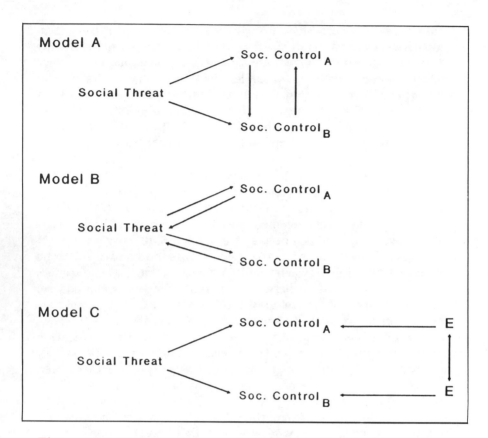

Figure 10-1 Modeling the causal structure underlying the relationship between forms of social control

model (figure 10.1, model B) postulates reciprocal effects between social threat and forms of social control. Tolnay and Beck (chapter 2) assume this model when they say that political disenfranchisement reduced the threat associated with the percentage of nonwhites, · thereby reducing the association between the percentage of non-whites and lynching.

A third source of covariation is through common causes. Forms of social control are caused by both unique and common factors. "Unique" means that the causes of one form are unrelated to the causes of others so that changes in the causes of one form yield variation in that form that is unrelated to variation in the other forms. Common causes that positively or negatively affect forms of control yield a positive covariation between them, and common causes that positively affect one and negatively affect the other yield a negative covariation between them. The same is true of correlated causes. If they positively affect each form of control and are themselves negatively correlated, then the two forms will negatively covary (see figure 10.1, model C).

This discussion is meant to highlight the problem that simple covariation, positive or negative, is insufficient to evaluate the functional-alternative or trade-off hypothesis. Covariation is the net effect of various causal processes. If one form of social control directly affects another form, this may well be obscured by the effect of common or correlated causes. For example, one version of the conflict threat hypothesis suggests that social threat positively affects various forms of social control, yielding positive covariations between them; this effect must be controlled in estimating the direct and indirect effects of one form on another. Conceptualizing this research issue in the language of causal modeling sensitizes us to these problems and directs our attention to specifying and estimating direct, indirect, and reciprocal causal effects. It also forces us to sharpen our conceptualization of the threat hypothesis. While both structural-functional and conflict theories generally and vaguely assume that different forms of control complement and substitute for each other, they do not clearly specify the causal processes and structures that yield these relationships.

Little Issues

By little issues I mean those that require little reconceptualization and are more or less resolvable through empirical research. While numerous such issues can be identified for each form of social control, I will discuss two that are relevant across forms of social control: the shape of the threat curve; and the relative effects of static levels of and changes in social structure on threat, and the differential impact of increases and decreases in threat on social control.

The shape of the threat curve. Research on the shape of the threat curve can be traced to the work of Blalock (1967) on the relationship between the relative size of minority groups and the perceived threat of the dominant group. He specified two nonlinear functional forms. As the percentage of minorities increases, the perceived economic threat of the dominant group increases at a decreasing rate and the perceived political threat of the dominant group increases at an increasing rate. Concerning the latter, Blalock argued that the perceived political threat of a dominant group is a multiplicative function of a minority's relative size, resources, and mobilization; this yields an increasing slope between any one of the three variables and the perceived threat of a dominant group. I will review the research support for this hypothesis in three areas: lynching, police expenditures, and fear of crime.

Regarding lynching, the evidence is mixed. Using Mississippi counties from 1889 to 1930, Reed (1972) reports that as percent black increases, the rate of lynching increases at an increasing rate with an inflection point at about eighty percent black. Using counties throughout the South from 1889 to 1930, Corzine et al. (1983) also report that the relationship between percent black and lynching shows an increasing slope. They further report that it is strongest in the Deep South, where blacks were most perceived as threatening, and specifically after the voter registration drives in the 1890s which accentuated racial conflict. Recently, Tolnay et al. (1989) challenge these findings. They report that empirical support for the power-threat hypothesis is contingent on a few outlier counties, a truncated sample, and an inappropriate measure of lynching. Correcting these "problems," they report no relationship between percent black and lynching in the border states and a linear one in the Deep South.

Regarding police expenditures, evidence for a nonlinear relationship is equally mixed. Using a sample of ninety nonsouthern cities over fifty thousand population, Jackson and Carroll (1981) report a nonlinear relationship between percent nonwhite and police expenditures for 1971 with two inflection points. From about zero to ten percent black, expenditures decrease; from that point to about fifty percent they accelerate; and from that point on they decrease. Jackson and Carroll (1981) argue that blacks do not become threatening until they reach a certain percentage of the population; from that point the threat accelerates until blacks become the majority and assume political power at which point the size of the black population is no longer a threat but a resource to local black authorities. Using a sample of all cities over fifty thousand for 1960, 1970, and 1980, Greenberg et al. (1985) challenge these findings. For nonsouthern cities, they report little evidence of a curvilinear effect and argue that Jackson and Carroll's findings are contingent on a few outlier cities. For the South they report a curvilinear effect for 1960 and 1970 and no effect at all for 1980. Updating her findings for 1980 and elaborating them by region, type of expenditure, city size, and decade, Jackson (1989) recently reports that the curvilinear effect is strongest for 1970, in cities over fifty thousand, for capital expenditures, and in the South. These findings are consistent with the threat hypothesis: blacks have traditionally been more of a threat in the South than elsewhere; racial confrontation was more intense in the 1970s than in the 1980s; large cities depend more on formal than informal social control; and federal funds to control urban disorder are allocated more for capital than salary expenditures.

Using twenty-six of the largest U.S. cities in the early 1960s to mid-1970s, Liska et al. (1982) examine the effect of the percentage of nonwhites on the fear of crime, controlling for crime rates. They report a curvilinear effect with two inflection points. An increase in the percentage of nonwhites shows no effect on fear until the percentage reaches about fifteen percent; after that point further increases in the percentage of nonwhites increases fear at an increasing rate until the percentage reaches about thirty-five percent, at which point fear stabilizes.

In sum, while research suggests a strong relationship between the percentage of nonwhites or blacks and different forms of social control, the exact functional form of the relationship remains unclear. There may, however, be some general similarities in the functional form of the relationship across forms of social control. An increase in the relative size of the minority population from zero to ten or fifteen percent may not be perceived as threatening; minority size may have a threshold below which it is simply ignored. For example, Jackson and Carroll (1981) report that the percentage has no effect on police expenditures until it reaches about ten percent. Reed (1972) and later Tolnay et al. (1989), using the Reed index of lynching, report that the percentage of blacks has little effect on lynching, a very serious act, until the percentage reaches about forty-five percent.

There may also be some systematic differences in the functional form of the relationship among forms of social control, such as police expenditures and lynching. As a minority population approaches and exceeds fifty percent, they frequently assume some degree of political power. To the new authorities, the size of the "minority" (the new majority) is more a resource than a threat. Hence, in political democracies, the relationship between the relative size of the minority and various forms of social control may weaken as the minority approaches fifty percent. This, of course, may not be the case, if the minority is partially disenfranchised, such as in the Reconstruction South, or if forms of control are not directly managed by authorities, such as lynching. Nonetheless, at some percentage point (forty to seventy-five percent) further increases in the relative size of the "minority," disadvantaged, or disenfranchised, population probably yields little increase in most forms of social control.

It thus seems reasonable to hypothesize that the relative size of the minority population must reach a certain proportion of the population before it is perceived as threatening by the majority. From that point further increases generate increases in perceived threat, linearly or even at an increasing rate, until some upper level is reached, at which point further increases in the size of the minority population yield no increase in the perceived threat of the majority. While the exact number and position of the inflection points may depend on the specific form of threat and control, the general functional form of the curve (e.g., third-degree polynomial) may operate across specific forms of threat and control.

Changes in threatening people, distributions, and acts. For the most part, research on social control associates threat with the absolute or relative size of certain classes of people (e.g., minorities), certain distributions of people (income inequality), and certain acts (crime); and research on social control uses change as a methodological tool to infer causality and ignores its substantive meaning. It may very well be that changes in the absolute or relative size of certain classes and distributions of people and of certain acts may be as or even more threatening than their absolute or relative size. For example, a crime rate of fifteen per thousand population may be more threatening than one of ten per thousand, but a change in the crime rate from five per thousand to ten per thousand may be even more threatening than a crime rate of fifteen per thousand.

In regards to police size and welfare, Chamlin (1989) addresses this issue. Using a large sample of U.S. cities, he reports that static measures of socioeconomic threat (percent black, racial segregation, property crime rates) show little effect on the change in police size from 1972 to 1982, but that changes in these measures show a substantial effect on the changes in police size from 1972 to 1982. He also reports (chapter 9) that static measures of socioeconomic threat and need (percent black and the unemployment rate) show little effect on changes in the AFDC rate from 1960 to 1970 and from 1970 to 1980, but that changes in these measures show substantial effects on changes in AFDC over both decades.

Related to this issue is the question of whether the causal processes underlying changes in social control are the same for the expansion and the contraction in social control. Studies tend to be cross-sectional and to focus on time periods of extreme expansion or contraction in social control. Variation in social control, whether brought about by expansion or contraction, is treated as variation.

Consequently, this research does not distinguish social processes that influence expansion from those that influence contraction.

For example, police size expanded tremendously from the late 1960s to the middle or late 1970s, and has stabilized and even decreased somewhat since then. Some of the strongest empirical support for the threat hypothesis comes from research on police size during the 1970s and some of the weakest support comes from that research during the 1980s. Perhaps the temper of the 1960s and early 1970s transformed a high percentage of nonwhites into a social threat, and by the late 1970s the temper or social climate again changed so that a high percentage of nonwhites no longer constituted a social threat. Hence, a high percentage of nonwhites sparked increases in police size in the late 1960s and middle 1970s but not in the late 1970s and 1980s. The decrease in police size that occurred in the late 1970s and 1980s may have been influenced more by financial considerations than social threat. Perhaps the expansion of police size is affected more by social threat than revenue, and the contraction of police size is affected more by revenue than threat.

I generally propose that social threat affects the expansion more than the contraction of social control; that is, increases in social threat generate increases in social control but decreases in social threat do not generate decreases in social control, particularly in organizational forms of control. Once established, internal processes of organizations maintain them. For example, a substantial reduction in crime may not lead to a reduction of the criminal justice system, or a substantial increase in the income of the poor may not lead to a decrease of the welfare system.

In sum, focusing on the cross-sectional variation among variables, researchers tend to ignore change. If they focus on change at all, they examine it as a methodological tool, ignoring its substantive meaning, and they examine general processes of change, rarely distinguishing the process of expansion from that of contraction.

Summary

Research on social control is dissipated across substantive forms of control. The focus of this book is threefold: to review the research on different forms of control, to bring together the work on different forms of control, and to refocus work from substantive forms to theoretical issues that cut across them. The third goal is both the most difficult and most important. It requires that researchers change their orientation from studying specific forms of social control to studying theoretical hypotheses and issues about general social structures and processes that cut across these forms of social control.

I focus on one such general hypothesis: the threat hypothesis. I discuss three types of issues: big issues or those that are more conceptual than empirical; middle-range issues or those that are both conceptual and empirical; and little issues or those that are more empirical than conceptual.

One big issue is that of embedding the threat hypothesis in a theory of structure and a theory of process. Clearly, threat research is not guided by a theory of social structure; instead, research links forms of social control to a smattering of interesting social structural variables. Some studies examine distributions of people (e.g., income inequality) assumed to threaten economic elites; others study actions (e.g., crime) assumed to threaten bureaucrats; and others still study social compositions (e.g., percent nonwhite) assumed to threaten majorities. Other than the assumption that some social structures, compositions, or formations are threatening to some people of power (economic elites, bureaucrats, and majorities), there is little conceptual or theoretical glue that holds these studies together. For example, which structures cause which structures, and which structures are subsumed by which structures? There is also no theory of process. Research simply assumes that some people of power perceive some actions, people, and distributions of people as threatening. It does not specify why some people of power perceive what specific actions, people, and distributions of people to be threatening, and how these perceptions lead to actions that influence the form and level of social control. Generally, embedding the threat hypothesis in theories of structure and process would go a long way toward integrating studies of social control and linking social structures, compositions, and formations to forms of social control.

One major middle-range issue is the relationship between forms of social control. Structural-functional theory suggests that many forms are functionally equivalent. As one increases, the other decreases. Conflict theory is somewhat more ambiguous. Assuming that forms of social control satisfy the interests of elites, it seems to imply, on the one hand, that as one form increases, others decrease; and assuming that all forms of social control respond to threat, it seems to imply, on the other hand, that all forms increase or decrease together. Some empirical research on the relationships between prison and mental asylum populations and between lynchings and legal executions in the South has appeared; but the findings are too inconsistent to resolve the issue.

I argue that the functional equivalent or trade-off hypothesis cannot even be addressed by bivariate correlations between forms of social control. It must be addressed within the context of a causal analysis whereby a bivariate relationship is partitioned into the direct effect of one form of control on another form, the indirect effect of one form of control on another form through its effect on threat, and the effect of common causes on both forms.

The third class of issues, deemed little issues, are predominantly empirical issues. I have discussed two: the functional form of the threat curve and the differential impact of increases and decreases of threat on forms of social control.

Research suggests a strong relationship between the relative size of the minority population and the perceived threat of the majority, but it provides mixed support for the functional form of that relationship. While the exact functional form may well be contingent on types of threat and forms of control, a general functional form may exist across various types of threat and forms of control. Research should focus on the shape of the threat curve and the extent to which the inflection points are contingent on the type of threat and form of control.

Researchers tend to focus on cross-sectional variation and ignore change. They treat change as a methodological tool and ignore its substantive meaning; yet, it seems reasonable to hypothesize that a rapid change in the crime rate, unemployment rate, and minority composition, for example, may be perceived as more threatening than a stable high level in them. Moreover, if researchers consider change at all, they assume that the same social processes underlie both the expansion and contraction of social control; yet, it seems reasonable to hypothesize that increases in threat affect expansion more than decreases in threat affect contraction.

Finally, social control research is organized around substantive forms of social control rather than around theoretical propositions and hypotheses. Researchers who study one form of control (e.g., welfare) are rarely familiar with theoretically similar research on another form of control (e.g., lynching); in a sense, social control research is dissipated into the study of specific forms of control. While general theories do stimulate some research in these substantive areas, this research does not feed back onto these theories; consequently, the theories of today are essentially the theories of the 1960s. This book brings together research on social control from a variety of substantive areas, ranging from lethal to beneficent controls, and tries to refocus research toward theoretical issues that cut across forms of social control.

Notes

Chapter 1

1. Part of this chapter is a revision and an extension of an article that first appeared in the *Annual Review of Sociology*, 1987.

Chapter 2

1. A recent article by Corzine et al. (1988) attempts to test the usefulness of Split Labor Market Theory as a framework for understanding southern lynchings. Unfortunately, they used the NAACP inventory of lynchings which is severely flawed, which makes their findings extremely doubtful. Furthermore, their measure of the presence of a cheap labor threat (#black tenant farmers/#white tenant farmers) is conceptually suspect, again undermining the usefulness of their findings.

2. Phillips (1987) has suggested that legal executions and lynchings were substitutable forms of lethal sanctioning in North Carolina after disenfranchisement. Subsequent investigation by Beck et al. (1989), however, found very little covariation, over time, in the use of legal executions and lynching in North Carolina and Georgia between 1882 and 1930.

3. Perhaps the most serious problem plaguing previous research concerned with southern lynchings has been the poor quality of publicly available data on lynchings, including the frequently used inventory compiled by the NAACP (1919, and annual supplements). Under a grant from the National Science Foundation (SES-8618123) we are preparing a refined inventory of lynch victims that includes information from the NAACP, the *Chicago Tribune*, and Tuskegee University inventories, plus verification of each incident by references from local and regional newspaper accounts.

4. An exception is the recent attempt by Corzine et al. (1988) to test the Split Labor Market Theory of black lynchings.

5. Some previous tests of the threat perspective of southern lynchings (e.g., Corzine et al. 1983) have included a control variable for the literacy of the white population. This, however, is not the same thing as positing *different motivations* for whites of different class positions.

Chapter 3

1. While there probably are some common sources of measurement error, so that not all of the common or shared variance between the two indexes reflects the underlying rates, using two substantially different measures of police homicide of citizens approximates the ideal strategy of controlling measurement error. To partially test this measurement assumption, we estimate various models, freeing and constraining the correlation between the measurement errors of the two indexes. Estimates of this correlation are very low (e.g., .03), and estimates of the model fit, x^2, do not differ between models where this correlation is assumed to be zero and where it is free to vary.

2. The Vital Statistics data are aggregated by county. We imputed city counts by multiplying the county count by the proportion of the city population to the county population in which the city is located. In only seven of the forty-five cities in our sample is the city located in more than one county, and in most of these the city is located primarily in one county.

3. Because citizen homicide of police is a rare event, rates should include more than one year. Hence, this index includes the same years (1975 to 1979) included in the police homicide of citizen index.

4. In computing these rates, the denominator can be the population of the offender category, the victim category, or the total population. After considerable deliberation, we used the total population, because a common denominator for all rates facilitates comparing the effects of different interracial and intraracial crimes. It is also theoretically appropriate. We are concerned with the extent to which a general threat of crime to the police is associated with various types of interracial and intraracial crime relative to the population, but not relative to the racial population from which either the offenders or victims are drawn. For example, if few blacks reside in a city, then a few crimes by these blacks standardized by the black population may yield a very high crime rate; but these few black crimes will have little effect on the threat of crime perceived by police.

5. Of twenty-six cities in the NCS, twenty-two are part of our sample of forty-five cities.

6. We estimated the equations using the logged and natural metrics of police homicide. The logged equations provide a better fit, although the pattern of structural coefficients is similar for the equations in logged and natural metrics; hence, the estimates of the logged equations are reported in the text and the estimates of the natural equations are noted in footnotes.

7. Although the properties (bias and efficiency) of ML estimates for small samples are not well known, our sample of forty-five cities is not large enough to ignore them. Consequently, we also use ILS methods to estimate the

structural-measurement model; however, because the ILS and ML estimates are very similar, we only report the ML estimates.

8. We also estimate a model using citizen homicide of police as the measure of threatening acts. Although a very rare act, the homicide of police may be particularly threatening to police. Even a few homicides of police over a series of years may be very threatening to the police. We estimate the equations twice, once standardizing the homicide of police by population and once standardizing by police size, as citizen homicide of police may have more impact in a small than in a large city or department. The effect of citizen homicide of police on police homicide of citizens is statistically insignificant. Citizen homicide of police may be just too rare an event to affect the perceived threat of police. Over the five-year period the median number of citizen homicides of police was 1.25 (0.25 per year) and fourteen of the forty-five cities experienced no such homicides.

9. We have also assumed that the threat hypothesis implies a relationship between the percentage of nonwhites and police homicide that is not contingent on any other variables. However, it might be argued that the presence of nonwhites is perceived to be more threatening by white than nonwhite police. Aggregated to the city level, the effect of percent nonwhite on police homicide should therefore increase with the percentage of the department that is white. We were able to collect data on the racial composition of the police department for only thirty of the forty-five cities sampled. However, only three departments were more than thirty percent nonwhite and only four were more than twenty percent nonwhite. This is not a characteristic of just our sample. Of a much larger sample of 109 cities, we were able to collect this information for seventy-nine cities, of which only four and six were over thirty percent and twenty percent nonwhite, respectively. Hence, this hypothesis simply may not be testable during the middle 1970s.

10. As for the aggregate model, a review of scattergrams and estimates of polynominal equations reveals no evidence of a departure from linearity. While there are some differences between the estimates of the equations in natural and logged metrics, the differences are small and the pattern of findings is exactly the same. Evidence of multicollinearity is, again, limited to model 4, where, as previously noted, the correlation between percent nonwhite and the homicide rate is strong. Again, while these are grounds for caution, they do not necessarily mean that the estimates of the models, especially the percent nonwhite coefficient, are necessarily biased. The estimated structural coefficient of percent nonwhite in model 4 is similar to those in models 1, 2, and 3 where the evidence for multicollinearity is minimal, and the estimated structural coefficients for percent nonwhite in all models are either 2.0 or 1.5 times their SEs.

11. There is some evidence of multicollinearity. The bivariate correlation between percent nonwhite and the NW-NW crime rate is .78. Again, while these are grounds for caution, they do not necessarily imply that the esti-

mates of the model are substantially biased due to multicollinearity. For the same reasons stated in footnote 10, there is considerable reason to believe that the bias in the estimates due to multicollinearity is minimal.

12. While we have emphasized threat in accounting for the relationship between the percentage of nonwhites and police homicide, threat may not be the only process underlying the relationship. Because of the general low status of nonwhites in contemporary American society, police may also feel less social constraint over their actions in neighborhoods and cities in which the percentage of nonwhites is relatively high. This may even operate through departmental policy. Sherman (1983) suggests that police department policies vary on the use of guns and that such policies affect police shootings; it seems quite plausible that the percentage of nonwhites may well affect these policies.

Chapter 4

1. Household victimizations included burglary, household larceny, and motor vehicle theft. Personal victimizations included rape, assault, robbery, and personal theft.

2. This variable is present only in the robbery and assault equations.

3. This variable is present only in the assault equations.

4. This variable is present only in the robbery and burglary equations.

5. This variable is present only in the assault equations.

6. Lower income was defined as those respondents with a family income of $5,999 or less. The middle-upper group was comprised of victims with family incomes of $6,000 or more. This division was based on poverty-level figures for 1974 and 1975. In 1974 the poverty level was defined as $5,038, and in 1975 it was defined as $5,500.

7. An interaction term for race and percent nonwhite was added to the lower-income equation, and although it was positive it was not significant.

8. Some recent research (Liska and Chamlin 1984; South and Messner 1986) would suggest that the positive effect of percent nonwhite on whites is due to an increase in interracial crime. However, when the offender's race was added to the equation for white victims, it was nonsignificant (b = .005; s.e. = .01).

Chapter 6

1. Because of missing arrest data, Liska and Chamlin (1984) also do not employ the full sample of cities. They use seventy-six of the 109 cities. We re-

estimated the equations using only their seventy-six cities. The findings are virtually identical to those reported in tables 6.1 through 6.4

2. Liska and Chamlin's (1984) measure of racial residential segregation, which was obtained from published work (Sorensen, Taeuber, and Hollingsworth 1975), refers to white-nonwhite segregation at the block level. Unfortunately, the only published source—which we are aware of—that reports measures of racial block-level segregation for 1980 reports only black-nonblack segregation (Choldin 1985). Although the correlation between nonwhite segregation in 1970 and black segregation in 1980 is strong (+ .78 p < .001), there may be some problems in comparing black segregation in 1980 to nonwhite segregation in 1970.

3. Because recent panel (Greenberg, Kessler, and Logan 1979) and time series (Chamlin 1988) analyses reveal no evidence that arrest rates affect crime rates, OLS regression techniques are used.

4. Following Liska and Chamlin (1984), we reestimate the equations deleting the percentage of families below the poverty level. The findings are virtually identical to those reported in tables 6.1 through 6.4.

Chapter 7

1. Several studies, however, question the use of the unemployment rate as the optimal dimension of labor market. See especially Melossi (1985), Lynch (1989), and Colvin (1990). Garland (1990) provides a broad overview of the major sociological theories of punishment.

2. Cohen and Tonry summarizes several studies of legal reform by observing "regardless of the type or locus of the procedural change, no appreciable changes were found in the use of prison; whatever system changes occurred were limited largely to modifications of case-processing procedures" (Cohen and Tonry 1983:438).

3. Jacobs elaborates further implications of the conflict perspective. States should differ in their repressiveness depending upon the extent to which their elites are victimized by crime. Thus, because elites are more likely to be victims of property than of violent crimes, the association between inequality and imprisonment should hold only for property crimes. Furthermore, regional variation in elite victimization should match regional variation in imprisonment. His multiple regression analysis provides some support for these hypotheses.

4. This application of structural theory illustrates how action and structural theories may be complementary rather than antagonistic. Giddens' (1982) theory of structuration attempts to amalgamate the two orientations at a general level. The more conventional approach is oppositional. See, for

example, the exchanges between Skocpol and Amenta (1985) and Quadagno (1985); Reiman (1982) with Greenberg and Humphries (1982).

5. Extant studies of criminal justice policy (e.g., Berk et al. 1977) find no evidence of a dominance of financial interests in prison policy formation. While certain businesses, such as convenience stores, depend upon criminal justice, for most business firms crime control does not rank as a pressing problem. Furthermore, to the extent firms substitute private security for state law enforcement (Bartel 1975), conflict theory may exaggerate the role of the criminal justice system in protecting elite property.

6. Substantial debate continues, however, over whether such reforms have reduced prison populations or simply widened the net of social control (Austin and Krisberg 1981). Conclusions are difficult to draw because until recently no systematic count of the numbers involved in noninstitutional treatments was available. There is some indication for the postwar U.S. that a tradeoff has taken place between prison and welfare expenditures (Grattet 1989) but not in controlled populations (Inverarity and Grattet 1989).

Chapter 9

1. Unfortunately, information about the number of black elected officials is not available for the 1960s, while race-related rioting virtually disappeared during the 1970s. Thus, I am unable to compare the relative impact of these two forms of racial insurgency on change in the AFDC recipient rate.

2. Because of data availability limitations, the years used in the calculation of the residual-change scores for the percentage of families below the poverty level are 1959, 1969, and 1979.

3. As is noted in the body of the text, AFDC transfers are best analyzed at the state level. However, rioting occurs in cities. Hence, it is possible that the relationship between rioting and the change in the level of the AFDC recipient rate might reflect, in part, the influence of some dimension of urbanism. In an effort to address this issue I reestimated the equations, including a measure of the change in the percentage of the population which is urban. The change in urbanism had no effect on the change in the AFDC recipient rate during the 1960s (or the 1970s). Moreover, rioting remains a significant predictor within the 1960 to 1970 change equation.

4. The value of Cook's D for Alaska is 35.3, indicating that it has a substantial influence on the parameter estimates. Specifically, the inclusion of Alaska would lead one to erroneously conclude that the change in poverty directly affects the change in the AFDC recipient rate during the 1960s (this problem does not arise when residual-change scores are used to measure change).

References

Chapter 1

Adamson, E. 1984. Toward a Marxian penology: Captive criminal populations as economic threats and resources. *Social Problems* 31:435-58.

Arvanites, Thomas M. 1988. The impact of state mental hospital deinstitutionalization on commitment for incompetency to stand trial. *Criminology* 26:307-320.

Bagozzi, Richard. 1977. Populism and lynching in Louisiana. (Comment on Inverarity, ASR April 1976) *American Sociological Review* 42:335-58.

Beck, E. M., James L. Massey, and Stewart E. Tolnay. 1989. The gallows, the mob, the vote: Lethal sanctioning of blacks in North Carolina and Georgia, 1982 to 1920. *Law and Society Review* 23:317-31.

Becker, Gary. 1968. Crime and punishment: An economic approach. *Journal of Political Economy* 76:169-217.

Becker, Howard. 1963. *Outsiders: Studies in the sociology of deviance.* New York: Free Press.

Beirne, Piers. 1979. Empiricism and the critique of Marxism on law and crime. *Social Problems* 26:373-85.

Ben-Yehuda, Nachman. 1980. The European witch craze of the fourteenth to seventeenth centuries: A sociologist's perspective. *American Journal of Sociology* 86:1-31.

Berk, Richard A. 1977. Proof? No. Evidence? No. A skeptic's comment on Inverarity's use of statistical inference. (Comment on Inverarity, ASR April 1976) *American Sociological Review* 42:625-55.

Berk, Richard, Sheldon L. Messinger, David Rauma, and J. E. Bercochea. 1983. Prisons as self-regulating systems: A comparison of historical patterns in California for male and female offenders. *Law and Society Review* 17:547-86.

Berk, Richard A., David Rauma, Sheldon L. Messinger, and Thomas F. Cooley. 1981. A test of the stability of punishment hypothesis: The case of California 1851-1970. *American Sociological Review* 46:805-29.

197

Black, Donald J., and Albert J. Reiss, Jr. 1970. Police control of juveniles. *American Sociological Review* 35:63-77.

Blalock, Hubert M., Jr. 1967. *Toward a theory of minority group relations.* New York: Wiley.

Blumstein, Alfred, and Jacqueline Cohen, 1973. A theory of the stability of punishment. *Journal of Criminal Law and Criminology* 64:198-207.

Blumstein, Alfred, Jacqueline J. Cohen, and David Nagin. 1978. *Deterrence and incapacitation: Estimating the effects of criminal sanctions on crime rates.* Washington, D.C.: National Academy of Sciences.

Blumstein, Alfred, and S. Moitra. 1979. Growing or stable incarceration rates: A comment on Cahalan's trends in incarceration in the United States since 1880. *Crime and Delinquency* 25:91-4.

Blumstein, Alfred, Jacqueline Cohen, and David Nagin. 1976. The dynamics of a homeostatic punishment process. *Journal of Criminal Law and Criminology* 67:317-34.

Bohrnsted, George W. 1977. Use of the multiple indicators multiple causes (MIMIC) model. (Comment on Inverarity, ASR April 1976). *American Sociological Review* 42:656-63.

Box, Steven, and Chris Hale. 1982. Economic crisis and the rising prisoner population in England and Wales. *Crime and Social Justice* 13:20-35.

Bureau of Justice Statistics. 1986. *State and federal prisoners, 1925-85.* Washington, D.C.: U.S. Department of Justice.

Carr-Hill, R. A., and N. H. Stern. 1979. *Crime, the police, and criminal statistics.* New York: Academic Press.

Center for Research on Criminal Justice. 1975. *The iron fist and the velvet glove: An analysis of the U.S. police.* Berkeley: Center for Research on Criminal Justice.

Chamlin, Mitchell B. 1987. General assistance among cities: An examination of need, economic threat, and benign neglect hypotheses. *Social Science Quarterly* 68:835-46.

———. 1989. A macro social analysis of change in police force size, 1972-1982. *The Sociological Quarterly* 30:615-24.

Chapman, Jeffrey I., Werner Hirsch, and Sidney Sonenblum. 1975. Crime prevention, the police production function and budgeting. *Public Finance* 30:197-215.

Connor, Walter. 1972. The manufacture of deviance: The case of the Soviet purge, 1936-1938. *American Sociological Review* 37:403-13.

Conrad, Peter, and Joseph W. Schneider. 1980. *Deviance and medicalization.*

St. Louis: C. V. Mosby.

Cook, Philip J. 1977. Punishment and crime: A critique of current findings concerning the preventive effect of criminal sanctions. *Law and Contemporary Problems* 41:164-204.

Cooley, Charles Horton. 1909. *Social organization*. New York: Scribner.

Corzine, Jay, James Creech, and Lin Corzine. 1983. Black concentration and lynchings in the South: Testing Blalock's power-threat hypothesis. *Social Forces* 61:774-96.

Currie, Elliot P. 1968. Crimes without criminals: Witchcraft and its control in renaissance Europe. *Law and Society Review* 3:7-32.

Davis, Nanette J., and Bo Anderson. 1983. *Social control: The production of deviance in the modern state*. New York: Irvington.

Dentler, Robert A., and Kai T. Erikson. 1959. The functions of deviance in groups. *Social Problems* 7:98-107.

Durkheim, Emile. 1938. *The rules of sociological method*. Translated by S. A. Solovay and J. H. Mueller, and edited by G. E. G. Catlin. Glencoe, Ill.: Free Press.

Ehrlich, Isaac. 1973. Participation in illegitimate activities: A theoretical and empirical investigation. *Journal of Political Economy* 81:521-64.

Erikson, Kai T. 1966. *Wayward puritans: A study in the sociology of deviance*. New York: Wiley.

Foucault, Michel. 1965. *Madness and civilization*. New York: Vintage.

Foucault, Michel. 1978. *Discipline and punish*. Translated by A. Sheridan. New York: Pantheon.

Fyfe, James J. 1982. *Readings on police use of deadly force*. Washington, D.C.: Police Foundation.

Galster, George C., and Laura H. Scaturo. 1985, The U.S. criminal justice system: Unemployment and the severity of punishment. *Journal of Research in Crime and Delinquency* 22:163-90.

Garofalo, James. 1979. Victimization and the fear of crime. *Journal of Research in Crime and Delinquency* 16:80-97.

Gibbs, Jack P. 1981. *Norms, deviance, and social control*. New York: Elsevier.

Greenberg, David F. 1977. The dynamics of oscillatory punishment processes. *Journal of Criminal Law and Criminology* 68:643-51.

Greenberg, David F. 1980. A critique of the immaculate conception: A comment on Beirne. *Social Problems* 27:476-77.

Greenberg, David, Ronald C. Kessler, and Colin Loftin. 1985. Social inequality and crime control. *Journal of Criminal Law and Criminology* 76:684 –704.

Harring, Sidney L. 1983. *Policing a class society.* New Brunswick, N.J.: Rutgers University Press.

Hicks, Alexander, and Duane Swank. 1983. Civil disorder, relief mobilization, and AFDC caseloads: A reexamination of the Piven and Cloward thesis. *American Journal of Political Science* 27:695-716.

Hirschi, Travis. 1969. *Causes of delinquency.* Los Angeles: University of California Press.

Ignatieff, Michael. 1978. *A just measure of pain: The penitentiary in the industrial revolution, 1850–1950.* New York: Pantheon.

Inverarity, James M. 1976. Populism and lynching on Louisiana, 1899–1986: A test of Erikson's theory of the relationship between boundary crises and repressive justice. *American Sociological Review* 41:262-80.

Inverarity, James, and Daniel McCarthy. 1988. Punishment and structure revised: Unemployment and imprisonment in the U.S., 1948-1984. *The Sociological Quarterly* 29:263-79.

Inverarity, James, and Ryken Grattet. 1989. Institutional responses to unemployment: A comparison of U.S. trends, 1948-1885, *Contemporary Crises* 13:351-70.

Isaac, Larry, and W. R. Kelly. 1981. Racial insurgency, the state, and welfare expansion: Local and national level evidence from the postwar United States. *American Journal of Sociology* 86:1348-86.

Jackson, Pamela I., and Leo Caroll. 1981. Race and the war on crime: The sociopolitical determinants of municipal police expenditures in 90 non-southern U.S. cities. *American Sociological Review* 46:290-305.

Jackson, Pamela I. *Minority group threat, crime, and policing.* 1989. New York: Praeger.

Jacobs, David. 1979. Inequality and police strength: Conflict theory and coercive control in metropolitan areas. *American Sociological Review* 44:913-25.

Jacobs, David. 1980. Marxism and the critique of empiricism: A comment on Beirne. *Social Problems* 27:467-70.

Jacobs, David, and D. Britt. 1979. Inequality and police use of deadly force: An empirical assessment of a conflict hypothesis. *Social Problems* 26:403 –12.

Jankovic, Ivan. 1977. Labor market and imprisonment. *Crime and Social*

Justice 8:17–37.

Jennings, Edward T. 1983. Racial insurgency, the state and welfare expansion: A critical comment and reanalysis. *American Journal of Sociology* 88: 1220–36.

Kania, Richard, and Wade C. Mackey. 1977. Police violence as a function of community characteristics. *Criminology* 27:27–48.

Kluegel, James, and Eliot R. Smith. 1981. Beliefs about stratification. *Annual Review of Sociology* 7:29–56.

Langan P. A., and L. A. Greenfeld. 1985. The prevalence of imprisonment. Washington D.C.: U.S. Department of Justice.

Lauderdale, Pat. 1976. Deviance and moral boundaries. *American Sociological Review* 41:660–76.

Lauderdale, Pat, J. Parker, P. Smith-Cunnien, and James Inverarity. 1984. External threat and the definition of deviance. *Journal of Personality and Social Psychology* 46:1058–68.

Lemert, Edwin M. 1951. *Social pathology.* New York: McGraw-Hill.

Liska, Allen E., and William F. Baccaglini. 1983. Fear of crime. In *Encyclopedia of crime and justice*, vol. 2, edited by Sanford H. Kadish. New York: Free Press.

Liska, Allen E., and Mitchell B. Chamlin. 1984. Social structure and crime control among macrosocial units. *American Journal of Sociology* 90:383 –95.

Liska, Allen E., Mitchell B. Chamlin, and Mark Reed. 1985. Testing the economic production and conflict models of crime control. *Social Forces* 63:119–38.

Liska, Allen E., Joseph J. Lawrence, and Michael Benson. 1981. Perspectives on the legal order: The capacity for social control. *American Journal of Sociology* 87:412–26.

Liska, Allen E. 1987. *Perspectives on deviance.* Englewood Cliffs, N.J.: Prentice-Hall.

Liska, Allen E., Joseph J. Lawrence, and Andrew Sanchirico. 1982. Fear of crime as a social fact. *Social Forces* 60:760–71.

Loftin, Colin and David McDowall. 1982. The police, crime and economic theory. *American Sociological Review* 47:393–401.

McPheters, L. R., and W. B. Stronge. 1974. Law enforcement expenditures and urban crime. *National Tax Journal* 27:633–44.

Melick, Mary E., Henry J. Steadman, and Joseph C. Cocozza. 1979. The medicalization of criminal behavior among mental patients. *Journal of Health and Social Behavior* 20:228-37.

Morrissey, Joseph P. 1982. Deinstitutionalizing the mentally ill: Processes, outcomes, and new directions. In *Deviance and mental illness.* Edited by Walter Gove. Beverly Hills: Sage.

Nye, F. Ivan. 1958. *Family relationships and delinquent behavior.* New York: Wiley.

Phillips, Charles David. 1987. Exploring relations among forms of social control: The lynching and execution of blacks in North Carolina, 1989-1981. *Law and Society Review* 21:361-74.

Phillips, Llad, and Harold L. Votey, Jr. 1981. *The economics of crime control.* Beverly Hills: Sage.

Piven, Frances F., and Richard A. Cloward. 1971. *Regulating the poor: The functions of public welfare.* New York: Vintage.

Pope, Whitney, and Charles Ragin. 1877. Mechanical solidarity, repressive justice, and lynchings in Louisiana. (Comment on Inverarity, ASR April 1976) *American Sociological Review* 42:2:363-68.

Quinney, Richard. 1977. *Class, state and crime.* New York: McKay.

Rauma, David. 1981a. Crime and punishment reconsidered: Some comments on Blumstein's stability of punishment hypothesis. *Journal of Criminal Law and Criminology* 72:1772-98.

Rauma, David. 1981b. A concluding note on the stability of punishment: Reply to Blumstein, Cohen, Moitra, and Nagin. *Journal of Criminal Law and Criminology* 72:1809-12.

Reed, John Sheldon. 1972. Percent black and lynching: A test of Blalock's theory. *Social Forces* 50:356-60.

Reiss, Albert J. 1951. Delinquency as a failure of personal and social controls. *American Sociological Review* 16:196-207.

Ross, E. A. 1901. *Social control.* New York: Macmillan.

Rothman, David J. 1971. *The discovery of the asylum.* Boston: Little, Brown & Company.

Rusche, George, and Otto Kirchheimer. 1939. *Punishment and social structure.* New York: Russell & Russell.

Scheff, Thomas. 1966. *Being mentally ill.* Chicago: Aldine.

Schmidt, P., and A. D. Witte. 1984. *An economic analysis of crime and justice.* New York: Academic Press.

Schram, Stanford F., and J. Patrick Turbett. 1983. Civil disorder and welfare

explosion: A two-step process. *American Sociological Review* 48:408
-14.

Scott, Robert A. 1976. Deviance, sanctions and integration in small scale
societies. *Social Forces* 54:603-20.

Sherman, Lawrence W., and Robert H. Langworthy. 1979. Measuring homicide
by police officers. *Journal of Criminal Law and Criminology* 70:546
-60.

Skogan, Wesley G., and Michael G. Maxfield. 1981. *Coping with crime: Individual and neighborhood reactions.* Beverly Hills: Sage.

Spitzer, Steven. 1975. Toward a Marxian theory of deviance. *Social Problems*
22:638-51.

Steadman, Henry J. 1979. *Beating a rap?* Chicago: University of Chicago Press.

Steadman, Henry J., John Mohahan, Barbara Dufee, Eliot Hartstone, and Dan
C. Robbins. 1984. The impact of state mental deinstitutionalization on
United States prison populations: 1968-1978. *Journal of Criminal
Law and Criminology* 75:474-90.

Stinchcombe, Arthur L. 1968. *Constructing social theories.* New York: Harcourt, Brace and World.

Stinchcombe, Arthur L., R. Adams, C. A. Heimer, K. L. Scheppele, T. Smith, and
D. G. Taylor. 1980. *Crime and punishment—Changing attitudes in
America.* Washington, D.C.: Jossey-Bass.

Sutherland, Edward. 1924. *Criminology.* Philadelphia: Lippincott.

Tolnay, Stewart E., E. M. Beck, and James L. Massey. 1989. Black lynching: The
power threat hypothesis revisted. *Social Forces* 67:605-23.

Turk, Austin. 1969. *Criminality and legal order.* Chicago: Rand McNally.

Wasserman, Ira. 1977. Southern violence and the political process. (Comment
on Inverarity, ASR April 1976) *American Sociological Review*
42:359-62.

Weicher, J. C. 1970. Determinants of central city expenditure: Some overlooked factors and problems. *National Tax Journal* 23:379-96.

Yeager, Matthew G. 1979. Unemployment and imprisonment. *Journal of
Criminal Law and Criminology* 70:586-88.

Yin, Peter. 1985. *Victimization and the aged.* Springfield, Ill.: Charles C.
Thomas.

Chapter 2

Ayers, Edward L. 1984. *Vengeance and justice: Crime and punishment in the 19th-century American South.* New York: Oxford University Press.

Bagozzi, Richard P. 1977. Populism and lynchings in Louisiana: Comment on Inverarity. *American Sociological Review* 42:355-58.

Beck, E. M., and Stewart E. Tolnay. 1990. The killing fields of the deep South: The market for cotton and the lynching of blacks, 1882-1930. *American Sociological Review* 55:526-39.

Beck, E. M., James L. Massey, and Stewart E. Tolnay. 1989. The gallows, the mob, the vote: Lethal sanctioning of blacks in North Carolina and Georgia, 1882 to 1930. *Law and Society Review* 23:317-31.

Blalock, Hubert M. 1967. *Toward a theory of minority-group relations.* New York: John Wiley.

———. 1989. Percent black and lynchings revisited. *Social Forces* 67:631-33.

Bloom, Jack M. 1987. *Class, race, and the civil rights movement.* Bloomington: Indiana University Press.

Bonacich, Edna. 1872. A theory of ethnic antagonism: The split labor market. *American Sociological Review* 37:547-59.

———. 1975. Abolition, the extension of slavery, and the position of free blacks: A study of split labor markets in the United States, 1830-1863. *American Journal of Sociology* 81:601-28.

Corzine, Jay, James Creech, and Lin Corzine. 1983. Black concentration and lynchings in the South: Testing Blalock's power-threat hypothesis. *Social Forces* 61:774-96.

Corzine, Jay, Lin Corzine, and James Creech. 1988. The tenant labor market and lynching in the South: A test of split labor market theory. *Sociological Inquiry* 58:261-78.

Ginsburg, Ralph. 1988. *100 years of lynchings.* Baltimore: Black Classics Press.

Henri, Florette. 1975. *Black migration: Movement North, 1900–1920.* Garden City: Anchor Press/Doubleday.

Hoffman, Frederick L. 1896. *Race traits and tendencies of the American negro.* New York: Macmillan Co.

Hovland, Carl I., and Robert R. Sears. 1940. Minor studies of aggression: Correlations of economic indices with lynchings. *Journal of Psychology* 9:301-10.

Inverarity, James M. 1976. Populism and lynching in Louisiana, 1889-1896: A test of Erikson's theory of the relationship between boundary crises and repressive justice. *American Sociological Review* 41:262-80.

Johnson, Charles S. 1941. *Statistical atlas of southern countries: Listing and analysis of socio-economic indices of 1,104 southern counties.* Chapel Hill: University of North Carolina Press.

Kousser, J. Morgan. 1974. *The shaping of southern politics: Suffrage restriction and the establishment of the one-party South.* New Haven: Yale University Press.

Massey, James L., and Martha A. Myers. 1989. Patterns of repressive social control in post-Reconstruction Georgia, 1882-1935. *Social Forces* 68: 458-88.

Mandle, Jay R. 1978. *The roots of black poverty: The southern plantation economy after the Civil War.* Durham: Duke University Press.

Mintz, Alexander. 1946. A re-examination of correlations between lynchings and economic indices. *Journal of Abnormal Social Psychology* 41: 154-60.

National Association for the Advancement of Colored People. [1919] 1969. *Thirty years of lynching in the United States, 1889-1918.* New York: NAACP.

Newby, I. A. 1965. *Jim Crow's defense: Anti-negro thought in America, 1900–1930.* Baton Rouge: Louisiana State University Press.

Phillips, Charles D. 1986. Social structure and social control: Modeling the discriminatory execution of blacks in Georgia and North Carolina, 1925-35. *Social Forces* 65:458-75.

————. 1987. Exploring relations among forms of social control: The lynching and execution of blacks in North Carolina. *Law and Society Review* 21:361-74.

Pope, Whitney, and Charles Ragin. 1977. Mechanical solidarity, repressive justice, and lynching in Louisiana: A commentary on Inverarity. *American Sociological Review* 42:363-69.

Quinney, Richard. 1977. *Class, state and crime.* New York: McKay.

Raper, Arthur. 1933. *The tragedy of lynching.* Chapel Hill: University of North Carolina Press.

Reed, John Shelton. 1972. Percent black and lynching: A test of Blalock's theory. *Social Forces* 50:356-60.

Shapiro, Herbert. 1988. *White violence and black response: From Reconstruction to Montgomery.* Amherst: The University of Massachusetts Press.

Smith, Lillian 1944. *Strange fruit: A novel.* New York: Reynal and Hitchcock.

Smith, William Benjamin. 1905. *The color line: A brief in behalf of the unborn.* New York: McClure, Phillips & Company.

Tolnay, Stewart E., and E. M. Beck. 1990. Black flight: Lethal violence and the great migration. *Social Science History* 14:347-70.

Tolnay, Stewart E., E. M. Beck, and James L. Massey. 1989a. Black lynchings: The power threat hypothesis revisited. *Social Forces* 67:605-23.

————. 1989b. Black competition and white vengeance: Legal execution of blacks as social control in the American South, 1890 to 1929. Unpublished Manuscript, Sociology Department, State University of New York at Albany.

Turk, Austin. 1969. *Criminality and legal order.* Chicago: Rand McNally.

U.S. Bureau of the Census. 1975. *Historical statistics of the United States: Colonial times to 1970.* Washington, D.C.: Government Printing Office.

Wasserman, Ira. 1977. Southern violence and the political process: Comment on Inverarity. *American Sociological Review* 42:359-62.

White, Walter [1929] 1969. *Rope and Faggot.* New York: Arno Press.

Williamson, Joel. 1984. *The crucible of race: Black-white relations in the American South since emancipation.* New York: Oxford University Press.

Woodward, C. Vann. 1966. *The strange career of Jim Crow.* Revised Edition, New York: Oxford University Press.

Young, Earle F. 1928-28. The relation of lynching to the size of political areas. *Sociology and Social Research* 12:348-53.

Chapter 3

Belsley, David A., Edwin Kuh, Roy E. Welsch. 1980. *Regression diagnostics.* New York: Wiley.

Blalock, Hubert M., Jr. 1967. *Toward a theory of minority group relations.* New York: Wiley.

Blau, Peter M. 1977. *Inequality and heterogeneity.* New York: Free Press.

Corzine, Jay, James Creech, Lin Corzine. 1983. Black concentration and lynchings in the South: Testing Blalock's power-threat hypothesis. *Social Forces* 61:774-96.

Federal Bureau of Investigation. 1972. *Uniform crime reports for the United*

States. Washington, D.C.: Government Printing Office.

Fischer, Claude. 1976. *The urban experience.* New York: Harcourt Brace Jovanovich.

Fischer, Joseph C., and Robert L. Mason. 1981. The analyses of multicollinear data in criminology. In *Methods in quantitative criminology*, edited by James Alan Fox. New York: Academic Press.

Fyfe, James J. 1982. *Readings on police use of deadly force.* Washington, D.C.: Police Foundation.

Fyfe, James J. 1980. Geographic correlates of police shootings: A micro analysis. *Journal of Research in Crime and Delinquency* 17:101–13.

Fyfe, James J. 1982. Race and extreme police-citizen violence. In *Police use of deadly force*, edited by James J. Fyfe. Washington, D.C.: Police Foundation.

Greenberg, David, Ronald C. Kessler, and Colin Loftin. 1985. Social inequality and crime control. *Journal of Criminal Law and Criminology* 76:684–704.

Hanushek, E. A., and J. E. Jackson. 1977. *Statistical methods for social scientists.* New York: Academic Press.

Hawkins, G., and P. Ward. 1970. Armed and disarmed police: Police firearms policy and levels of violence. *Journal of Research in Crime and Delinquency* 7:188–97.

Inverarity, James M. 1976. Populism and lynching in Louisiana, 1889–1896: A test of Erikson's theory of the relationship between boundary crises and repressive justice. *American Sociological Review* 41:262–80.

Jackson, Pamela I., and Leo Carroll. 1981. Race and the war on crime: The sociopolitical determinants of municipal police expenditures in 90 non-southern U.S. cities. *American Sociological Review* 46:290–305.

Jackson, Pamela I. 1986. Black visibility, city size, and social control. *The Sociological Quarterly* 27:185–203.

Jackson, Pamela I. 1989. *Minority group threat, crime, and policing: Social context and social control.* New York: Praeger.

Jacobs, David. 1979. Inequality and police strength: Conflict theory and coercive control in metropolitan areas. *American Sociological Review* 44:913–25.

Jacobs, David, and David Britt. 1979. Inequality and police use of deadly force: An empirical assessment of a conflict hypothesis. *Social Problems* 26:403–12.

Kania, Richard, and Wade C. Mackey. 1977. Police violence as a function of community characteristics. *Criminology* 27:27-48.

Langworthy, Robert H. 1986. Police shooting and criminal homicide: The temporal relationship. *Journal of Quantitative Criminology* 2:377-88.

Lester, David. 1982. Civilians who kill police officers and police officers who kill civilians: A comparison of American cities. *Journal of Police Science and Administration* 10:384-87.

Liska, Allen E., Joseph J. Lawrence, and Michael Benson. 1981. Perspectives on the legal order: The capacity for social control. *American Journal of Sociology* 87:412-26.

Liska, Allen E., Joseph J. Lawrence, and Andrew Sanchirico. 1982. Fear of crime as a social fact. *Social Forces* 60:760-71.

Liska, Allen E., and Mitchell B. Chamlin. 1984. Social structures and crime control among macrosocial units. *American Journal of Sociology* 90: 388-95.

Lizotte, Allan J., and David J. Bordua. 1980. Firearms ownership for sport and protection. *American Sociological Review* 45:229-43.

Matulia, Kenneth J. 1985. *A balance of forces.* Washington, D.C.: International Association of Chiefs of Police.

Milton, Catherine, Jeanne Wahl Halleck, James Lardner, and Gary L. Abrecht. 1977. *Police use of deadly force.* Washington, D.C.: Police Foundation.

National Center for Health Statistics. 1966-76. *Vital statistics of the United States.* Washington, D.C.: Government Printing Office.

National Crime Survey. 1973-75. *Criminal victimization surveys in American cities.* Washington, D.C.: U.S. Department of Justice.

New York Times Index. 1973. The New York Times Company 60:1496.

Reed, John S. 1972. Percent black and lynching: A test of Blalock's theory. *Social Forces* 50:356-60.

Robin, Gerald D. 1963. Justifiable homicide by police officers. *Journal of Criminal Law, Criminology and Police Science* 54:225-31.

Sherman, Lawrence W. 1983. Reducing police gun use: Critical events, administrative policy, and organizational change. In *Control in the police organization,* edited by Maurice Punch. Boston: MIT Press.

Sherman, Lawrence, and Robert H. Langworthy. 1979. Measuring homicide by police officers. *Journal of Criminal Law and Criminology* 70:546-60.

Sorenson, Annemette, Karl E. Taeuber, and Leslie J. Hollingsworth, Jr. 1975. Indexes of racial residential segregation for 109 cities in the United

States, 1940-1970. *Sociological Focus* 8:125-42.

Swigert, Victoria, and Ronald A. Farrell. 1976. *Murder, inequality and the law: Differential treatment in the legal process.* Lexington, M.A.: D. C. Heath.

Tolnay, Stewart E., E. M. Beck, and James L. Massey. 1989. Black lynchings: The power threat hypothesis revisited. *Social Forces* 57:605-23.

Turk, Austin T. 1969. *Criminality and legal order.* Chicago: Rand McNally.

Chapter 4

Black, Donald J. 1970. Production of crime rates. *American Sociological Review* 35:733-48.

_____. 1971. The social organization of arrest. *Stanford Law Review* 23:1087 -111.

Black, Donald, J. and Albert J. Reiss Jr. 1970. Police control of juveniles. *American Sociological Review* 35:63-77.

Blumstein, Alfred. 1982. On the racial disproportionality of United States' prison populations. *Journal of Criminal Law and Criminology* 73:1259-281.

Cohen, Lawrence E., and James R. Kluegel. 1978. Determinants of juvenile court dispositions: Ascriptive and achieved factors in two metropolitan courts. *American Sociological Review* 43:162-76.

Conklin, John E. 1971. Criminal environment and support for the law. *Law and Society Review* 6:247-65.

_____. 1975. *The impact of crime.* New York: Macmillan.

Elliott, Delbert S., and Suzanne S. Ageton. 1980. Reconciling race and class differences in self-reported and official estimates of delinquency. *American Sociological Review* 45:95-110.

Elliott, Delbert S., and David Huizinga. 1983. Social class and delinquent behavior in a national youth panel. *Criminology* 21:149-77.

Gottfredson, Michael R., and Don M. Gottfredson. 1980. *Decision-making in criminal justice: Toward the rational exercise of discretion.* Cambridge, Ma.: Ballinger.

Gottfredson, Michael R., and Michael J. Hindelang. 1979. A study of the behavior of law. *American Sociological Review* 44:3-18.

Gottfredson, Stephen D., Barbara D. Warner, and Ralph B. Taylor. 1988. Conflict and consensus about criminal justice in Maryland. In *Public atti-*

tudes to sentencing: Surveys from five countries, edited by Mike Hough and Nigel Walker. Brookfield, Vt.: Gower.

Greenberg, David F. 1983. Reflections on the justice model debate. *Contemporary Crises* 7:313–27.

Greenberg, David F., Ronald C. Kessler, and Colin Loftin. 1985. Social inequality and crime control. *Journal of Criminal Law and Criminology* 76: 684–704.

Hagan, John. 1974. Extra-legal attributes and criminal sentencing: An assessment of a sociological viewpoint. *Law and Society Review* 8:357–83.

Hanushek, Eric A., and John E. Jackson. 1977. *Statistical methods for social scientists.* New York: Academic Press.

Hindelang, Michael J. 1976. *Criminal victimization in eight American cities: A descriptive analysis of common theft and assault.* Cambridge, Mass.: Ballinger.

————. 1978. Race and involvement in common law personal crimes. *American Sociological Review* 43:93–109.

Hindelang, Michael J., and Michael Gottfredson. 1976. The victim's decision not to invoke the criminal justice process. In *Criminal justice and the victim,* edited by W. F. McDonald. Beverly Hills: Sage.

Jackson, Pamela I., and Leo Carroll. 1981. Race and the war on crime: The sociopolitical determinants of municipal police expenditures in 90 non-southern U.S. cities. *American Sociological Review* 46:290–305.

Jacobs, David. 1979. Inequality and police strength: Conflict theory and coercive control in metropolitan areas. *American Sociological Review* 44: 913–25.

Langan, Patrick A. 1985. Racism on trial: New evidence to explain the racial composition of prisons in the United States. *Journal of Criminal Law and Criminology* 76:666–83.

Levi, M., and S. Jones. 1985. Public and police perceptions of crime seriousness in England and Wales. *British Journal of Criminology* 25:234–50.

Liska, Allen E., and Mitchell B. Chamlin. 1984. Social structure and crime control among macrosocial units. *American Journal of Sociology* 90:383 –95.

Liska, Allen E., Mitchell B. Chamlin, and Mark D. Reed. 1985. Testing the economic production and conflict models of crime control. *Social Forces* 64:119–38.

Liska, Allen E., Joseph J. Lawrence, and Michael Benson. 1981. Perspectives on the legal order: The capacity for social control. *American Journal of*

Sociology 87:413-26.

Liska, Allen E., and Mark Tausig. 1979. Theoretical interpretations of social class and racial differentials in legal decision-making for juveniles. *The Sociological Quarterly* 20:197-207.

Lundman, Richard J. 1980. *Police behavior: A sociological perspective.* New York: Oxford University Press.

Lundman, Richard J., Richard E. Sykes, and John P. Clark. 1978. Police control of juveniles: A replication. *Journal of Research in Crime and Delinquency* 15:74-91.

Macoby, Eleanor E., Joseph P. Johnson, and Russell M. Church. 1958. Community integration and the social control of juvenile delinquency. *Journal of Social Issues* 14:38-51.

Pindyck, Robert S., and Daniel L. Rubinfeld. 1981. *Econometric models and economic forecasts.* 2d ed. New York: McGraw-Hill.

Pruitt, Charles R., and James Q. Wilson. 1983. A longitudinal study of the effect of race on sentencing. *Law and Society Review* 17:613-35.

Reiss, Albert J., Jr. 1971. *The police and the public.* New Haven: Yale University Press.

Rossi, Peter H., Emily Waite, Christine E. Bose, and Richard E. Berk. 1974. The seriousness of crimes: Normative structure and individual differences. *American Sociological Review* 39:224-37.

Sampson, Robert J. 1985. Structural sources of variation in race-age specific rates of offending across major U.S. cities. *Criminology* 23:647-74.

Sellin, Thorsten, and Marvin E. Wolfgang. 1964. *The measurement of delinquency.* New York: John Wiley and Sons.

Smith, Douglas A. 1986. The neighborhood context of police behavior. In *Communities and Crime,* edited by Albert J. Reiss, Jr., and Michael Tonry. Chicago: University of Chicago Press.

South, Scott J., and Steven F. Messner. 1986. Structural determinants of intergroup association: Interracial marriage and crime. *American Journal of Sociology* 91:1409-30.

Turk, Austin T. 1969. *Criminality and legal order.* Chicago: Rand McNally.

Williams, Kirk R., and Susan Drake. 1980. Social structure, crime and criminalization: An empirical examination of the conflict perspective. *The Sociological Quarterly* 21:563-75.

Chapter 5

Becker, Gary. 1968. Crime and punishment: An economic approach. *Journal of Political Economy* March/April: 169-217.

Becker, Howard. 1963. *Outsiders: studies in the sociology of deviance.* New York: Macmillan.

Blalock, Hubert. 1967. *Toward a theory of minority group relations.* New York: Wiley.

Blau, Judith R., and Peter M. Blau. 1982. Metropolitan structure and violent crime. *American Sociological Review* 47:114-28.

Boggs, Sarah L. 1965. Urban crime patterns. *American Sociological Review* 30:899-905.

Brantingham, Paul, and Patricia Brantingham. 1984. *Patterns in crime.* New York: Macmillan.

Brazer, Harvey E. 1959. *City expenditures in the United States.* Occasional paper #66. New York: National Bureau of Economic Research.

Button, James W. 1978. *Black violence: Political impact of the 1960s riots.* New Jersey: Princeton University Press.

Carroll, Leo, and Pamela Irving Jackson. 1983. Inequality, opportunity, and crime rates in central cities. *Criminology* 21(2):178-94.

Cohen, Lawrence E., and Marcus Felson. 1979. Social change and crime rate trends. *American Sociological Review* 44:588-607.

Community Relations Service. 1973, 1974. *Annual report of the community relations service.* Washington, D.C.: U.S. Government Printing Office.

Fegan, Joseph R., and Harlan Hahn. 1973. *Ghetto revolts: The politics of violence in American cities.* New York: Macmillan.

Fischer, Claude S. 1984. *The urban experience. 2d ed.* San Diego: Harcourt Brace Jovanovich.

Gastil, R. D. 1971. Homicide and a regional culture of violence. *American Sociological Review* 36:412-17.

Garofalo, James. 1979. Victimization and the fear of crime. *Journal of Research in Crime and Delinquency* 16:80-97.

Gove, Walter. 1975. *The labeling of deviance: Evaluating a perspective.* New York: John Wiley.

Greenberg, David F., Ronald C. Kessler, and Colin Loftin. 1983. The effect of police employment on crime. *Criminology* 21(3):375-94.

Greenwood, Michael J., and Walter J. Wadycki. 1973. Crime rates and public expenditures for police protection: Their interaction. *Review of Social Economy* 31:138-51.

Hackney, S. 1969. Southern violence. *American Historical Review* 74:906-25.

Hagedorn, John M., with Perry Macon. 1988. *People and folks: Gangs, crime and the underclass in a rustbelt city.* Chicage: Lake View Press.

Harries, Keith D. 1971. The geography of American crime, 1968. *Journal of Geography* 70:204-13.

———. 1974. *The geography of crime and justice.* New York: McGraw-Hill.

Harring, Sidney L. 1983. *Policing a class society.* New Jersey: Rutgers University Press.

Heinz, A., H. Jacob, and R. L. Lineberry, eds. 1983. *Crime in city politics.* New York: Longman.

Jackson, Pamela Irving. 1984. Opportunity and crime: A function of city size. *Sociology and Social Research* 62(2):172-93.

———. 1985. Ethnicity, region, and public fiscal commitment to policing. *Justice Quarterly* 2(2):167-94.

———. 1986. Black visibility, city size, and social control. *Sociological Quarterly* 27(2):185-203.

———. 1989. *Minority group threat, crime, and policing: Social context and social control.* New York: Praeger.

Jackson, Pamela Irving, and Leo Carroll. 1981. Race and the war on crime: The sociopolitical determinants of municipal police expenditures in 90 U.S. cities. *American Sociological Review* 46:290-305.

Jacobs, David. 1979. Inequality and police strength: Conflict theory and coercive control in metropolitan areas. *American Sociological Review* 44: 912-25.

———. 1982. Inequality and economic crime. *Sociology and Social Research* 66:12-28.

Johnson, David R. 1979. *Policing the urban underworld.* Philadelphia: Temple University Press.

Kowalski, G. S., R. L. Dittman, Jr., and W. L. Bung. 1980. Spatial distribution of criminal offenses by states, 1970-1976. *Journal of Research in Crime and Delinquency* 17:4-25.

Larson, Richard C. 1972. *Urban police patrol analysis.* Boston: MIT Press.

Lemert, Edwin. 1951. *Social pathology.* New York: McGraw-Hill.

Liska, Allen E. 1987. A critical examination of macro perspectives on crime control. In *Annual review of sociology*, vol. 13, edited by W. Richard Scott and James F. Short. Palo Alto, CA: Annual Reviews.

Liska, Allen E., and William F. Baccaglini 1983. Fear of crime. In *Encyclopedia of crime and justice* vol. 2. edited by Sanford H. Kadish. New York: Free Press.

Liska, Allen E., and Mitchell B. Chamlin. 1984. Social structure and crime control among macrosocial units. *American Journal of Sociology* 90(2):383-95.

Liska, Allen E., Mitchell B. Chamlin, and Mark D. Reed. 1985. Testing the economic production and conflict models of crime control. *Social Forces* 64(1):119-38.

Liska, Allen E., Joseph J. Lawrence, and Michael Benson. 1981. Perspectives on the legal order: The capacity for social control. *American Journal of Sociology* 87:413-26.

Liska, Allen E., Joseph J. Lawrence, and Andrew Sanchirico. 1982. Fear of crime as a social fact. *Social Forces* 60(30):760-70.

Lizotte, Alan J., and David J. Bordua. 1980. Firearms ownership for sport and protection. *American Sociological Review* 45:229-43.

Loftin, Colin, and Robert Hill. 1974. Regional subculture of violence: An examination of the Gastil-Hackney thesis. *American Sociological Review* 39:714-24.

Loftin, Colin, and David McDowall. 1982. The police, crime, and economic theory: An assessment. *American Sociological Review* 47:393-401.

Mansfield, Roger, Leroy C. Gould, and J. Zvi Namewirth. 1974. A socioeconomic model for the prediction of societal rates of property theft. *Social Forces* 52:462-72.

Mayhew, Bruce H., and Robert L. Levinger. 1976. Size and the density of interaction in human aggregates. *American Journal of Sociology* 82:86-110.

McPheters, Lee R., and William B. Stronge. 1974. Law enforcement expenditures and urban crime. *National Tax Journal* 27:633-44.

Miller, Walter. 1958. Lower-class culture as a generating milieu of gang delinquency. *Journal of Social Issues* 14:5-19.

Ogburn, W. F. 1935. Factors in variation of crime among cities. *Journal of the American Statistical Association* 30:12-20. Washington, D.C.: U.S. Government Printing Office.

Pyle, Gerald F. 1976. Geographic perspectives in crime and the impact of anticrime legislation. In *Urban policymaking and metropolitan dynamics:*

A comparative geographic analysis, edited by John S. Adams. Cambridge, Mass.: Ballinger.

Quinney, Richard. 1970. *The social reality of crime*. Boston: Little, Brown & Company.

Reppetto, Thomas, 1974. *Residential crime*. Cambridge, Mass.: Ballinger.

Rubinstein, Jonathan. 1973. *City police*. New York: Farrar, Straus and Giroux.

Schur, Edwin. 1972. *Labeling deviant behavior*. New York: Harper and Row.

Shaw, Clifford R., and Henry D. McKay. 1942. *Juvenile delinquency and urban areas*. Chicago: University of Chicago Press.

Silver, Alan. 1967. The demand for order in civil society: A review of some themes in the history of urban crime, police, and riot. In *The police: Six sociological essays*, edited by David J. Bordua. New York: John Wiley.

Skolnick, Jerome H. 1967. *Justice without trial: Law enforcement in a democratic society*. New York: Wiley.

Skolnick, Jerome H., and David H. Bayley. 1986. *The new blue line: Police innovation in six American cities*. New York: Free Press.

Spitzer, Steven. 1981. The political economy of policing. In *Crime* and *capitalism*, edited by David Greenberg. Palo Alto, Calif.: Mayfield Press.

Turk, Austin T. 1969. *Criminality and the legal order*. Chicago: Rand McNally.

Weicher, John C. 1970. Determinants of central city expenditures: Some overlooked factors and problems. *National Tax Journal* 23(4):379-96.

Westley, William A. 1970. *Violence and the police: A sociological study of law, custom, and morality*. Cambridge, Mass.: MIT Press.

Wilson, James Q., and George L. Kelling. 1989. Making neighborhoods safe. *The Atlantic Monthly* February:46-52.

Wilson, O. W. 1941. *Distribution of police patrol force*. Publication 74. Chicago: Public Administration Service.

_____. 1972. *Police administration*. 3d ed. New York: McGraw-Hill.

Wilson, William Julius. 1987. *The truly disadvantaged: The inner city, the underclass, and public policy*. Chicago: University of Chicago Press.

Wirth, Louis. 1938. Urbanism as a way of life. *American Journal of Sociology* 44:1-24.

Wolfgang, Marvin E. 1968. Urban Crime. In *The metropolitan enigma*, edited by J. Q. Wilson. Cambridge: Harvard University Press.

Zelinsky, Wilbur. 1973. *The cultural geography of the United States*. Englewood Cliffs, N.J.: Prentice-Hall.

Chapter 6

Becker, Gary S. 1968. Crime and punishment: An economic approach. *Journal of Political Economy* 76:169–217.

Belsley, David A., Edwin Kuh, and Roy E. Welsch. 1980. *Regression diagnostics: Identifying influential data and sources of collinearity.* New York: Wiley.

Blau, Peter M. 1977. *Inequality and heterogeneity.* New York: Free Press.

Blauner, Robert. 1972. *Racial oppression in America.* New York: Harper and Row.

Bonger, Willem. 1916. *Criminality and economic conditions.* Boston: Little, Brown & Company.

Chambliss, William J., and Robert B. Seidman. 1982. *Law, order, and power.* Reading, Mass.: Addison-Wesley.

Chamlin, Mitchell B. 1988. Crimes and arrests: An autoregressive integrated moving average (ARIMA) approach. *Journal of Quantitative Criminology* 4:247–58.

———. 1989. A macro social analysis of change in police size, 1972–1982: Controlling for static and dynamic influences. *The Sociological Quarterly* 30:615–24.

Choldin, Harvey. 1985. *Cities and suburbs.* New York: McGraw-Hill.

Federal Bureau of Investigation. 1982. *Uniform crime reports.* Washington, D.C.: U.S. Government Printing Office.

Fischer, Claude S. 1976. *The urban experience.* New York: Harcourt Brace Jovanovich.

Gove, Walter R., Michael Hughes, and Michael Geerken. 1985. Are uniform crime reports a valid indicator of the index crimes? An affirmative answer with minor qualifications. *Criminology* 23:451–501.

Greenberg, David F., Ronald C. Kessler, and Charles H. Logan. 1979. A panel model of crime rates and arrest rates. *American Sociological Review* 44:843–50.

Greenberg, David F., Ronald C. Kessler, and Colin Loftin. 1985. Social inequality and crime control. *The Journal of Criminal Law and Criminology* 76:684–704.

Jackson, Pamela Irving. 1985. Ethnicity, region, and public fiscal commitment to policing. *Justice Quarterly* 2:185-203.

———. 1989. *Minority group threat, crime, and policing.* New York: Praeger.

Jackson, Pamela Irving, and Leo Carroll. 1981. Race and the war on crime: The sociopolitical determinants of municipal expenditures in 90 non-southern cities. *American Sociological Review* 46:290-305.

Jacobs, David. 1979. Inequality and police strength: Conflict and coercive control in metropolitan areas. *American Sociological Review* 44:913-24.

Liska, Allen E., and Mitchell B. Chamlin. 1984. Social structure and crime control among macrosocial units. *American Journal of Sociology* 90:383-95.

Liska, Allen E., Joseph L. Lawrence, and Michael Benson. 1981. Perspectives on the legal order: The capacity for social control. *American Journal of Sociology* 87:413-26.

McCleary, Richard, Barbara C. Nienstedt, and James M. Ervin. 1982. Uniform crime reports as organizational outcomes: Three time series experiments. *Social Problems* 29:361-72.

Piven, Frances Fox, and Richard A. Cloward. 1971. *Regulating the poor: The functions of public welfare.* New York: Vintage.

———. 1987. The historical sources of the contemporary relief debate. In *The mean season: The attack on the welfare state*, edited by Fred Block, Richard A. Cloward, Barbara Ehrenreich, and Frances Fox Piven. New York: Pantheon Books.

Sorensen, Annemette, Karl E. Taeuber, and Leslie J. Hollingsworth, Jr. 1975. Indexes of racial residential segregation for 109 cities in the United States. *Sociological Focus* 8:124-42.

Spitzer, Steven. 1975. Toward a Marxian theory of deviance. *Social Problems* 22:638-51.

Turk, Austin T. 1969. *Criminality and legal order.* Chicago: Rand McNally.

Chapter 7

Adamson, Christopher R. 1983. Punishment after slavery: Southern penal systems, 1865-1880. *Social Problems* 30:555-69.

Austin, James, and Barry Krisberg. 1981. Wider, stronger and different nets: The dialectics of criminal justice reform. *Journal of Research in Crime and Delinquency* 18:165-96.

Ayers, Edward. 1984. *Crime and punishment in the nineteenth-century American South.* New York: Oxford University Press.

Balbus, Issac. 1973. *The dialectics of legal repression: Black rebels before the American criminal courts.* New York: Russell Sage.

Bartel, Ann P. 1975. An analysis of firm demand for protection against crime. *Journal of Legal Studies* 4:443-78.

Berk, Richard A., Harold Brackman, and Selma Lesser. 1977. *A measure of justice: An empirical study of changes in the California penal code, 1955-1971.* New York: Academic Press.

Berk, Richard A., Sheldon L. Messinger, David Rauma, and John E. Berecochea. 1983. Prisons as self-regulating systems: A comparison of historical patterns in California for male and female offenders. *Law and Society Review* 17:547-86.

Block, Fred. 1977. The ruling class does not rule. *Socialist Revolution* 33:6-28.

Blumstein, Alfred. 1988. Prison populations: A system out of control? *In Crime and Justice: An Annual Review of Research* vol. 9 edited by Michael Torny and Norval Morris. Chicago: University of Chicago Press.

Box, Steven. 1987. *Recession, crime and punishment.* Totawa, N.J.: Barnes and Noble.

Box, Steven, and Chris Hale. 1985. Unemployment imprisonment and prison overcrowding. *Contemporary Crisis* 9:209-28.

Bridges, George S., and Robert D. Crutchfield. 1988. Law, social standing, and racial disparities in imprisonment. *Social Forces* 66:699-724.

Burawoy, Michael. 1976. The functions and reproduction of migrant labor: Comparative material from southern Africa and the United States. *American Journal of Sociology* 81:1050-87.

Carroll, Leo, and Claire P. Cornell. 1985. Racial composition, sentencing reforms and rates of incarceration 1970-1980. *Justice Quarterly* 2:473 -90.

Coates, Robert B., Alden D. Miller, and Lloyd E. Ohlin. 1978. *Diversity in a youth correctional system.* Cambridge, Mass. Ballinger.

Cohen, Jacqueline, and Michael H. Tonry. 1983. Sentencing reforms and their impact. In *Research in sentencing: The search for reform,* vol. 2., edited by Alfred Blumstein et al. Washington, D.C.: National Academy Press.

Cohen, William. 1976. Negro involuntary servitude in the South, 1865-1940: A preliminary analysis. *Journal of Social History* 32:31-60.

Colvin, Mark. 1990. Labor markets, industrial monopolization, welfare and imprisonment: Evidence from a cross-section of U.S. counties. *The Sociological Quarterly* 31:441-57.

Cullen, Francis T., Gregory A. Clark, and John F. Wozniak. 1985. Explaining the get tough movement: Can the public be blamed? *Federal Probation* 69:16-24.

Darrow, Clarence. [1902] 1957. Address to the prisoners in the Cook County jail. In *Attorney for the damned*, edited by Arthur Weinberg. New York: Simon and Schuster.

Davis, Allison, Burleigh B. Gardner, and Mary Gardner. 1941. *Deep south*. Chicago: University of Chicago Press.

de Haan, Willem. 1990. *The politics of redress: Crime punishment and penal abolition*. London: Unwin Hyman.

Dickson, Donald T. 1968. Bureaucracy and morality: An organizational perspective on a moral crusade. *Social Problems* 16:143-56.

Elster, Jon. 1984. *Ulysses and the sirens: Studies in rationality and irrationality*. Rev. ed. Cambridge: Cambridge University Press.

Epstein, Jayson. 1977. *Agency of fear: Opiates and political power in America*. New York: Putnam.

Feeley, Malcom M., and Austin D. Sarat. 1980. *The policy dilemma: Federal crime policy and the law enforcement assistance administration*. Minneapolis: University of Minnesota Press.

Garland, David. 1985. *Punishment and welfare A history of penal strategies*. Borkfield, Vt.: Gower.

——. 1990. *Punishment and modern society: A study in social theory*. Chicago: University of Chicago Press.

Giddens, Anthony. 1982. Action, structure and power. In *Profiles and critiques in social theory*, edited by Anthony Giddens. Berkeley: University of California Press.

Gottfredson, Stephen D., Barbara D. Warner, and Ralph B. Taylor. 1988. Conflict and consensus about criminal justice in Maryland. In *Public Attitudes Toward Sentencing*, edited by Nigel Walker and Mike Hough. Brookfield, Vt.: Gower.

Grattet, T. Ryken. 1989. Institutions and public welfare: Alternative models of social control? Paper presented at the American Sociological Association meetings, San Francisco.

Greenberg, David F. 1977. The dynamics of oscillatory punishment processes. *Journal of Criminal Law and Criminology* 68:643-51.

——. 1980. Penal sanctions in Poland: A test of alternative modesl. *Social Problems* 28:194-204.

Greenberg, David F., and Drew Humphries. 1982. Economic crises and the justice model: A skeptical view. *Crime and Delinquency* 28:601-09.

Guttman, Herbert G. 1975. *Slavery and the numbers game: A critique of time on the cross.* Urbana: University of Illinois Press.

Hagan, John. 1982. The corporate advantage: A study of the involvement of corporate and individual victims in a criminal justice system. *Social Forces* 60:994–1022.

Hale, Chris. 1989. Unemployment, imprisonment, and the stability of punishment hypothesis: Some results using cointegration and error correction modesl. *Journal of Quantitative Criminology* 5:169–86.

Hay, Douglas. 1975. Property, authority, and the criminal law. In *Albion's fatal tree: Crime and justice and eighteenth-century England,* edited by Douglas Hay, Peter Linebaugh, John G. Rule, E. P. Thompson, and Cal Winslow. London: Allen Lane.

Heidenheimer, A. J., H. Heclo, and C. T. Adams. 1983. *Comparative public policy: The politics of social choice in Europe and America.* 2d ed. New York: St. Martin's Press.

Hodson, Randy, and Robert L. Kaufman. 1982. Economic dualism: A critical review. *American Sociological Review* 47:727–39.

Humphries, Drew, and David Greenberg. 1981. The dialectics of crime control. In *Crime and capitalism,* edited by David Greenberg. Palo Alto: Mayfield.

Inverarity, James, and Rykken Grattet. 1989. Institutional responese to unemployment: A comparison of U.S. trends, 1948–1985. *Contemporary Crises* 13:351–70.

Inverarity, James, and Daniel McCarthy. 1988. *Punishment and social structure revisited: Unemployment and imprisonment in the U.S., 1948–1984. Sociological Quarterly* 29:263–79.

Inverarity, James, and Lucky Tedrow. 1990. Does unemployment directly affect imprisonment?: Evidence from a pooled-cross section and time series analysis of U.S. states, 1974–1986. Paper presented at the Meeting of the American Sociological Association, Washington, D.C.

Jacobs, David. 1978. Inequality and the legal order: An ecological test of the conflict view. *Social Problems* 25:515–25.

Jankovic, Ivan. 1977. Labor market and imprisonment. *Crime and Social Justice* 8:17–31.

Laffargue, Bernard, and Thierry Godefroy. 1989. Economic cycles and punishment: Unemployment and imprisonment: A time series study, France 1920–1985. *Contemporary Crises* 13:371–404.

Langan, Patrick A. 1989. *Felony sentences in state courts, 1986.* Washington, D.C.: Department of Justice.

Lea, J. 1979. Discipline and capitalist development. In *Capitalism and the rule of law*, edited by Bob Fine. London: Hutchinson.

Lerman, Paul. 1982. *Deinstitutionalization and the welfare state*. New Brunswick, N.J.: Rutgers University Press.

Linebaugh, P. 1976. Karl Marx, the theft of wood, and working class composition: A contribution to the current debate. *Crime and Social Justice* 6:5–16.

Link, Christopher T., and Neal Shover. 1986. The origins of criminal sentencing reforms. *Justice Quarterly* 3:329–41.

Liska, Allen E., Joseph J. Lawrence, and Andrew Sanchirico. 1982. Fear of crime as a social fact. *Social Forces* 60:760–70.

Liska, Allen E., and William F. Baccaglini. 1990. Feeling safe by comparison: Crime in the newspapers. *Social Problems* 37:360–74.

Lynch, Michael J. 1989. The extraction of surplus value, crime and punishment: A preliminary analysis. *Contemporary Crises* 12:329–44.

Melossi, Dario. 1985. Punishment and social action: Changing vocabularies of punitive motive within a political business cycle. *Current Perspectives in Social Theory* 6:169–97.

Michalowski, R. J., and M. A. Pearson. 1990. Punishment and social structure at the state level: A cross-sectional comparison of 1970 and 1980. *Journal of Research in Crime and Delinquency* 27:52–78.

Myers, Samuel L., Jr., and William J. Sabol. 1987. Business cycles and racial disparities in punishment. *Contemporary Policy Issues* 5:46–58.

Petchesky, Rosalind P. 1981. At hard labor: Penal confinement and production in nineteenth-century America. In *Crime and capitalism*, edited by David Greenberg. Palo Alto: Mayfield.

Piandiani, John A. 1988. The crime control corps: An invisible New Deal program. *British Journal of Sociology* 33:348–58.

Piven, F. F., and R. A. Cloward. 1971. *Regulating the poor: The functions of public welfare*. New York: Vintage Books.

Platt, Anthony. 1974. The triumph of benevolence: The origins of the juvenile justice system in the United States. In *Criminal justice in America*, edited by Richard Quinney. Boston: Little, Brown & Company.

Quadagno, Jill. 1985. Two models of welfare state development: Reply to Skocpol and Amenta. *American Sociological Review* 50:575–78.

———. 1988. *The transformation of old age security: Class and politics in the American welfare state*. Chicago: University of Chicago Press.

Ransom, Roger L., and Richard Sutch. 1977. *One kind of freedom: The economic consequences of emancipation.* Cambridge: Cambridge University Press.

Reiman, Jeffrey H. 1982. Marxist explanations and radical misinterpretations: A reply to Greenberg and Humphries. *Crime and Delinquency* 28:610-17.

Riley, Pamela J., and Vicki M. Rose. 1980. Public vs. elite opinion on correctional reform: Implications for social control. *Journal of Criminal Justice* 8:345-56.

Rothman, David. 1971. *The discovery of the asylum: Social order and disorder in the new republic.* Boston: Little, Brown & Company.

Rusche, G., and O. Kirchheimer. [1939] 1968. *Punishment and social structure.* New York: Russell and Russell.

Rutherford, Andrew. 1984. *Prisons and the process of justice: The reductionist challenge.* London: Heinemann.

Sabol, William J. 1989. Racially disproportionate prison populations in the U.S.: An overview of historical patterns and review of competing issues. *Contemporary Crises* 13:405-32.

Scheingold, Stuart A. 1984. *The politics of law and order: Street crime and public policy.* New York: Longman.

Schervish, Paul G. 1983. *The structural determinants of unemployment.* New York: Academic Press.

Scull, Andrew. 1977. *Decarceration: community treatment and the deviant: A radical view.* Englewood Cliffs, N.J.: Prentice-Hall.

———. 1982. Community corrections: Panacea, progress or pretense? In *The Politics of Informal Justice.* Vol. 1, edited by Richard L. Abel. New York: Academic Press.

Shelden, Randall G. 1981. Convict leasing: An application of the Rusche-Kirchheimer thesis to penal changes in Tennessee, 1830-1915. In *Crime and Capitalism,* edited by David Greenberg. Palo Alto: Mayfield.

Sherman, Michael, and Gordon Hawkins. 1981. *Imprisonment in America: Choosing the future.* Chicago: University of Chicago Press.

Skocpol T., and E. Amenta. 1985. Did capitalists shape social security? *American Sociological Review* 50:572-75.

———. 1986. States and social policies. *Annual Review of Sociology* 12:131-57.

Sutton, John. 1987. Doing time: Dynamics of imprisonment in the reformist state. *American Sociological Review* 52:612-30.

Taggart, William A. 1989. Redefining the power of the federal judiciary: The impact of court-ordered prison reform on state expenditures of corrections. *Law and Society Review* 23:241-72.

Taylor, D. Garth, Kim L. Scheppele, and Arthur L. Stinchcombe. 1979. Salience of crime and support for harsher penalties. *Social Problems* 26:413-24.

Thompson, E. P. 1975 *Whigs and hunters: The origins of the black act.* New York: Pantheon.

Unnever, James D., and Larry H. Hembroff. 1988. The prediction of racial/ethnic sentencing disparities: An expectation states approach. *Journal of Research in Crime and Delinquency* 25:53-82.

Wilson, James Q. 1975. *Thinking about crime.* New York: Vintage.

Wright, Gavin. 1986. *Old South, new South: Revolutions in the southern economy since the Civil War.* New York: Basic Books.

Zimring, Franklin E., and Gordon Hawkins. 1986. *Capital punishment and the American agenda.* Cambridge: Cambridge University Press.

Chapter 8

Abramson, Marc F. 1972. Criminalization of mentally disordered behavior: Possible side effects of the mental health law. *Hospital and Community Psychiatry* 23:101-05.

Arvanites, Thomas M. 1990. A comparison of civil patients and incompetent defendants: Pre and post deinstitutionalization. *Bulletin of the American Academy of Psychiatry and Law* 18:393-404.

_____. 1988. The impact of state mental hospital deinstitutionalization on commitments for incompetency to stand trial. *Criminology* 26:307-20.

_____. 1989. The differential impact of deinstitutionalization on white and nonwhite defendants found incompetent to stand trial. *Bulletin of the American Academy of Psychiatry and Law* 17:311-20.

Biles, David, and Glen Mulligan, 1973. Mad or bad? The enduring dilemma. *British Journal of Criminology* 13:275-79.

Bonovitz, Jennifer, and Jay Bonovitz. 1981. Diverson of the mentally ill into the criminal justice system: The police intervention perspective. *American Journal of Psychiatry* (138)7:973-76.

Bonovitz, Jennifer, and Edward Guy. 1979. Impact of restrictive civil commitment prison procedures on prison psychiatric services. *American Journal of Psychiatry* 136(8):1045-48.

Burt, Robert, and Norval Morris. 1972. A plea for the absolution of the incompetency plea. *University of Chicago Law Review* Fall:55–95.

Cocozza, Joseph, Mary Melick, and Henry J. Steadman. 1978. Trends in violent crime among ex-mental patients. *Criminology* 16:317–34.

Conrad, Peter, and John Schneider, 1980. *Deviance and medicalization: From badness to sickness*, St. Louis: Mosby.

Dickey, Walter. 1980. Incompetency and the non-dangerous mentally ill client. *Criminal Law Bulletin* (January/February):22–40.

Drope v. Missouri, 420 U.S. 162 (1975).

Dusky v. United States, 362 U.S. 402 (1960).

Geller, Jeffrey, and Eric Lster. 1978. The process of criminal commitment for pre-trial psychiatric examination: An evaluation. *American Journal of Psychiatry* 135:53–60.

Grob, G. N. 1970. The state hospital in the mid-nineteenth century in America: A social analysis. *In Social psychology and mental health*, edited by H. Wechsler, L. Solomon, and B. Kramer. New York: Holt, Rinehart and Winston.

Group for the Advancement of Psychiatry. 1974. Misuse of psychiatry in criminal courts: Competency to stand trial. Vol. 8, Report No. 89.

Gudeman, Howard. 1981. Legal sanctions and clinicians. *Clinical Psychologist* (Winter):15–17.

Heryford v. Parker, 396 F.2d. 393 (10th, Cir. 1968).

Kaplan, Leonard V. 1978. State control of deviant behavior: A critical essay of Scull's critique of community treatment and deinstitutionalization. *Arizona Law Review* 20:189–212.

Kiesler, C. A. 1982. Public and professional myths about mental hospitalization: An empirical reassessment of policy related beliefs. *American Psychologist* 37:1323–39.

Kiesler, C., T. McGuire, D. Mechanic, L. Mosher, S. Nelson, F. Newman, R. Rich, H. Schulberg. 1983. Federal mental health policymaking: An assessment of deinstitutionalization. *American Psychologist* 38:1291–97.

Kittrie, Nicholas. 1971. *The right to be different*. Baltimore: Johns Hopkins University Press.

Lamb, H. R., and R. Grant, 1982. The Mentally ill in an urban jail. *Archives of General Psychiatry* 39:17–22.

Lessard v. Schmidt, 349 F. Supp. 1078 (E.D. Wis. 1972).

Melick, Mary, Henry J. Steadman, and Joseph Cocozza. 1979. The medicalization of criminal behavior among mental patients. *Journal of Health and Social Behavior* 20:228-37.

Monahan, John, Cynthia Caldeira, and Herbert D. Friedlander. 1979. Police and the mentally ill: A comparison of committed and arrested persons. *International Journal of Law and Psychiatry* 2:509-18.

Morrissey, Joseph P. 1982. Deinstitutionalizing the mentally ill: Processes, outcomes and new directions. In *Deviance and mental illness*, edited by Walter Gove. Beverly Hills: Sage.

National Institute of Mental Health. 1989. *Additions and Resident Patients at End of Year, State and County Mental Hospitals: 1987*. Division of Biometry and Applied Sciences, Survey and Reports Branch, Washington, D.C.

_____. 1986. *State and county mental hospitals: United States 1973-1983 and 1983-1984*. Division of Biometry and Applied Sciences, Survey and Reports Branch Statistical, Note 176. Washington, D.C.

_____. 1983. *State and county mental hospitals, 1979-1980 and 1980-1982*. Division of Biometry and Applied Sciences, Survey and Reports Branch Statistical, Note 165. Washington D.C.

New York State Office of Mental Health. 1983. *Criminal commitments to psychiatric centers*. Bureau of Special Projects Research. Albany, N.Y.

Pate v. Robinson, 383 U.S. 375 (1966).

Penrose, L. 1939. Mental disease and crime: Outline of a comparative study of European statistics. *British Journal of Medical Psychology*. 18:1-13.

Pogrebin, M. R., and R. M. Regoli. 1985. Mentally disordered persons in jail. *Journal of Community Psychology*, 13:409-12.

Pollock, S. 1974. Forensic psychiatry: A specialty. *Bulletin of the American Academy of Psychiatry and Law* 2:1-6.

Roche, A. 1978. *Frontiers of psychiatry*. Nutley, N.J.: Hoffman LaRiche.

Roesch, Ronald, and Stephen Golding. 1980. *Competency to stand trial*. Urbana, Ill.: University of Illinois Press.

Rothman, David. 1971. *The discovery of the asylum*. Boston: Little, Brown & Company.

Rouse v. Cameron, 373 F.2d 451 (D.C. Cir. 1966).

Scull, Andrew. 1977. Madness and segregative control in the rise of the insane asylum. *Social Problems* 24:337-51.

_____. 1977. *Decarceration*. Englewood Cliffs, N.J.: Prentice-Hall.

Shah, Saleem. 1981. Legal and mental health system interaction: Major developments and research needs. *International Journal of Law and Psy-*

chiatry 4:219-70.

Steadman, Henry J., and Joseph Cocozza. 1978. Selective reporting and the public's misconception of the criminally insane. *Public Opinion Quarterly* 41:523-33.

Steadman, Henry J., Joseph J. Cocozza, and Mary Melick. 1978. Explaining the increased arrest rates among mental patients: The changing clientele of state hospitals. *American Journal of Psychiatry* 135(7):816-20.

Steadman, Henry J., John Monahan, Barbara Duffee, Eliot Hartstone, and Pam Robbins. 1984. The impact of state mental deinstitutionalization on United States prison populations: 1968-1978. *Journal of Criminal Law & Criminology* 75(2):474-90.

Steadman, Henry J. 1979. *Beating a rap?* Chicago: University of Chicago Press.

Steadman, Henry J., Marilyn J. Rosenstein, Robin L. Macaskill, and Ronald W. Manderscheild. 11988. A profile of mentally disordered offenders admitted to patient psychiatric services in the U.S. *Law and Human Behavior* 12:91-99.

Swank, G. E., and D. Winer. 1976. Occurrence of psychiatric disorder in a country prison. *American Journal of Psychiatry* 133:1331-36.

Swisher v. United States, 237 F. Supp. 291 (1965).

Szasz, Thomas, 1970. *The Manufacture of madness.* New York: Harper and Row.

Teplin, Linda A. 1984. Criminalizing mental disorder: The comparative arrest rate of the mentally ill. *American Psychologist* 39:794-813.

Wyatt v. Stickney, 325 F. Supp. 781 (M.D. 1971).

Winick Bruce. 1983. Incompetent to stand trial. In *Mentally disordered offenders: Perspectives from the law and social sciences*, edited by John Monahan and Henry J. Steadman. New York: Plenum.

Chapter 9

Albritton, Robert B. 1979a. Social amelioration through mass insurgency? A reexamination of the Piven and Cloward thesis. *American Political Science Review* 73:1003-11.

———. 1979b. A reply to Piven and Cloward. *American Political Science Review* 73:1020-23.

Belsley, David A., Edwin Kuh, and Roy E. Welsch. 1980. *Regression diagnostics: Identifying influential data and sources of collinearity.* New York: Wiley.

Betz, Michael, 1974. Riots and welfare: Are they related? *Social Problems* 21: 345–55.

Blalock, Hubert M., Jr. 1967. *Toward a theory of minority-group relations*. New York: Wiley.

Bohrnstedt, George W. 1969. Observations on the measurement of change. In *Sociological methodology*, edited by E. F. Borgatta and G. W. Bohrnstedt. San Francisco: Jossey-Bass.

Bursik, Robert J., Jr., and Jim Webb. 1982. Community change and patterns of delinquency. *American Journal of Sociology* 88:24–42.

Chamlin, Mitchell B. 1987. General assistance among cities: An examination of the need, economic threat, and benign neglect hypotheses. *Social Science Quarterly* 68:835–46.

Cook, R. Dennis, and Sanford Weisberg. 1982. Criticism and influence analysis in regression. In *Sociological methodology*, edited by S. Leinhardt. San Francisco: Jossey-Bass.

Ganz, Alexander, and Thomas O'Brien. 1973. The city: Sandbox, reservation, or dynamo? *Public Policy* 21:107–23.

Greenberg, David F., Ronald C. Kessler, and Colin Loftin. 1985. Social inequality and crime control. *The Journal of Criminal Law & Criminology* 76:684–704.

Gronbjerg, Kristen A. 1977. *Mass society and the extension of welfare, 1960–1970*. Chicago: University of Chicago Press.

Guest, Avery M. 1977. The functional reorganization of the metropolis. *Pacific Sociological Review* 20:553–67.

Hanushek, Eric A., and John E. Jackson. 1977. *Statistical methods for social sciences*. New York: Academic Press.

Henry, Charles P. 1987. Racial factors in the 1982 California gubernatorial campaign: Why Bradley lost. In *The new black politics*, edited by M. R. Preston, L. J. Henderson, Jr., and P. L. Puryear. New York: Longman.

Hicks, Alexander, and Duane H. Swank. 1983. Civil disorder, relief mobilization, and AFDC caseloads: A reexamination of the Piven and Cloward thesis. *American Journal of Political Science* 27:696–716.

Isaac, Larry, and William Kelly. 1981. Racial insurgency, the state, and welfare expansion: Local and national evidence from postwar United States. *American Journal of Sociology* 86:1348–86.

Jackson, Pamela Irving. 1989. *Minority group threat, crime, and policing*. New York: Praeger

Jackson, Pamela Irving, and Leo Carroll. 1981. Race and the war on crime: The sociopolitical determinants of municipal police expenditures in 90 non-southern cities. *American Sociological Review* 46:290–305.

Jennings, Edward T., Jr. 1983. Racial insurgency, the state, and welfare expansion: A critical comment and reanalysis. *American Journal of Sociology* 88:1220–36.

Karsarda, John D. 1978. Urbanization, community, and the metropolitan problem. In *The handbook of contemporary urban life*, edited by D. Street and Associates. San Francisco: Jossey-Bass.

Kinder, Donald R., and David O. Sears. 1981. Prejudice and politics: Symbolic racism versus racial threats to the good life. *Journal of Personality and Social Psychology* 40:414–31.

Liska, Allen E., and Mitchell B. Chamlin. 1984. Social structure and crime control among macrosocial units. *American Journal of Sociology* 90:383 –95.

Liska, Allen E., Mitchell B. Chamlin, and Mark D. Reed. 1985. Testing the economic production and conflict models of crime control. *Social Forces* 64:119–38.

Liska, Allen E., Joseph J. Lawrence, and Michael Benson. 1981. Perspectives on the legal order: The capacity for social control. *American Journal of Sociology* 87:413–26.

Piven, Frances Fox, and Richard A. Cloward. 1971. *Regulating the poor: The functions of public welfare*. New York: Vintage.

———. 1979. Electoral instability, civil disorder, and relief rises: A reply to Albritton. *American Political Science Review* 73:1012–19.

Schiller, Bradley R. 1973. *The economics of poverty and discrimination*. Englewood Cliffs, N.J.: Prentice-Hall.

Schram, Stanford F., and J. Patrick Turbett. 1983. Civil disorder and the welfare expansion: A two-step process. *American Sociological Review* 48: 408–14.

The New York Ties. 1965–1969. *The New York Times index*. New York: The New York Times Company.

U.S. Bureau of the Census. 1983. *County and city data book. Washington, D.C.: U.S. Government Printing Office.*

———. 1972. *County and city data book*. Washington, D.C.: U.S. Government Printing Office.

———. 1983. *County and city data book*. Washington, D.C.: U.S. Government Printing Office.

———. 1970–1980. *Statistical abstract of the United States*. Washington, D.C.:

U.S. Government Printing Office.

Wilensky, Harold L. 1975. *The welfare state and equity.* Berkeley and Los Angeles: University of California Press.

Wilensky, Harold L., and Charles N. Lebeaux. 1965. *Industrial society and social welfare.* New York: Free Press.

Wilson, William J. 1987. *The truly disadvantaged.* Chicago: University of Chicago Press.

Winegarden, C. R. 1973. The welfare explosion: Determinants of the size and growth of the AFDC population. *American Journal of Economics and Sociology* 32:245–56.

Chapter 10

Adamson, E. 1984. Toward a Marxian penology: Captive criminal populations as economic threats and resources. *Social Problems* 31:435–58.

Arvanites, Thomas M. 1988. The impact of state mental hospital deinstitutionalization on commitment for incompetency to stand trial. *Criminology* 26:307–20.

Beck, E. M., James L. Massey, and Stewart E. Tolnay. 1989. The gallows, the mob, the vote: Lethal sanctioning by blacks in North Carolina and Georgia, 1982 to 1930. *Law and Society Review* 23:317–31.

Beirne, Piers. 1979. Empiricism and the critique of Marxism on law and crime. *Social Problems* 26:373–85.

Berk, Richard A., David Rauma, Sheldon Messinger, and Thomas F. Cooley. 1981. A test of the stability of punishment hypothesis: The case of California 1851–1970. *American Sociological Review* 46:805–29.

Biles, D., and G. Mulligan. 1973. Mad or bad: The enduring dilemma. *British Journal of Criminology* 13:275–79.

Black, Donald J., and Albert J. Reiss, Jr. 1970. Police control of juveniles. *American Sociological Review* 35:63–77.

Blalock, Hubert M., Jr. 1967. *Toward a theory of minority group relations.* New York: Wiley.

Bonacich, Edna. 1975. Abolition, the extension of slavery, and the position of split labor markets in the United States. 1830–1863. *American Journal of Sociology* 81:601–28.

Box, Steven, and Chris Hale. 1982. Economic crisis and the rising prisoner population in England and Wales. *Crime and Social Justice* 13:20–35.

Chamlin, Mitchell B. 1989. A macro social analysis of change in police size, 1972–1982: Controlling for static and dynamic influences. *The Sociological Quarterly* 30:615-24.

Connor, Walter D. 1972. The manufacture of deviance: The case of the Soviet purge, 1936–1938. *American Sociological Review* 37:403-13.

Conrad, Peter, and Joseph W. Schneider. 1980. *Deviance and medicalization*. St. Louis: C. V. Mosby.

Corzine, Jay, James Creech, and Lin Corzine. 1983. Black concentration and lynchings in the South: Testing Blalock's power-threat hypothesis. *Social Forces* 61:774-96.

Erikson, Kai T. 1966. *Wayward puritans: A study in the sociology of deviance*. New York: Wiley.

Foucault, Michel. 1965. *Madness and civilization*. New York: Vintage.

Foucault, Michel. 1978. *Discipline and punish*. (Translated by A. Sheridan. New York: Pantheon.

Fyfe, James J. 1982. *Readings on police use of deadly force*. Washington, D.C.: Police Foundation.

Galster, George C., and Laure H. Scaturo. 1985. The U.S. criminal justice system: Unemployment and the severity of punishment. *Journal of Research in Crime and Delinquency* 22:163-90.

Garofalo, James. 1979. Victimization and the fear of crime. *Journal of Research in Crime and Delinquency* 16:80-97.

Grabosky, Peter N. 1980. Rates of imprisonment and psychiatric hospitalization in the United States. *Social Indicators Research* 7:63-70.

Greenberg, David F. 1977. The dynamics of oscillatory punishment processes. *Journal of Criminal Law and Criminology* 68:643-51.

Greenberg, David, Ronald C. Kessler and Colin Loftin. 1985. Social inequality and crime control. *Journal of Criminal Law and Criminology* 76:684 -704.

Harring, S. L. 1983. *Policing a class society*. New Brunswick, N.J.: Rutgers University Press.

Hicks, Alexander, and Duane H. Swank. 1983. Civil disorder, relief mobilization, and AFDC caseloads: A reexamination of the Piven and Cloward thesis. *American Political Science Review* 27:692-716.

Ignatieff, Michael. 1978. *A just measure of pain: The penitentiary in the industrial revolution, 1850–1950*. New York: Pantheon.

Inverarity, James M. 1976. Populism and lynching in Louisiana, 1889-1986: A test of Erikson's theory of the relationship between boundary cirses and repressive justice. *American Sociological Review* 41:262-80.

Inverarity, James, and Ryken Grattet. 1989. Institutional responses to unemployment: A comparison of U.S. trends, 1948-1985. *Contemporary Crises* 13:351-70.

Inverarity, James, and Daniel McCarthy. 1988. Punishment and social structure revised: Unemployment and imprisonment in the U.S., 1948-1984. *Sociological Quarterly* 29:263-79.

Isaac, Larry, and W. R. Kelly. 1981. Racial insurgency, the state, and welfare expansion: Local and national level evidence from the postwar United States. *American Journal of Sociology* 86:1348-86.

Jackson, Pamela I., and Leo Carroll. 1981. Race and the war on crime: The sociopolitical determinants of municipal police expenditures in 90 non-southern U.S. cities. *American Sociological Review* 46:290-305.

Jackson, Pamela I. 1989. *Minority group threat, crime, and policing.* New York: Praeger.

Jacobs, David. 1979. Inequality and police strength: Conflict theory and coercive control in metropolitan areas. *American Sociological Review* 44: 913-25.

Jacobs, David, and D. Britt. 1979. Inequality and police use of deadly force: An empirical assessment of a conflict hypothesis. *Social Problems* 26: 403-12.

Jankovic, Ivan. 1977. Labor market and imprisonment. *Crime and Social Justice* 8:17-37.

Liska, Allen E., and Mitchell B. Chamlin. 1984. Social structure and crime control among macrosocial units. *American Journal of Sociology* 90:383 -95.

Liska, Allen E., Mitchell B. Chamlin, and Mark Reed. 1985. Testing the economic production and conflict models of crime control. *Social Forces* 63:119-38.

Liska, Allen E., Joseph J. Lawrence, and Michel Benson. 1981. Perspectives on the legal order: The capacity for social control. *American Journal of Sociology* 87:412-26.

Liska, Allen E., Joseph J. Lawrence, and Andrew Sanchirico. 1982. Fear of crime as a social fact. *Social Forces* 60:760-71.

Massey, James L., and Martha Myers. 1989. Patterns of repressive social control in post-Reconstruction Georgia, 1882-1935. *Social Forces* 68: 458-88.

Melick, Mary E., Henry J. Steadman, and Joseph C. Cocozza. 1979. The medicalization of criminal behavior among mental patients. *Journal of Health and Social Behavior* 20:228-37.

Morrissey, Joseph P. Deinstitutionalizing the mentally ill: Process, outcomes, and new directions. In *Deviance and mental illness*, edited by Walter Gove. Beverly Hills: Sage.

Penrose, L. 1939. Mental disease and crime: Outline of a comparative study of European statistics. *British Journal of Medical Psychology* 28:1-15.

Phillips, Charles D. 1986. Social structure and social control: Modeling the discriminatory execution of blacks in Georgia and North Carolina, 1925-35. *Social Forces* 65:458-75.

Phillips, Charles D. 1987. Exploring relations among forms of social control: The lynching and execution of blacks in North Carolina, 1889-1918. *Law and Society Review* 21:361-74.

Piven, Frances F., and Richard A. Cloward. 1971. *Regulating the poor: The functions of public welfare.* New York: Vintage.

Quinney, Richard. 1977. *Class, state and crime.* New York: McKay.

Reed, John Shelton. 1972. Percent black and lynching: A test of Blalock's theory. *Social Forces* 50:356-60.

Rothman, David J. 1971. *The discovery of the asylum.* Boston: Little, Brown & Company.

Rusche, Georg, and Otto Kirchheimer. 1939. *Punishment and social structure.* New York: Russell & Russell.

Schram, Stanford, F., and Patrick J. Turbett. 1983. Civil disorder and welfare explosion: A two-step process. *American Sociological Review* 48:408 -14.

Sherman, Lawrence W., and Robert H. Langworthy. 1979. Measuring homicide by police officers. *Journal of Criminal Law and Criminology* 70:546 -60.

Skogan, Wesley G., and Michael G. Maxfield. 1981. *Coping with crime: Individual and neighborhood reactions.* Beverly Hills: Sage.

Spitzer, Steven. 1975. Toward a Marxian theory of deviance. *Social Problems* 22:638-51.

Steadman, Henry J. 1979. *Beating a rap?* Chicago: University of Chicago Press.

Tolnay, Stewart E., E. M. Beck, and James L. Massey. 1989. Black lynchings: The power threat hypothesis revisited. *Social Forces* 67:605-23.

Turk, Austin T. 1969. *Criminality and legal order.* Chicago: Rand McNally.

Yeager, Matthew G. 1979. Unemployment and imprisonment. *Journal of*

Criminal Law and Criminology 70:586–88.

Yin, Peter. 1985. *Victimization and the aged.* Springfield, Ill.: Charles C. Thomas.

List of Contributors

Thomas M. Arvanites is a member of the Department of Sociology at Villanova University. He earned his Ph.D. at the State University of New York at Albany. Dr. Arvanites has written several articles on the criminalization of the mentally ill. Currently, he is examining the relative effects of economic and crime data on the level of coercive control in the United States.

E. M. Beck is associate professor of sociology at the University of Georgia. He received his Ph.D. in sociology from the University of Tennessee. His current research focuses on the political economy of racial violence, in particular the relationship between economic changes in the status of the white lower class and violence against blacks.

Mitchell B. Chamlin is an associate professor of sociology at the University of Oklahoma. He received his Ph.D. in sociology from the State University of New York at Albany in 1985. He is currently engaged in longitudinal analyses of alternative styles of social control within Oklahoma city and Chicago.

James Inverarity is an associate professor of sociology at Western Washington University. He received his Ph.D. from Stanford University. In addition to ongoing research on race, unemployment, and imprisonment he is working on a revisioin of *Law and Society*.

Pamela Irving Jackson is professor and chair of the Sociology Department and director of the Justice Studies Program at Rhode Island College. She holds a Ph.D. in sociology from Brown University and recently served a three-year stint as associate editor of the *American Sociological Review*. Her work investigating the bases of collective support for social control has been published in several articles in major professional journals, including *Justice Quarterly* and the *American Sociological Review*, and in her recent book, *Minority Group Threat, Crime, and Policing: Social Context and Social Control*. Currently, her research focuses on the influence of postindustrial economic development and urban decline on youth gangs and street crime.

Allen E. Liska received his Ph.D. from the University of Wisconsin-Madison in 1974, and he is presently a professor of sociology at the State University of New York at Albany. His research has focused both on social psychology, studying the impact of attitudes on behavior, and on social deviance, studying interpersonal theories of deviance and macro theories of social control. He has served on the editorial boards of the *Social Psychology Quarterly and Criminology;* on the council of the social psychology section of the American Sociological Association; and as chair of the crime, law and deviance section of the American Sociological Association. Recently, he has examined how broad patterns of social control and the fear of crime are shaped and structured by the social composition of macrosocial units. This work has appeared in the leading journals of sociology and is presently being integrated into a book.

Stewart E. Tolnay is associate professor of sociology and director of the Center for Social and Demographic Analysis at the State University of New York at Albany. He received his Ph.D. in sociology from the University of Washington. His research has been concentrated in two primary areas: the causes and consequences of racial violence in the American South, and fertility transitions in historical populations.

Barbara D. Warner received her Ph.D. in 1989 from the State University of New York at Albany. She is presently an assistant professor of sociology at the University of Kentucky. Her research interests are on the neighborhood-level determinants of both crime and crime control.

Jiang Yu completed his Ph.D. in sociology at the State University of New York at Albany. His areas of concentration include social deviance, criminology, and social control. Besides teaching courses in juvenile delinquency, sociological theory, and criminology, he has been working as a research scientist and project coordinator of the Problem Drinker Driver Project at the New York State Division of Alcoholism and Alcohol Abuse.

Index